THE STORY OF

NEW YORK: 1833-1928

BY

FRANK M. O'BRIEN

WITH AN INTRODUCTION BY
EDWARD PAGE MITCHELL
ILLUSTRATIONS AND FACSIMILES

NEW EDITION

D. APPLETON AND COMPANY
NEW YORK :: LONDON :: MCMXXVIII

William T. Dewart
President of *The Sun*.

O'Brien, Frank Michael, 1875–

The story of the Sun. New York, 1833–1918. By Frank M. O'Brien; with an introduction by Edward Page Mitchell, illustrations and facsimiles... New York, London, D. Appleton and company, 1928.

xviii p., 1 l., 305 p. front., plates, ports., facsims. 21 cm.

1. The Sun, New York. 2. Dana, Charles Anderson, 1819–1897. I. Title.

THE STORY OF
The Sun
NEW EDITION

PRINTED IN THE UNITED STATES OF AMERICA

THIS NEW EDITION IS DEDICATED TO

WILLIAM THOMPSON DEWART

THROUGH WHOSE COURAGE, VISION AND ENTERPRISE "THE SUN" REMAINS IN THE HANDS OF THOSE WHO MAKE IT

PREFACE TO THE NEW EDITION

It is nearly ten years since Mr. Mitchell, then the editor of the Sun, *wrote the following introduction to the first edition of this book. Death claimed that greatest of all* Sun *men on January 22, 1927. I regret that this volume lacks his impressions of the last decade, knowing with what approving interest he watched the course of the* Sun, *particularly after his close friend Mr. Dewart had mutualized the ownership of the paper. At no period in the half-century of his connection with the* Sun *was Mr. Mitchell more devoted to it than in the final year of his life.*

FRANK M. O'BRIEN

New York

INTRODUCTION TO THE FIRST EDITION

It is truer, perhaps, of a newspaper than of most other complex things in the world that the whole may be greater than the sum of all its parts. In any daily paper worth a moment's consideration the least fancifully inclined observer will discern an individuality apart from and in a degree independent of the dozens or hundreds or thousands of personal values entering at a given time into the composite of its grey pages.

This entity of the institution, as distinguished from the human beings actually engaged in carrying it on, this fact of the newspaper's possession of a separate countenance, a spirit or soul differentiating it from all others of its kind, is recognized either consciously or unconsciously by both the more or less unimportant workers who help to make it and by their silent partners who support it by buying and reading it. Its loyal friends and intelligent critics outside the establishment, the Old Subscriber and the Constant Reader, form the habit of attributing to the newspaper, as to an individual, qualities and powers beneficent or maleficent or merely foolish, according to their mood or digestion. They credit it with traits of character quite as distinct as belong to any man or woman of their acquaintance. They personify it, moreover, without much knowledge, if any, of the people directing and producing it; and, often and naturally, without any particular concern about who and what these people may be.

On their own side, the makers of the paper are accustomed to individualize it as vividly as a crew does the ship. They know better than anybody else not only how far each personal factor, each element of the composite, is modified and influenced in its workings by the other personal factors associated in the production, but also the extent to which all the personal units are influenced and modified by something not listed in the office directory or visible upon the payroll; something that was there before they came and will be there after they go.

Of course, that which has given persistent idiosyncrasy to a newspaper like the *Sun,* for example, is accumulated tradition. That which has made the whole count for more than the sum total of its parts, in the *Sun's* case as in the case of its esteemed contemporaries, is the heritage of method and expedient, the increment of standardized skill and localized imagination contributed through many years to the fund of the paper by the forgotten worker as well as by the remembered.

The manner of growth of the great newspaper's well-defined and continuous character, distinguishing it from all the rest of the offspring of the printing press, a development sometimes not radically affected by changes of personnel, of ownership, of exterior conditions and fashions set by the popular taste, is a subject over which journalistic metaphysics might easily exert itself to the verge of boredom. Fortunately there has been found a much better way to deal with the attractive theme.

The *Sun* is eighty-five years old as this book [the first edition] goes to press. In telling its intimate story, from the September Tuesday which saw the beginning of Mr. Day's intrepid and epochal experiment, throughout the days of the Beaches, of Dana, of Laffan, and of Reick to the time of Mr. Munsey's purchase of the property in the summer of 1916, Mr. O'Brien has done what has never been undertaken before, so far as is known to the writer of this introduction, for any newspaper with a career of considerable span.

There have been general histories of Journalism, presenting casually the main facts of evolution and progress in the special instance. There have been satisfactory narratives of journalistic episodes, reasonably accurate accounts of certain aspects or dynastic periods of newspaper experience, excellent portrait biographies or autobiographies of journalists of genius and high achievement, with the eminent man usually in strong light in the foreground and his newspaper seldom nearer than the middle distance. But here, probably for the first time in literature of this sort, we have a real biography of a newspaper itself, covering the whole range of its existence, exhibiting every function of its organism, illustrating every quality that has been conspicuous in the successive stages of its growth. The *Sun* is the hero of Mr. O'Brien's *Story of "The Sun."* The human participants figure in their incidental relation to the main thread of its life and activities. They do their parts, big or little, as they pass in interesting procession. When they have done their parts they disappear, as in real life, and the story goes on, just as the *Sun* has gone on, without them except as they may have left their personal impress on the newspaper's structure or its superficial decoration.

During no small part of its four score and five years of intelligent interest in the world's thoughts and doings it has been the *Sun's* fortune to be regarded as in a somewhat exceptional sense the newspaper man's newspaper. If in truth it has merited in any degree this peculiar distinction in the eyes of its professional brethren it must have been by reason of originality of initiative and soundness of method; perhaps by a chronic indifference to those ancient conventions of news importance or of editorial phraseology which, when systematically observed, are apt to result in a pale, dull, or even stupid uniformity of product. Mr. Dana wrote more than half a century ago to one of his associates, "Your articles have stirred up the animals, which you as well as I recognize as one of the great ends of life." Sometimes he borrowed Titania's wand; sometimes he used a red hot poker. Not only in that great editor's time but also in the time of his predecessors and successors the *Sun* has held it to be a duty and a joy to assist to the best of its ability in the discouragement of anything like lethargy in the menagerie. Perhaps, again, that was one of the things that helped to make it the newspaper man's newspaper.

However this may be, it seems certain that to the students of the theory and practice of journalism, now happily so numerous in the land, the chronicler of one highly individual newspaper's deeds and ways is affording an object lesson of practical value, a textbook of technical usefulness, as well as a store of authoritative history, entertaining anecdote, and suggestive professional information. And a much wider audience than is made up of newspaper workers present or to come will find that the story of a newspaper which Mr. O'Brien has told with wit and knowledge in the pages that follow becomes naturally and inevitably a swift and charming picture of the town in which that newspaper is published throughout the period of its service to that town—the most interesting period in the existence of the most interesting city of the world.

It is a fine thing for the *Sun*, by all who have worked for it in its own spirit beloved, I believe, like a creature of flesh and blood and living intelligence and human virtues and failings, that through Mr. Munsey's wish it should have found in a son of its own schooling a biographer and interpreter so sympathetically responsive to its best traditions.

EDWARD P. MITCHELL

New York, 1918

CONTENTS

ILLUSTRATIONS

THE STORY OF "THE SUN"

CHAPTER I

SUNRISE AT 222 WILLIAM STREET

Benjamin H. Day, with No Capital Except Youth and Courage, Establishes the First Permanent Penny Newspaper.—The Curious First Number Entirely His Own Work.

IN the early thirties of last century the only newspapers in the city of New York were six-cent journals whose reading matter was adapted to the politics of men, and whose only appeal to women was their size, perfectly suited to deep pantry shelves.

Dave Ramsey, a compositor on one of these sixpennies, the *Journal of Commerce,* had an obsession. It was that a penny paper, to be called the *Sun,* would be a success in a city full of persons whose interest was in humanity in general, rather than in politics, and whose pantry shelves were of negligible width. Why his mind fastened on the *Sun* as the name of this child of his vision is not known; perhaps it was because there was a daily in London bearing that title. It was a short name, easily written, easily spoken, easily remembered.

Benjamin H. Day, another printer, worked beside Dave Ramsey in 1830. Ramsey reiterated his idea to his neighbor so often that Day came to believe in it, although it is doubtful whether he had the great faith that possessed Ramsey. Now that due credit has been given to Ramsey for the idea of the penny *Sun*, he passes out of the record, for he never attempted to put his project into execution.

Nor was Day's enthusiasm for a penny *Sun* so big that he plunged into it at once. He was a business man rather than a visionary. With the savings from his wages as a compositor he went into the job-printing business in a small way. He still met his old chums and still talked of the *Sun*, but it is likely that he never would have come to start it if it had not been for the cholera.

There was an epidemic of this plague in New York in 1832. It killed more than 35,000 people in that year and added to the depression of business already caused by financial disturbances and a wretched banking system. The job-printing trade suffered with other industries, and Day decided that he needed a newspaper—not to reform, not to uplift, not to arouse, but to push the printing business of Benjamin H. Day. Incidentally he might add luster to the fame of the President, Andrew Jackson, or uphold the hands of the Mayor of New York, Gideon Lee; but his prime purpose was to get the work of printing handbills for John Smith, the grocer, or letterheads for Richard Robinson, the dealer in hay. Incidentally he might become rich and powerful, but for the time being he needed work at his trade.

Ben Day was only twenty-three years old. He was the son of Henry Day, a hatter of West Springfield, Massachusetts, and Mary Ely Day; and sixth in descent from his first American ancestor, Robert Day. Shortly after the establishment of the Springfield *Republican* by Samuel Bowles, in 1824, young Day went into the office of that paper, then a weekly, to learn the printer's trade. That was two years before the birth of the second and greater Samuel Bowles, who was later to make the *Republican*, as a daily, one of the greatest of American newspapers.

Day learned well his trade from Sam Bowles. When he was twenty, and a first-class compositor, he went to New York, and worked at the case in the offices of the *Evening Post*, the *Journal of Commerce*, and the *Commercial Advertiser*. He married, when he was twenty-one, Miss Eveline Shepard. At the time of the *Sun's* founding Mr. Day lived, with his wife and their infant son, Henry, at 75 Duane Street, only a few blocks from the newspaper offices.

The idea of a penny paper was not new. In Philadelphia, the *Cent* had had a brief, inglorious existence. In Boston, the *Bostonian* had failed to attract the cultured readers of the modern Athens. Eight months before Day's hour arrived, the *Morning Post* had braved it in New York, selling first at two cents and later at one cent, but even with Horace Greeley as one of the founders it lasted only three weeks.

When Ben Day sounded his friends, particularly the printers, as to their opinion of his project, they cited the doleful fate of the other penny journals. He drew, or had designed, a headline for the *Sun* that was to be, and took it about to his cronies. A. S. Abell, a printer on the *Mercantile Advertiser*, poked the most fun at him. A penny paper, indeed! But this same Abell lived to stop scoffing, to found another *Sun*—this one in Baltimore—and to buy a half-million-dollar estate out of the profits of it. He was the second beneficiary of the penny *Sun* idea.

William M. Swain, another journeyman printer, also made light of Day's ambition. He lived to be Day's foreman, and later to own the Philadelphia *Public Ledger*. He told Day that the penny *Sun* would ruin him. As Day had not much enthusiasm at the outset, surely his friends did not add to it, unless by kindling his stubbornness.

As for capital, he had none at all, in the money sense. He did have a printing press, hardly improved from the machine of Benjamin Franklin's day, some job paper and plenty of type. The press would throw off two hundred impressions an hour at full speed, man power. He hired a room, 12 by 16 feet, in the building at 222 William Street. That building was still there, in the shadow of the Brooklyn Bridge approach, when the *Sun* celebrated its fiftieth anniversary in 1883; but a six-story factory is on the site to-day.

There is no question as to the general authorship of the first paper. Day was proprietor, publisher, editor, chief pressman, and mailing clerk. He stayed up all the night before that fateful Tuesday, September 3, 1833, setting with his own hands some advertisements that were regularly appearing in the six-cent papers, for he wanted to make a show of prosperity.

He also wrote, or clipped from some out-of-town newspaper, a poem that would fill nearly a column. He rewrote news items from the West and South—some of them not more than a month old. As for the snappy local news of the day, he bought, in the small hours of that Tuesday morning, a copy of the *Courier and Enquirer,* the livest of the six-cent papers, took it to the single room in William Street, clipped out or rewrote the police-court items, and set them up himself. A boy, whose name is unknown to fame, assisted him at devil's work. A journeyman printer, Parmlee, helped with the press when the last quoin had been made tight in the fourth and last of the little pages.

The sun was well up in the sky before its namesake of New York came slowly, hesitatingly, almost sadly, up over the horizon of journalism—never to set!

But young Mr. Day, wiping the ink from his hands at noon, and waiting in doubt to see whether the public would buy the thousand *Suns* he had printed, could not foresee this. Neither could he know that, by this humble effort to exalt his printing business, he had driven a knife into the heart of ancient journalism.

The size of the first *Sun* was 11¼ × 8 inches, not a great deal bigger than a sheet of commercial letter paper, and considerably less than one-quarter the size of a page of the *Sun* of to-day. Compared with the first *Sun,* the present newspaper is about forty times larger. The type was a good, plain face of agate, with some verse on the last page in nonpareil.

An almost perfect reprint of the first *Sun* was issued as a supplement to the paper on its twentieth birthday, in 1853, and again—to the number of about 140,000 copies—on its fiftieth birthday, in 1883. Many of the persons who treasure the replicas of 1883 believe them to be original first numbers, as they were not labeled "Presented gratuitously to the subscribers of the *Sun,*" as was the issue of 1853. Hardly a month passes by but the

Sun receives one of them from some proud owner. It is easy, however, to tell the reprint from the original, for Mr. Day in his haste committed an error at the masthead of the editorial or second page of the first number. The date line there reads "September 3, 1832," while in the reprints it is "September 3, 1833," as it should have been, but wasn't, in the original. And there are minor typographical differences, invisible to the layman.

Of the thousand, or fewer, copies of the first *Sun*, only five are known to exist—one in the bound file of the *Sun's* first year, held jealously in the *Sun's* safe; one in the private library of the late Edward Page Mitchell; one in the Public Library at Fifth Avenue and Forty-second Street, New York; and two in the library of the American Type Founders Company, Jersey City.

There were three columns on each of the four pages. At the top of the first column on the front page was a modest announcement of the *Sun's* ambitions:

> The object of this paper is to lay before the public, at a price within the means of every one, all the news of the day, and at the same time afford an advantageous medium for advertising.

It was added that the subscription in advance was three dollars a year, and that yearly advertisers were to be accommodated with ten lines every day for thirty dollars per annum—ten cents a day, or one cent a line. That was the old fashion of advertising. The friendly merchant bought thirty dollars' worth of space, say in December, and inserted an advertisement of his fur coats or snow shovels. The same advertisement might be in the paper the following July, for the newspapers made no effort to coördinate the needs of the seller and the buyer. So long as the merchant kept his name regularly in print, he felt that was enough.

The leading article on the first page was a semi-humorous story about an Irish captain and his duels. It was flanked by a piece of reprint concerning microscopic carved toys. There was a paragraph about a Vermont boy so addicted to whistling that he fell ill of it. Mr. Day's apprentice may have needed this warning.

The front-page advertising, culled from other newspapers and printed for effect, consisted of the notices of steamship sailings. In one of these Commodore Vanderbilt offered to carry passengers from New York to Hartford, by daylight, for one dollar, on his splendid low-pressure steamboat *Water Witch.* Cornelius Vanderbilt was then thirty-nine years old, and had made the boat line between New York and New Brunswick, New Jersey, pay him forty thousand dollars a year. When the *Sun* started, the Commodore was at the height of his activity, and he stuck to the water for thirty years afterward, until he had acccumulated something like forty million dollars.

E. K. Collins had not yet established his famous Dramatic line of clipper ships between New York and Liverpool, but he advertised the "very fast sailing coppered ship *Nashville* for New Orleans." He was only thirty years old then.

Cooks were advertised for by private families living in Broadway, near Canal Street—pretty far uptown to live at that day—and in Temple Street, near Liberty, pretty far down town now.

On the second page was a bit of real news, the melancholy suicide of a young Bostonian of "engaging manners and amiable disposition," in Webb's Congress Hall, a hotel. There were also two local anecdotes; a paragraph to the effect that "the city is nearly full of strangers from all parts of this country and Europe"; nine police-court items, nearly all concerning trivial assaults; news of murders committed in Florida, at Easton, Pennsylvania, and at Columbus, Ohio; a report of an earthquake at Charlottesville, Virginia, and a few lines of stray news from Mexico.

The third page had the arrivals and clearances at the port of New York, a joke about the cholera in New Orleans, a line to say that the same disease had appeared in the City of Mexico, an item about an insurrection in the Ohio penitentiary, a marriage announcement, a death notice, some ship and auction advertisements, and the offer of a reward of $1,000 for the recovery of $13,600 stolen from the mail stage between Boston and Lynn and the arrest of the thieves.

The last page carried a poem, "A Noon Scene," but the atmosphere was of the Elysian Fields over in Hoboken rather than of midday in the city. Another good filler was the banknote table, copied from a six-cent contemporary. The quotations indicated that not much of the bank currency of the day was accepted at par.

The rest of the page was filled with borrowed advertising. The Globe Insurance Company, of which John Jacob Astor was a director, announced that it had a capital of a million dollars. The North River Insurance Company, whose directorate included William B. Astor, declared its willingness to insure against fire and against "loss or damage by inland navigation." At that time

BENJAMIN H. DAY
Founder of *The Sun*.

the boilers of river steamboats had an unpleasant trick of blowing up; hence Commodore Vanderbilt's mention of the low pressure of the *Water Witch.* John A. Dix, then Secretary of State of the State of New York, and later to be the hero of the "shoot him on the spot" order, advertised an election. Castleton House Academy, on Staten Island, offered to teach and board young gentlemen at twenty-five dollars a quarter.

Such was the first *Sun.* Part of it was stale news, rewritten. Part was borrowed advertising. It is doubtful whether even the police-court items were original, although they were the most human things in the issue, the most likely to appeal to the readers whom Day hoped to reach—people to whom the purchase of a paper at six cents was impossible, and to whom windy, monotonous political discussions were a bore.

In those early thirties, daily journalism had not advanced very far. Men were willing, but means and methods were weak.

The frailness of the early dailies was largely due to the fact that their publishers looked almost entirely to advertising for the support of the papers. On the other hand, the editors were politicians or highbrows who thought more of a speech by Lord Piccadilly on empire than of a good street tragedy; more of an essay by Lady Geraldine Glue than of a first-class report of a kidnaping.

Another great obstacle to success—one for which neither editor nor publisher was responsible—was the lack of facilities for the transmission of news. Fulton launched the *Clermont* twenty-six years before Day launched the *Sun,* but even in Day's time steamships were nothing to brag of, and the first of them was yet to cross the Atlantic. When the *Sun* was born, the most important railroad in America was thirty-four miles long, from Bordentown to South Amboy, New Jersey. There was no telegraph; the mails were prehistorically slow.

It was hard to get out a successful daily newspaper without daily news. A weekly would have sufficed for the information that came in, by sailing ship and stage, from Europe and Washington and Boston. Ben Day was the first man to reconcile himself to an almost impossible situation. He did so by the simple method of using what news was nearest at hand—the incidental happenings of New York life.

CHAPTER II

THE FIELD OF THE LITTLE "SUN"

A Very Small Metropolis Which Day and His Partner, Wisner, Awoke by Printing Small Human Pieces About Small Human Beings and Having Boys Cry the Paper in the Streets.

HOW far could the little *Sun* hope to throw its beam in a stodgy if not naughty world? The circulation of all the dailies in New York at the time was less than thirty thousand. The seven morning and four evening papers all sold at six cents a copy, shared the field thus:

MORNING PAPERS

Morning Courier and New York Enquirer	4,500
Democratic Chronicle	4,000
New York Standard	2,400
New York Journal of Commerce	2,300
New York Gazette and General Advertiser	1,500
New York Daily Advertiser	1,400
Mercantile Advertiser and New York Advocate	1,200

EVENING PAPERS

Evening Post	3,000
Evening Star	2,500
New York Commercial Advertiser	2,100
New York American	1,600
Total	26,500

New York was the American metropolis, but it was a small city, measured by the towns of to-day. Of its quarter of a million population, only eight or ten thousand lived above Twenty-third Street. Washington Square, now the residence district farthest down town, had just been adopted as a park; before that it had been the Potter's Field. In 1833 rich New Yorkers were putting up some fine residences there—of which a good many still stand.

Wall Street was already the financial center, with its Merchants' Exchange, banks, brokers, and insurance companies. Canal Street was pretty well filled with retail stores. Third Avenue had been macadamized from the Bowery to Harlem. The down-town streets were paved, and some were lighted with gas at seven dollars a thousand cubic feet.

Columbia College, in the square bounded by Murray, Barclay, Church, and Chapel Streets, had a hundred students. James Kent was professor of law in the Columbia of that day, and Charles Anthon was professor of Greek and Latin. A rival seat of learning, the University of the City of New York, chartered two years earlier, was temporarily housed at 12 Chambers Street, with a certain Samuel F. B. Morse as professor of sculpture and painting. There were twelve schools, harboring six thousand pupils, whose welfare was guarded by the Public School Society of New York, Lindley Murray, secretary. The National Academy of Design, incorporated five years before, guided the budding artist in Clinton Hall, and Mr. Morse was its president, while it had for its professor of mythology one William Cullen Bryant.

Albert Gallatin was president of the National Bank,

at 13 Wall Street. Often at the end of his day's work he would walk around to the small shop in William Street where his young friend Delmonico, the confectioner, was trying to interest the gourmets of the city in his French cooking. Gideon Lee, besides being mayor, was president of the Leather Manufacturers' Bank at 334 Pearl Street. He was the last mayor of New York to be appointed by the common council, for Dix's advertisement in the first *Sun* called an election by which the people of the city gained the right to elect a mayor by popular vote.

A list of the solid citizens of the New York of that year would include Peter Schermerhorn, Nicholas Fish, Robert Lenox, Sheppard Knapp, Samuel Swartwout, Henry Beekman, Henry Delafield, John Mason, William Paulding, David S. Kennedy, Jacob Lorillard, David Lydig, Seth Grosvenor, Elisha Riggs, John Delafield, Peter A. Jay, C. V. S. Roosevelt, Robert Ray, Preserved Fish, Morris Ketchum, Rufus Prime, Philip Hone, William Vail, Gilbert Coutant, and Mortimer Livingston.

These men and their fellows ran the banks and the big business of that day. They read the six-cent papers, mostly those which warned the public that Andrew Jackson was driving the country to the devil. It would be years before the *Sun* would bring the light of common, everyday things into their dignified lives—if it ever did so. Day, the printer, did not look to them to read his paper, although he hoped for some small part of their advertising.

It was a small New York upon which the timid *Sun* threw its still smaller beam. The mass of the people had not been interested in newspapers, because the newspapers brought nothing into their lives but the drone of American and foreign politics. A majority of them were in sympathy with Tammany Hall, particularly since 1821, when the property qualification was removed from the franchise through Democratic effort.

New York had literary publications other than the six-cent papers. The *Knickerbocker Magazine* was founded in January of 1833, with Charles Hoffman, assistant editor of the *American Magazine*, as editor. Among the contributors engaged were William Cullen Bryant and James K. Paulding. The subscription list, it was proudly announced, had no fewer than eight hundred names on it. The *Mechanics' Magazine*, the *Sporting Magazine*, the *American Ploughboy*, the *Journal of Public Morals*, and the *Youth's Temperance Lecturer* were among the periodicals that contended for public favor.

Bryant was a busy man, for he was the chief editor of the *Evening Post* as well as a magazine contributor and a teacher. Fame had come to him early, for "Thanatopsis" was published when he was twenty-three, and "To a Water-fowl" appeared a year later, in 1818. Now, in his thirties, he was no longer the delicate youth, the dreamy poet. One April day in 1831, Bryant and William L. Stone, one of the editors of the *Commercial Advertiser*, had a rare fight in front of the City Hall, the poet beginning it with a cowskin whip swung at Stone's head, and the spectators ending it after Stone had seized the whip. These two were editors of sixpenny "respectables."

Irving and Cooper, Bryant and Halleck, Nathaniel P. Willis and George P. Morris were the largest figures of intellectual New York. In 1833, Irving returned from Europe after a visit that had lasted seventeen years. He was then fifty, and had written his best books. Cooper, half a dozen years younger, had long since basked in the glory that came to him with the publication of *The Spy*, *The Pilot*, and *The Last of the Mohicans*. He and Irving were guests at every cultured function.

Prescott was finishing his first work, *The History of Ferdinand and Isabella*. Bancroft was beginning his *History of the United States*. George Ticknor had written his *Life of Lafayette*. Hawthorne had published only *Fanshawe* and some of the *Twice Told Tales*. Poe was struggling along in Baltimore. Holmes, a medical student, had written a few poems. Dr. John William Draper, later to write his great *History of the Intellectual Development of Europe*, arrived from Liverpool that year to make New York his home.

Longfellow was professor of modern languages at Bowdoin, and unknown to fame as a poet. Whittier had written *Legends of New England* and *Moll Pitcher*. Emerson was in England. Richard Henry Dana and Motley were at Harvard. Thoreau was helping his father to make lead pencils. Parkman, Lowell, and Herman Melville were schoolboys.

Away off in Buffalo was a boy of fourteen who clerked in his uncle's general store by day, selling steel traps to Seneca braves, and by night read Latin, Greek, poetry, history, and the speeches of Andrew Jackson. His name was Charles Anderson Dana.

The leading newspaperman of the day in New York was James Watson Webb, a son of the General Webb who held the Bible upon which Washington took the oath of office as first president. J. Watson Webb had been in the army and, as a journalist, was never for peace at any price. He united the *Morning Courier* and the *Enquirer,* and established a daily horse express between New York and Washington, which is said to have cost $25,000 a month, in order to get news from Congress and the White House twenty-four hours before his rivals.

Webb was famed as a fighter. He had a row with Duff Green in Washington in 1830. In January, 1836, he thrashed James Gordon Bennett in Wall Street. He incited a mob to drive Wood, a singer, from the stage of the Park Theater. In 1838 he sent a challenge to Representative Cilley, of Maine, a classmate of Longfellow and Hawthorne at Bowdoin. Cilley refused to fight, on the ground that he had made no personal reflections on Webb's character; whereupon Representative Graves, of Kentucky, who carried the card for Webb, challenged Cilley for himself, as was the custom. They fought with rifles on the Annapolis Road, and Cilley was killed at the third shot.

In 1842 Webb fought a duel with Representative Marshall, of Kentucky, and not only was wounded, but on his return to New York was sentenced to two years in prison "for leaving the State with the intention of giving or receiving a challenge." At the end of two weeks, however, he was pardoned.

Having deserted Jackson and become a Whig, Webb continued to own and edit the *Courier and Enquirer* until 1861, when it was merged with the *World.* His quarrels, all of political origin, brought prestige to his paper. Ben Day had no dueling pistols. His only chance to advertise the *Sun* was by its own light and its popular price.

Beyond Webb, Day had no lively journalist with whom to contend at the outset, and Webb probably did not dream that the *Sun* would be worthy of a joust. Perhaps fortunately for Day, Horace Greeley had just failed in his attempt to run a one-cent paper. This was the *Morning Post*, which Greeley started in January, 1833, with Francis V. Story, a fellow printer, as his partner, and with a capital of $150. In spite of Greeley's ability it ran for three weeks only.

When George W. Wisner, a young printer who was out of work, applied to the *Sun* for a job, Day told him that he would give him four dollars a week if he would get up early every day and attend the police court, which held its sessions from 4 A.M. on. The people of the city were quite as human then as they are to-day. Unregenerate mortals got drunk and fought in the streets. Others stole shoes. The worst of all beat their wives. Wisner was to be the Balzac of the daybreak court in a year when Balzac himself was writing his *Droll Stories*.

The second issue of the *Sun* continued the typographical error of the day before. The year in the date line of the second page was "1832." The big news in this paper was under date of Plymouth, England, August 1, and it told of the capture of Lisbon by Admiral Napier on July 25. Day—or perhaps it was Wisner—wrote an editorial article about it:

> To us as Americans there can be little of interest in the triumph of one member of a royal family of

Europe over another; and although we can but rejoice at the downfall of the modern Nero who so lately filled the Portuguese throne, yet if rumor speak the truth the victorious Pedro is no better than he should be.

Theatrical advertising appeared in this number, the Park Theater announcing the comedy of "Rip Van Winkle," as redramatized by Mr. Hackett, who played Rip. Mr. Gale was playing "Mazeppa" at the Bowery. Perhaps these advertisements were borrowed from a six-cent paper, but there was one "help wanted" advertisement that was not borrowed. It was the upshot of Day's own idea, destined to bring another revolution in newspaper methods:

> TO THE UNEMPLOYED—A number of steady men can find employment by vending this paper. A liberal discount is allowed to those who buy to sell again.

Before that day there had been no newsboys; no papers were sold in the streets. The big, blanket political organs that masqueraded as newspapers were either sold over the counter or delivered by carriers to the homes of the subscribers. Most of the publishers considered it undignified even to angle for new subscribers, and one of them boasted that his great circulation of perhaps two thousand had come unsolicited.

The first unemployed person to apply for a job selling *Suns* in the streets was a ten-year-old boy, Bernard Flaherty, born in Cork. Years afterward two continents knew him as Barney Williams, Irish comedian, hero of "The Emerald Ring" and "The Connie Soogah," and at one time manager of Wallack's old Broadway Theater.

When Day got some regular subscribers, he sent carriers on routes. He charged them sixty-seven cents a hundred, cash, or seventy-five cents on credit. The first of these carriers was Sam Messenger, who delivered the *Sun* in the Fulton Market district, and who later became a rich livery-stable keeper. Live lads like these, carrying out Day's idea, wrought the greatest change in journalism that ever had been made, for they brought the paper to the people.

On the third day of the *Sun's* life, with Wisner at the pen and Barney Flaherty "hollering" in the startled streets, the editor expressed his yearning that something would happen:

> We newspaper people thrive best on the calamities of others. Give us one of your real Moscow fires, or your Waterloo battlefields; let a Napoleon be dashing with his legions through the world, overturning the thrones of a thousand years and deluging the world with blood and tears; and then we of the types are in our glory.

The yearner had to wait thirty years for another Waterloo, but he got his "real Moscow fire" in about two years, and so close that it singed his eyebrows.

The big story on the first page of the fourth issue of the *Sun* was a conversation between Envy and Candor in regard to the beauties of a Miss H, perhaps a fictitious person. But on the second page, at the head of the editorial column, was a real editorial article approving the course of the British government in freeing the slaves in the West Indies:

> We supposed that the eyes of men were but half open to this case. We imagined that the slave would have to toil on for years and *purchase* what in justice was already *his own.* We did not once dream that light had so far progressed as to prepare the British nation for the colossal stride in justice and humanity and benevolence which they are about to make. The abolition of West Indian slavery will form a brilliant era in the annals of the world. It will circle with a halo of imperishable glory the brows of the transcendent spirits who wield the present destinies of the British Empire.
>
> Would to Heaven that the honor of leading the way in this godlike enterprise had been reserved to our own country! But as the opportunity for this is passed, we trust we shall at least avoid the everlasting disgrace of long refusing to imitate so bright and glorious an example.

Thus the *Sun* came out for the freedom of the slave twenty-eight years before that freedom was to be accomplished in the United States through war. The *Sun* was the *Sun* of Day, but the hand was the hand of Wisner. That young man was an Abolitionist before the word was coined.

"Wisner was a pretty smart young fellow," said Mr. Day nearly fifty years afterward, "but he and I never agreed. I was rather Democratic in my notions. Wisner, whenever he got a chance, was always sticking in his damned little Abolitionist articles." On September 10, Mr. Day printed an editorial grieving over the existence of slavery, but hitting at the methods of the Abolitionists.

The *Sun* was a week old before it contained dramatic

criticism, its first subject in that field being the appearance of Mr. and Mrs. Wood at the Park Theater in "Cinderella," a comic opera. The paper's first animal story was printed on September 12, recording the fact that on the previous Sunday about sixty wild pigeons stayed in a tree at the Battery nearly half an hour.

On September 14, the *Sun* printed its first illustration—a two-column cut of "Herschel's Forty-Feet Telescope." This was Sir W. Herschel, then dead some ten years, and the telescope was on his grounds at Slough, near Windsor, England. Another knighted Herschel with another telescope in a far land was to play a big part in the fortunes of the *Sun,* but that comes later. In the issue with the cut of the telescope was a paragraph about a rumor that Fanny Kemble, who had just captivated American theatergoers, had been married to Pierce Butler, of Philadelphia—as, indeed, she had.

Broadway seems to have had its lure as early as 1833, for in the *Sun* of September 17, on the first page is a plaint by "Citizen":

> They talk of the pleasures of the country, but would to God I had never been persuaded to leave the labor of the city for such woful pleasures. Oh, Broadway, Broadway! In an evil hour did I forsake thee for verdant walks and flowery landscapes and that there tiresome piece of made water. What walk is so agreeable as a walk through the streets of New York? What landscape more flowery than those of the print-shops? And what water was made by man equal to the Hudson?

This was followed by uplifting little essays on "Suicide" and "Robespierre." The chief news of the day—

that John Quincy Adams had accepted a nomination from the Anti-Masons—was on an inside page. What was possibly of more interest to the readers, it was announced that thereafter a ton of coal would be 2,000 pounds instead of 2,240—Lackawanna, broken and sifted, $6.50 a ton.

On Saturday, September 21, when it was only eighteen days old, the *Sun* adopted a new headline. The letters remained the same, but the eagle device of the first issue was supplanted by the solar orb rising over hills and sea. This design was used only until December 2, when its place was taken by a third emblem—a printing press shedding symbolical effulgence upon the earth.

The *Sun's* first book notice appeared on September 23, when it acknowledged the sixtieth volume of the *Family Library* (Harper), this being a biography of Charlemagne by G. P. R. James. "It treats of a most important period in the history of France." The *Sun* had little space then for book reviews or politics. Of its attitude toward the great financial fight then being waged, this lone paragraph gives a good view:

> The *Globe* of Monday contains in six columns the reasons which prompted the President to remove the public deposits from the United States Bank, which were read to his assembled cabinet on the 18th inst.

Nicholas Biddle and his friends could fill other papers with arguments, but the *Sun* kept its space for police items, stories of authenticated ghosts, and yarns about the late Emperor Napoleon. The removal of William J. Duane as secretary of the treasury got two lines on a page where a big shark caught off Barnstable got three

THE  SUN.

NUMBER 1.] NEW YORK, TUESDAY, SEPTEMBER 3, 1833. [PRICE ONE PENNY.

PUBLISHED DAILY,

AN IRISH CAPTAIN.

THE FIRST ISSUE OF "THE SUN"
September 3, 1833.

lines, and the feeding of the anaconda at the American Museum a quarter of a column. Miss Susan Allen, who bought a cigar on Broadway and was arrested when she smoked it while she danced in the street, was featured more prominently than the expected visit to New York of Mr. Henry Clay, after whom millions of cigars were to be named. For the satisfaction of universal curiosity it must be reported that Miss Allen was discharged.

On October 1 of that same year, 1833, the *Sun* came out for better fire-fighting apparatus, urging that the engines should be drawn by horses, as in London. In the same issue it assailed the gambling house in Park Row and scorned the allegation of Colonel Hamilton, a British traveler, that the toothbrush was unknown in America. Slowly the paper was getting better, printing more local news; and it could afford to, for the penny *Sun* idea had taken hold of New York, and the sales were larger every week.

Wisner was stretching the police-court pieces out to nearly two columns. Now and then, perhaps when Mr. Day was away fishing, the reporter would slip in an Abolition paragraph or a gloomy poem on the horrors of slavery. But he was so valuable that, while his chief did not raise his salary of four dollars a week, he offered him half the paper, the same to be paid for out of the profits. And so, in January of 1834, Wisner became a half owner of the *Sun*. Benton, another *Sun* printer, also wanted an interest, and left when he could not get it.

Before it was two months old the *Sun* had begun to take an interest in aëronautics. It printed a full column, October 16, 1833, on the subject of Durant's balloon ascensions, and quoted Napoleon as saying that the only insurmountable difficulty of the balloon in war was the impossibility of guiding its course. "This difficulty Dr. Durant is now endeavoring to obviate." And the *Sun* added:

> May we not therefore look to the time, in perspective, when our atmosphere will be traversed with as much facility as our waters?

The union printers were lively even in the first days of the *Sun,* which announced, on October 21, 1833, that the *Journal of Commerce* paid its journeymen only ten dollars a week, and added:

> The proprietors of other morning papers cheerfully pay twelve dollars. Therefore, the office of the *Journal of Commerce* is what printers term a rat office—and the term "rat," with the followers of the same profession with Faust, Franklin, and Stanhope, is a most odious term.

At the end of its first month the *Sun* was getting more and more advertising. Its news was lively enough, considering the times. Rum, the cholera in Mexico, assassinations in the South, the police court, the tour of Henry Clay, and poems by Walter Scott were its long suit. The circulation of the little paper was now about twelve hundred copies, and the future seemed promising, even if Mr. Day did print, at suspiciously frequent intervals, articles inveighing against the debtors'-prison law.

The Astor House was at first to be called the Park Hotel, for the *Sun* of October 29, 1833, announced editorially:

THE PARK HOTEL—Mr. W. B. Astor gives notice that he will receive proposals for building the long-contemplated hotel in Broadway, between Barclay and Vesey Streets.

The *Sun* blew its own horn for the first time on November 9, 1833.

Its success is now beyond question, and it has exceeded the most sanguine anticipations of its publishers in its circulation and advertising patronage. Scarcely two months has it existed in the typographical firmament, and it has a daily circulation of upward of two thousand copies, besides a steadily increasing advertising patronage. Although of a character (we hope) deserving the encouragement of all classes of society, it is more especially valuable to those who cannot well afford to incur the expense of subscribing to a "blanket-sheet" and paying ten dollars per annum.

In conclusion we may be permitted to remark that the penny press, by diffusing useful knowledge among the operative classes of society, is effecting the march of intelligence to a greater degree than any other mode of instruction.

The same article called attention to the fact that the "penny" papers of England were really two-cent papers. The *Sun's* price had been announced as "one penny" on the earliest numbers, but on October 8, when it was a little more than a month old, the legend was changed to read: "Price one cent."

The *Sun* ran its first serial in the third month of its existence. This was *The Life of Davy Crockett,* dictated or authorized by the frontiersman himself. It must have been a relief to the readers to get away from the usual dull reprint from foreign papers that had been filling the *Sun's* first page. In those days the first pages were always the dullest, but Crockett's lively stories about bear hunts enlivened the *Sun*.

Other celebrities were often mentioned. Aaron Burr, now old and feeble, was writing his memoirs. Martin Van Buren had taken lodgings at the City Hotel. The Siamese Twins were arrested in the South for beating a man. "Mr. Clay arrived in town last evening and attended the new opera." This was "Fra Diavolo," in which Mr. and Mrs. Wood sang at the Park Theater.

On December 5, 1833, the *Sun* printed the longest news piece it had ever put in type—the message of President Jackson to the Congress. This took up three of the four pages, and crowded out nearly all the advertising.

On December 17, in the fourth month of its life, the *Sun* announced that it had procured "a machine press, on which one thousand impressions can be taken in an hour. The daily circulation is now nearly *four thousand.*" It was a happy Christmas for Day and Wisner. The *Sun* surely was shining!

The paper retained its original size and shape during the whole of 1834, and rarely printed more than four pages. As it grew older, it published more and more local items and developed greater interest in local affairs. The first page was taken up with advertising and reprint. A state election might have taken place the day before, but on page 1 the *Sun* worshipers looked for a bit of fiction or history. What were the fortunes of William L. Marcy as compared to a two-column thriller,

"The Idiot's Revenge," or "Captain Chicken and Gentle Sophia"?

The headlines were all small, and most of them italics. Here are samples:

INGRATITUDE OF A CAT

PERSONALITY OF NAPOLEON

WONDERFUL ANTICS OF FLEAS

BROUGHT TO IT BY RUM

The news paragraphs were sometimes models of condensation:

PICKPOCKETS—On Friday night a Gentleman lost $100 at the Opera and then $25 at Tammany Hall.

The Hon. Daniel Webster will leave town this morning for Washington.

James G. Bennett has become sole proprietor and editor of the Philadelphia *Courier*.

Colonel Crockett, it is expected, will visit the Bowery Theater this evening.

RUMOR—It was rumored in Washington on the 6th that a duel would take place the next day between two members of the House.

SUDDEN DEATH—Ann McDonough, of Washington Street, attempted to drink a pint of rum on a wager, on Wednesday afternoon last. Before it was half swallowed Ann was a corpse. Served her right.

> Bayington, the murderer, we learn by a contemporary, was formerly employed in this city on the *Journal of Commerce*. No wonder he came to an untimely fate.
>
> DUEL—We understand that a duel was fought at Hoboken on Friday morning last between a gentleman of Canada and a French gentleman of this city, in which the latter was wounded. The parties should be arrested.
>
> LAMENTABLE DEATH—The camelopard shipped at Calcutta for New York died the day after it was embarked. "We could have better spared a better" *crittur,* as Shakespeare doesn't say.

The *Sun,* although read largely by Jacksonians, did not take the side of any political party. It favored national and state economy and city cleanliness. It dismissed the New York Legislature of 1843 thus:

> The Legislature of this State closed its arduous duties yesterday. It has increased the number of our banks and fixed a heavy load of debt upon posterity.

Nothing more. If the readers wanted more they could fly to the ample bosoms of the sixpennies; but apparently they were satisfied, for in April of 1834 the *Sun's* circulation reached eight thousand, and Colonel Webb, of the *Courier and Enquirer,* was bemoaning the success of "penny trash." The *Sun* replied to him by saying that the public had been "imposed upon by ten-dollar trash long enough." The *Journal of Commerce* also slanged the *Sun,* which promptly announced that the *Journal* was conducted by "a company of rich, aristocratical men," and that it would take sides with any party to gain a subscriber.

The influence of Partner Wisner, the Abolitionist, was evident in many pages of the *Sun*. On June 23, 1834, it printed a piece about Martin Palmer, who was "pelted down with stones in Wall Street on suspicion of being a runaway slave," and paid its respects to Boudinot, a southerner in New York who was reputed to be a tracker of runaways. It was he who had set the crowd after the black:

> The man who will do this will do anything; he would dance on his mother's grave; he would invade the sacred precincts of the tomb and rob a corpse of its windingsheet; he has no SOUL. It is said that this useless fellow is about to commence a suit against us for libel. Try it, Mr. Boudinot!

During the anti-abolition riots of that year the *Sun* took a firm stand against the disturbers, although there is little doubt that many of them were its own readers.

The paper made a vigorous little crusade against the evils of the Bridewell in City Hall Park, where dozens of wretches suffered in the filth of the debtors' prison. The *Sun* was a live wire when the cholera reappeared, and it put to rout the sixpenny papers which tried to make out that the disease was not cholera, but "summer complaint." Incidentally, the advertising columns of that day, in nearly all the papers, were filled with patent "cholera cures."

The *Sun* had an eye for urban refinement, too, and begged the aldermen to see to it that pigs were prevented from roaming in City Hall Park. In the matter of silver forks, then a novelty, it was more conservative, as the following paragraph, printed in November, 1834, would indicate:

> EXTREME NICETY—The author of the *Book of Etiquette,* recently printed in London, says: "Silver forks are now common at every respectable table, and for my part I cannot see how it is possible to eat a dinner comfortably without them." The booby ought to be compelled to cut his beefsteak with a piece of old barrelhoop on a wooden trencher.

Almost every newspaper editor in that era had a theater feud at one day or another. The *Sun's* quarrel was with Farren, the manager of the Bowery, where Forrest was playing. So the *Sun* said:

> DAMN THE YANKEES—We are informed by a correspondent (though we have not seen the announcement ourselves) that Farren, the chap who damned the Yankees so lustily the other day, and who is now under bonds for a gross outrage on a respectable butcher near the Bowery Theater, is intending to make his appearance on the Bowery stage THIS EVENING!

Five hundred citizens gathered at the theater that night, waited until nine o'clock, and then charged through the doors, breaking up the performance of "Metamora." The *Sun* described it:

> The supernumeraries scud from behind the scenes like quails—the stock actors' teeth chattered—*Oceana* looked imploringly at the good-for-nothing

Yankees—*Nahmeeoke* trembled—*Guy of Godalwin* turned on his heel, and *Metamora* coolly shouldered his tomahawk and walked off the stage.

The management announced that Farren was discharged. The Mayor of New York and Edwin Forrest made conciliatory speeches, and the crowd went away.

The attacks of Colonel Stone, editor of the six-cent *Commercial,* aroused the *Sun* to retaliate in kind. A column about the colonel ended thus:

> He was then again cowskinned by Mr. Bryant of the *Post,* and was most unpoetically flogged near the American Hotel. He has always been the slave of avarice, cowardice, and meanness. . . . The next time he sees fit to attack the penny press we hope he will confine himself to facts.

It must be said of Colonel Stone that he was a man of literary and political attainments. He was editor of the *Commercial Advertiser* for more than twenty years.

The colonel did not reform to the *Sun's* liking at once, but the feud lessened, and presently it was the *Transcript*—a penny paper which sprang up when the *Sun's* success was assured—to which the *Sun* took its biggest cudgels. One of the *Transcript's* editors, it said, had passed a bogus three-dollar bill on the Bank of Troy. Another walked "on both sides of the street, like a two-penny postman." But, added the *Sun,* "we never let personalities creep in."

The New York *Times*—not the present *Times*—had also started up, and it dared to boast of a circulation "greater than any in the city except the *Courier.*" Said the *Sun:*

> If the daily circulation of the *Sun* be not larger than that of the *Times* and *Courier* both, then may we be hung up by the ears and flogged to death with a rattlesnake's skin.

The *Sun* took no risk in this. By November of 1834 its circulation was above ten thousand. On December 3, it published the President's message in full and circulated fifteen thousand copies. At the beginning of 1835 it announced a new press—a Napier, built by R. Hoe and Company—new type, and a bigger paper, circulating twenty thousand. The print paper was to cost four-fifths of a cent a copy, but the *Sun* was getting lots of advertising. With the increase in size, that New Year's Day, the *Sun* adopted the motto, "It Shines for All," which it used for seventy years. This motto doubtless was suggested by the sign of the famous Rising Sun Tavern, or Howard's Inn, which then stood at the junction of Bedford and Jamaica turnpikes, in East New York. The sign, which was in front of the tavern as early as 1776, was supported on posts near the road and bore a rude picture of a rising sun and the motto which Day adopted.

As prosperity came, the news columns improved. The sensational was not the only pabulum fed to the reader. Beside the story of a duel between two midshipmen he would find a review of the Burr autobiography, just out. Gossip about Fanny Kemble's quarrel with her father—the *Sun* was vexed with the actress because she said that New York audiences were made up of butchers—would appear next to a staid report of the doings of Congress.

The success of Mr. Day's paper was so great that every printer and newspaperman in New York longed to run a penny journal. On June 22, 1835, the paper's name appeared at the head of the editorial column on page 2 as the *True Sun,* although on the first page the bold headline *THE SUN,* remained as usual. An editorial note said:

> We have changed our inside head to *True Sun* for reasons which will hereafter be made known.

On the following day the *True Sun* title was entirely missing, and its absence was explained in an editorial article as follows:

> Having understood on Wednesday [June 21] that a daily paper was about being issued in this city as nearly like our own as it could be got up, under the title of the *True Sun,* for the avowed purpose of benefiting the proprietors at our expense, we yesterday changed our inside title, being determined to place an injunction upon any such piratical proceedings. Yesterday morning the anticipated *Sun* made its appearance, and at first sight we immediately abandoned our intention of defending ourselves legally, being convinced that it is a mere catchpenny second-hand concern which (had it our whole list of patronage) would in one month be among the "Things that were." It is published by William F. Short and edited by Stephen B. Butler, who announces that his "politics are Whig."

On June 28, six days after the *True Sun's* first appearance, the *Sun* announced the failure of the pretender. The *True Sun's* proprietors, it said, "have concluded to abandon their piratical course."

Another *True Sun* was issued by Benjamin H. Day in

1840, two years after he sold the *Sun* to Moses Y. Beach. A third *True Sun*, established by former employees of the *Sun* on March 20, 1843, ran for more than a year. A daily called the *Citizen and True Sun*, started in 1845, had a short life.

When a contemporary did not fail the *Sun* poked fun at it:

> MAJOR NOAH'S SINGULARITY—The *Evening Star* of yesterday comes out in favor of the French, lottery, gambling, and phrenology for ladies. Is the man crazy?

For their attacks on Attree, the editor of the *Transcript*, Messrs. Day and Wisner got themselves indicted for criminal libel. They took it calmly:

> Bigger men than we have passed through that ordeal. There is Major Noah, the Grand Mogul of the editorial tribe, who has not only been indicted, but, we believe, placed at the bar. Then there's Colonel Webb, no longer ago than last autumn he was indicted by the grand jury of Delaware County. The colonel, it is said, didn't consider this a fair business transaction, and, brushing up the mahogany pistol, he took his coach and hounds, drove up to good old Delaware, and bid defiance to the whole posse comitatus of the county. The greatest men in the country have some time in the course of their lives been indicted.

A few weeks later, when Attree, who had left the *Transcript* to write "horribles" for the *Courier*, was terribly beaten in the street, the *Sun* denounced the assault and tried to expose the assailants.

In February, 1835, a few days after the indictment of the partners, Mr. Wisner was challenged to a duel by a quack dentist whose medicines the *Sun* had exposed. The *Sun* announced editorially that Wisner accepted the challenge, and that, having the choice of weapons, he chose syringes charged with the dentist's own medicine, the distance five paces. No duel!

It would seem that the *Sun* owners sought a challenge from the fiery James Watson Webb of the mahogany pistol, for they made many a dig at his sixpenny paper. Here is a sample:

> OUTRAGEOUS—The *Courier and Enquirer* of Saturday morning is just twice as large as its usual size. The sheet is now large enough for a blanket and two pairs of pillow-cases, and it contains, in printers' language, 698,300 ems—equal to eight volumes of the ordinary-sized novels of the present day. If the reading matter were printed in pica type and put in one unbroken line, it would reach from Nova Zembla to Terra del Fuego. Such a paper is an insult to a civilized community.

A little later, when Colonel Webb's paper boasted of "the largest circulation," the *Sun* offered to bet the colonel a thousand dollars—the money to go to the Washington Monument Association—that the *Sun* had a circulation twice as great as that of the big sixpenny daily.

It must not be thought, however, that the *Sun* did not attempt to treat the serious matters of the day. It handled them very well, considering the lack of facilities. The war crisis with France, happily dispelled; the amazing project of the Erie Railroad to build a line as far west as Chautauqua County, New York; the antiabolitionist riot and the little religious rows; the ambitions of Daniel Webster; and the approach of Halley's comet—all these had their half column or so.

When Matthias the Prophet, the Dowie of that day, was brought to trial in White Plains, Westchester County, on a charge of having poisoned a Mr. Elijah Pierson, the *Sun* sent a reporter to that then distant court. It is possible that this reporter was Benjamin H. Day himself. At any rate, Day attended the trial, and there met a man who that very summer made the *Sun* the talk of the world and brought to the young paper the largest circulation of any daily.

CHAPTER III

RICHARD ADAMS LOCKE'S MOON HOAX

A Magnificent Fake Which Deceived Two Continents, Brought to the "Sun" the Largest Circulation in the World and, in Edgar Allan Poe's Opinion, Established Penny Papers.

THE man whom Day met at the murder trial in White Plains was Richard Adams Locke, a reporter who was destined to kick up more dust than perhaps any other man of his profession. As he comes on the stage, we must let his predecessor, George W. Wisner, pass into the wings.

When Wisner's health became poor, in the summer of 1835, he expressed a desire to get away from New York. Mr. Day paid him five thousand dollars for his interest in the paper and he went west and settled at Pontiac, Michigan. There his health improved, his fortune increased, and he was at one time a member of the Michigan Legislature.

When Day found that Locke was the best reporter attending the trial of Matthias the Prophet, he hired him to write a series of articles on the religious fakir. These, the first "feature stories" that ever appeared in the *Sun,* were printed on the front page.

A few weeks later, while the Matthias articles were still being sold on the streets in pamphlet form, Locke went to Day and told him that his boss, Colonel Webb of the *Courier and Enquirer,* had discharged him for working for the *Sun* "on the side." Wisner was about to leave the paper, and Day was glad to hire Locke, for he needed an editorial writer. Twelve dollars a week was the alluring wage, and Locke accepted it.

Locke was then thirty-five—ten years senior to his employer. Let his contemporary, Edgar Allan Poe, describe him:

> He is about five feet seven inches in height, symmetrically formed; there is an air of distinction about his whole person—the *air noble* of genius. His face is strongly pitted by the smallpox, and, perhaps from the same cause, there is a marked obliquity in the eyes; a certain calm, clear *luminousness*, however, about these latter amply compensates for the defect, and the forehead is truly beautiful in its intellectuality. I am acquainted with no person possessing so fine a forehead as Mr. Locke.

Locke was nine years older than Poe, who at this time had most of his fame ahead of him. Poe was quick to recognize the quality of Locke's writings; indeed, the poet saw, perhaps more clearly than others of that period, that America was full of good writers—a fact of which the general public was neglectful. This was Poe's tribute to Locke's literary gift:

> His prose style is noticeable for its concision, luminosity, completeness—each quality in its proper place. He has that *method* so generally characteristic of genius proper. Everything he writes is a model in its peculiar way, serving just the purposes intended and nothing to spare.

The *Sun's* new writer was a collateral descendant of John Locke, the English philosopher of the seventeenth

Richard Adams Locke
Author of "The Moon Hoax."

Bernard Flaherty
The Sun's first newsboy.

THE SUN.

The First Instalment of "The Moon Hoax"

century. He was born on September 22, 1800, but his birthplace was not New York, as his contemporary biographers wrote. It was East Brent, Somersetshire, England. His early American friends concealed this fact when writing of Locke, for they feared that his English birth (all the wounds of war had not healed) would keep him out of some of the literary clubs. He was educated by his mother and by private tutors until he was nineteen, when he entered Cambridge. While still a student he contributed to the *Bee*, the *Imperial Magazine*, and other English publications. When he left Cambridge he had the hardihood to start the London *Republican*, the title of which describes its purpose. This was a failure, for London declined to warm to the theories of American democracy, no matter how scholarly their expression.

Abandoning the *Republican*, young Locke devoted himself to literature and science. He ran a periodical called the *Cornucopia* for about six months, but it was not a financial success, and in 1832, with his wife and infant daughter, he went to New York. Colonel Webb put him at work on his paper.

While he lived in London, Locke was a regular reader of the Edinburgh *New Philosophical Journal*, and he brought some copies of it to America. One of these, an issue of 1826, contained an article by Dr. Thomas Dick, of Dundee, suggesting the feasibility of communicating with the moon by means of great stone symbols on the face of the earth. The people of the moon—if there were any—would fathom the diagrams and reply in a similar way. Dr. Dick explained afterward that he wrote this piece with the idea of satirizing a certain coterie of eccentric German astronomers.

Now it happened that Sir John Frederick William Herschel, the greatest astronomer of his time, and the son of the celebrated astronomer Sir William Herschel, went to South Africa in January, 1834, and established an observatory at Feldhausen, near Cape Town, with the intention of completing his survey of the sidereal heavens by examining the southern skies as he had swept the northern, thus to make the first telescopic survey of the whole surface of the visible heavens.

Locke knew about Sir John and his mission and he laid a plan before Mr. Day. It was a plot as well as a plan, and the first angle of the plot appeared on the second page of the *Sun* on August 21, 1835:

> CELESTIAL DISCOVERIES—The Edinburgh *Courant* says—"We have just learnt from an eminent publisher in this city that Sir John Herschel, at the Cape of Good Hope, has made some astronomical discoveries of the most wonderful description, by means of an immense telescope of an entirely new principle."

Nothing further appeared until Tuesday, August 25, when three columns of the *Sun's* first page took the newspaper and scientific worlds by the ears. Those were not the days of big type. The *Sun's* heading read:

GREAT ASTRONOMICAL DISCOVERIES

LATELY MADE
BY SIR JOHN HERSCHEL, LL.D., F.R.S., &C.

At the Cape of Good Hope.

[*From Supplement to the Edinburgh Journal of Science.*]

It may as well be said here that although there had been an Edinburgh *Journal of Science,* it ceased to exist several years before 1835. The periodical to which Dr. Dick, of Dundee, contributed his moon theories was, in a way, the successor to the *Journal of Science,* but it was called the *New Philosophical Journal.* The likeness of names was not great, but enough to cause some confusion. It is also noteworthy that the sly Locke credited to a supplement, rather than to the *Journal of Science* itself, the revelations which he that day began to pour before the eyes of *Sun* readers. Thus he started:

> In this unusual addition to our *Journal* we have the happiness of making known to the British public, and thence to the whole civilized world, recent discoveries in astronomy which will build an imperishable monument to the age in which we live, and confer upon the present generation of the human race proud distinction through all future time.

After solemnly dwelling on the awe which mortal man must feel upon peering into the secrets of the sky, the article declared that Sir John

> paused several hours before he commenced his observations, that he might prepare his own mind for discoveries which he knew would fill the minds of myriads of his fellow men with astonishment.

It continued:

> And well might he pause! From the hour the first human pair opened their eyes to the glories of the blue firmament above them, there has been no accession to human knowledge at all comparable in

sublime interest to that which he has been the honored agent in supplying. Well might he pause! He was about to become the sole depository of wondrous secrets which had been hid from the eyes of all men that had lived since the birth of time.

At the end of a half column of glorification, the writer got down to brass tacks:

To render our enthusiasm intelligible, we will state at once that by means of a telescope, of vast dimensions and an entirely new principle, the younger Herschel, at his observatory in the southern hemisphere, has already made the most extraordinary discoveries in every plant of our solar system; has discovered planets in other solar systems; has obtained a distinct view of objects in the moon, fully equal to that which the unaided eye commands of terrestrial objects at the distance of one hundred yards; has affirmatively settled the question whether this satellite be inhabited, and by what orders of beings; has firmly established a new theory of cometary phenomena; and has solved or corrected nearly every leading problem of mathematical astronomy.

And where was the *Journal of Science* getting this mine of astronomical revelation for its supplement? The mystery is explained at once:

We are indebted to the devoted friendship of Dr. Andrew Grant, the pupil of the elder, and for several years past the inseparable coadjutor of the younger Herschel. The amanuensis of the latter at the Cape of Good Hope, and the indefatigable superintendent of his telescope during the whole period of its construction and operations, Dr. Grant has been able to supply us with intelligence equal in general interest at least to that which Dr. Herschel himself has transmitted to the Royal Society.

Regarding the illustrations which, according to the implications of the text, accompanied the supplement, the writer was specific. Most of them, he stated, were copies of

> drawings taken in the observatory by Herbert Home, Esq., who accompanied the last powerful series of reflectors from London to the Cape. The engraving of the belts of Jupiter is a reduced copy of an imperial folio drawing by Dr. Herschel himself. The segment of the inner ring of Saturn is from a large drawing by Dr. Grant.

A history of Sir William Herschel's work and a description of his telescopes took up a column of the *Sun*, and on top of this came the details—as the *Journal* printed them—of Sir John's plans to outdo his father by revolutionary methods and a greater telescope.

Details of the casting of a great lens came next. It was 24 feet in diameter, and weighed nearly 15,000 pounds after it was polished; its estimated magnifying power was 42,000 times. As he saw it safely started on its way to Africa, Sir John "expressed confidence in his ultimate ability to study even the entomology of the moon, in case she contained insects upon her surface."

Thus ended the first installment of the story. Where had the *Sun* got the *Journal of Science* supplement? An editorial article answered that "it was very politely furnished us by a medical gentleman immediately from Scotland, in consequence of a paragraph which appeared on Friday last from the Edinburgh *Courant.*" The article added:

> The portion which we publish to-day is introductory to celestial discoveries of higher and more universal interest than any, in any science yet known to the human race. Now indeed it may be said that we live in an age of discovery.

It cannot be said that the whole town buzzed with excitement that day. Perhaps this first installment was a bit over the heads of most readers; it was so technical, so foreign. But in Nassau and Ann Streets, wherever two newspapermen were gathered together, there was buzzing enough.

Nearly four columns of the revelations appeared on the following day—August 26, 1835. This time the reading public came trooping into camp, for the *Sun's* reprint of the *Journal of Science* supplement got beyond the stage of preliminaries and predictions, and began to tell of what was to be seen on the moon. Let us plunge in at about the point where the public plunged:

> The specimen of lunar vegetation, however, which they had already seen, had decided a question of too exciting an interest to induce them to retard its exit. It had demonstrated that the moon has an atmosphere constituted similarly to our own, and capable of sustaining organized and, therefore, most probably, animal life.

A column farther on, in a wonderful valley of this wonderful moon, life at last burst upon the seers:

> In the shade of the woods on the southeastern side we beheld continuous herds of brown quadrupeds,

having all the external characteristics of the bison, but more diminutive than any species of the *bos* genus in our natural history. Its tail was like that of our *bos grunniens;* but in its semicircular horns, the hump on its shoulders, the depth of its dewlap, and the length of its shaggy hair, it closely resembled the species to which I have compared it.

It had, however, one widely distinctive feature, which we afterward found common to nearly every lunar quadruped we have discovered; namely, a remarkable fleshy appendage over the eyes, crossing the whole breadth of the forehead and united to the ears. We could most distinctly perceive this hairy veil, which was shaped like the upper front outline of the cap known to the ladies as Mary Queen of Scots cap, lifted and lowered by means of the ears. It immediately occurred to the acute mind of Dr. Herschel that this was a providential contrivance to protect the eyes of the animal from the great extremes of light and darkness to which all the inhabitants of our side of the moon are periodically subjected.

The next animal perceived would be classed on earth as a monster. It was a bluish lead color, about the size of a goat, with a head and beard like him, and a *single horn,* slightly inclined forward from the perpendicular. The female was destitute of the horn and beard, but had a much longer tail. It was gregarious, and chiefly abounded on the acclivitous glades of the woods. In elegance of symmetry it rivaled the antelope, and like him it seemed an agile, sprightly creature, running with great speed and springing from the green turf with all the unaccountable antics of the young lamb or kitten.

This beautiful creature afforded us the most exquisite amusement. The mimicry of its movements upon our white-painted canvas was as faithful and luminous as that of animals within a few yards of a camera obscura when seen pictured upon its tympan. Frequently, when attempting to put our fingers upon its beard, it would suddenly bound away into oblivion, as if conscious of our earthly impertinence; but then others would appear, whom we could not prevent nibbling the herbage, say or do what we would to them.

So, at last, the people of earth knew something concrete about the live things of the moon. Goats with beards were there, and every New Yorker knew goats, for they fed upon the rocky hills of Harlem. And the moon had birds, too:

> On examining the center of this delightful valley we found a large, branching river, abounding with lovely islands and water-birds of numerous kinds. A species of gray pelican was the most numerous, but black and white cranes, with unreasonably long legs and bill, were also quite common. . . . Near the upper extremity of one of these islands we obtained a glimpse of a strange amphibious creature of a spherical form, which rolled with great velocity across the pebbly beach, and was lost sight of in the strong current which set off from this angle of the island.

At this point clouds intervened, and the Herschel party had to call it a day. But it had been a big day and nobody who read the *Sun* wondered that the astronomers tossed off "congratulatory bumpers of the best 'East India particular,' and named this place of wonders the Valley of the Unicorn." So ended the *Sun* story of

August 26, but an editorial paragraph assured the patrons of the paper that on the morrow there would be a treat even richer.

What did the other papers say? In the language of a later and less elegant period, most of them ate it up. The *Daily Advertiser* declared:

> No article has appeared for years that will command so general a perusal and publication. Sir John has added a stock of knowledge to the present age that will immortalize his name and place it high on the page of science.

The *Mercantile Advertiser,* knowing that its lofty readers were unlikely to see the moon revelations in the lowly *Sun,* hastened to begin reprinting the articles in full, with the remark that the document appeared to have intrinsic evidence of authenticity.

The *Times,* a daily then only a year old, and destined to live only eighteen months more—later, of course, the title was used by a successful daily—said that everything in the *Sun* story was probable and plausible, and had an "air of intense verisimilitude."

The New York *Sunday News* advised the incredulous to be patient:

> Our doubts and incredulity may be a wrong to the learned astronomer, and the circumstances of this wonderful discovery may be correct.

The *Courier and Enquirer* said nothing at all. Like the *Journal of Commerce,* it hated the *Sun* for a lucky upstart. Both of these sixpenny respectables stood silent, with their axes behind their backs.

The *Herald,* then about four months old, said not a word about the moon story. In fact, that was a period in which it said nothing at all about any subject, for the fire of that summer had unfortunately wiped out its plant. On the very days when the moon stories appeared, Mr. Bennett stood cracking his knuckles in front of his new establishment, the basement of 202 Broadway, trying to hurry the men who were installing a double-cylinder press. Being a wise person, he advertised his progress in the *Sun.* It may have vexed him to see the circulation of the *Sun*—which he had imitated in character and price—bound higher and higher as he stood helpless.

The third installment of the literary treasure introduced to *Sun* readers new and important regions of the moon—the Vagabond Mountains, the Lake of Death, craters of extinct volcanoes twenty-eight hundred feet high, and twelve luxuriant forests divided by open plains "in which waved an ocean of verdure, and which were probably prairies like those of North America." The details were satisfying:

> Dr. Herschel has classified not less than thirty-eight species of forest trees and nearly twice this number of plants, found in this tract alone, which are widely different to those found in more equatorial latitudes. Of animals he classified nine species of mammalia and five of oviparia. Among the former is a small kind of reindeer, the elk, the moose, the horned bear, and the biped beaver.
>
> The last resembles the beaver of the earth in every other respect than its destitution of a tail and its invariable habit of walking upon only two feet. It

> carries its young in its arms, like a human being, and walks with an easy, gliding motion. Its huts are constructed better and higher than those of many tribes of human savages, and from the appearance of smoke in nearly all of them there is no doubt of its being acquainted with the use of fire.

The largest lake described was 266 miles long and 193 wide, shaped like the Bay of Bengal, and studded with volcanic islands. One island in a large bay was pinnacled with quartz crystals as brilliant as fire. Near by roamed zebras three feet high. Golden and blue pheasants strutted about.

The *Sun* of Friday, August 28, 1835, was a notable issue. Not yet two years old, Mr. Day's newspaper had the satisfaction of announcing that it had achieved the largest circulation of any daily in the world. It had, it said, 15,440 regular subscribers in New York and 700 in Brooklyn, and it sold 2,000 in the streets and 1,220 out of town—a grand total of 19,360 copies, as against the 17,000 circulation of the London *Times*. The double-cylinder Napier press in the building at Nassau and Spruce Streets—later the home of the *Tribune*, and to which the *Sun* had moved on August 3—had to run ten hours a day to satisfy the public demand. People waited with more or less patience until three o'clock in the afternoon to read about the moon.

That very issue contained the most sensational installment of all the moon series, for through that mystic chain which included Dr. Grant, the supplement of the Edinburgh *Journal of Science*, the "medical gentleman immediately from Scotland," and the *Sun*, public curiosity as to the presence of human creatures on the orb of night was satisfied at last. The astronomers, according to this scholarly narrative, were looking upon cliffs and crags of a new part of the moon:

> But whilst gazing upon them in a perspective of about half a mile we were thrilled with astonishment to perceive four successive flocks of large winged creatures, wholly unlike any kind of birds, descend with a slow, even motion from the cliffs on the western side and alight upon the plain. They were first noticed by Dr. Herschel, who exclaimed:
>
> "Now, gentlemen, my theories against your proofs, which you have often found a pretty even bet, we have here something worth looking at. I was confident that if ever we found beings in human shape it would be in this longitude, and that they would be provided by their Creator with some extraordinary powers of locomotion. First, exchange for my Number D."
>
> This lens, being soon introduced, gave us a fine half-mile distance; and we counted three parties of these creatures, of twelve, nine, and fifteen in each, walking erect toward a small wood near the base of the eastern precipices. Certainly they were like human beings, for their wings had now disappeared, and their attitude in walking was both erect and dignified.
>
> Having observed them at this distance for some minutes, we introduced lens H.*z*., which brought them to the apparent proximity of eighty yards—the highest clear magnitude we possessed until the latter end of March, when we effected an improvement in the gas burners.
>
> About half of the first party had passed beyond our canvas; but of all the others we had a perfectly

distinct and deliberate view. They averaged four feet in height, were covered, except on the face, with short and glossy copper-colored hair, and had wings composed of a thin membrane, without hair, lying snugly upon their backs, from the top of the shoulders to the calves of the legs.

The face, which was of a yellowish flesh-color, was a slight improvement upon that of the large orang-utan, being more open and intelligent in its expression, and having a much greater expanse of forehead. The mouth, however, was very prominent, though somewhat relieved by a thick beard upon the lower jaw, and by lips far more human than those of any species of the *Simia* genus.

In general symmetry of body and limbs they were infinitely superior to the orang-utan; so much so that, but for their long wings, Lieutenant Drummond said they would look as well on a parade-ground as some of the old cockney militia. The hair on the head was a darker color than that of the body, closely curled, but apparently not woolly, and arranged in two curious semi-circles over the temples of the forehead. Their feet could only be seen as they were alternately lifted in walking; but from what we could see of them in so transient a view, they appeared thin and very protuberant at the heel.

Whilst passing across the canvas, and whenever we afterward saw them, these creatures were evidently engaged in conversation; their gesticulation, more particularly the varied actions of the hands and arms, appeared impassioned and emphatic.

The next view we obtained of them was still more favorable. It was on the borders of a little lake, or expanded stream, which we then for the first time perceived running down the valley to the large lake,

> and having on its eastern margin a small wood. Some of these creatures had crossed this water and were lying like spread eagles on the skirts of the wood.
>
> We could then perceive that their wings possessed great expansion, and were similar in structure to those of the bat, being a semi-transparent membrane expanded in curvilineal divisions by means of straight radii, united at the back by the dorsal integuments.
>
> Our further observation of the habits of these creatures, who were of both sexes, led to results so very remarkable that I prefer they should be first laid before the public in Dr. Herschel's own work, where I have reason to know that they are fully and faithfully stated, however incredulously they may be received. . . .
>
> The three families then almost simultaneously spread their wings, and were lost in the dark confines of the canvas before we had time to breathe from our paralyzing astonishment. We scientifically denominated them the *vespertilio-homo*, or man-bat; and they are doubtless innocent and happy creatures, notwithstanding some of their amusements would but ill comport with our terrestrial notions of decorum.

New York now stopped its discussion of human slavery, the high cost of living—apples cost as much as four cents apiece in Wall Street—and other familiar topics, and devoted its talking hours to the man-bats of the moon. The *Sun* was stormed by people who wanted back numbers of the stories, and flooded with demands by mail. As the text of the *Journal of Science* article indicated that the original narrative had been illustrated, there was a cry for pictures. Locke's graphic descriptions did not satisfy all the readers.

Mr. Day was busy with the paper and its overworked press, but he gave Mr. Locke a free hand, and that scholar took to Norris and Baker, lithographers, in the Union Building, Wall Street, the drawings which had been intrusted to his care by the "medical gentleman immediately from Scotland." Mr. Baker, described by the *Sun* as quite the most talented lithographic artist of the city, worked day and night on his delightful task, that the illustrations might be ready when the *Sun's* press should have turned out, in the hours when it was not printing *Suns*, a pamphlet containing the astronomical discoveries.

"Dr. Herschel's great work," said the *Sun*, "is preparing for publication at ten guineas sterling, or fifty dollars; and we shall give all the popular substance of it for twelve or thirteen cents." The pamphlets were to be sold two for a quarter; the lithographs at twenty-five cents for the set.

The conclusion of this astounding narrative, which totaled eleven thousand words, was printed on August 31. In the valley of the temple a new set of man-bats was found:

> We had no opportunity of seeing them actually engaged in any work of industry or art; and, so far as we could judge, they spent their happy hours in collecting various fruits in the woods, in eating, flying, bathing, and loitering about upon the summits of precipices.

A deputation from Yale College hurried to the steamboat and came to New York to see the wonderful supplement.

Harriet Martineau, who was touring America at the time, wrote in her *Sketches of Western Travel* that the ladies of Springfield, Massachusetts, subscribed to a fund to send missionaries to the benighted luminary. When the *Sun* articles reached Paris, they were at once translated into illustrated pamphlets, and the caricaturists of the Paris newspapers drew pictures of the man-bats going through the streets singing *"Au clair de la lune."* London, Edinburgh, and Glasgow made haste to issue editions of the work.

Meanwhile, of course, Sir John Herschel was busy with his telescope at the Cape, all unaware of his expanded fame in the north. Caleb Weeks, of Jamaica, Long Island, the Adam Forepaugh of his day, was setting out for South Africa to get a supply of giraffes for his menagerie, and he had the honor of laying in the great astronomer's hand a clean copy of the pamphlet. To say that Sir John was amazed at the *Sun's* enterprise would be putting it mildly. When he had read the story through, he went to Caleb Weeks and said that he was overcome; that he never could hope to live up to the fame that had been heaped upon him.

In New York, meanwhile, Richard Adams Locke had spilled the beans. There was a reporter named Finn, once employed by the *Sun*, but later a scribe for the *Journal of Commerce*. He and Locke were friends. One afternoon Gerard Hallock, who was David Hale's partner in the proprietorship of the *Journal of Commerce*, called Finn to his office and told him to get extra copies of the *Sun* containing the moon story, as the

Journal had decided, in justice to its readers, that it must reprint it.

Perhaps at the *Sun* office, perhaps in the taproom of the Washington Hotel, Finn met Locke, and told him of the work on which he was engaged, and said that, as the moon story was already being put into type at the *Journal* office, it was likely that it would be printed on the morrow.

"Don't print it right away," said Locke. "I wrote it myself."

The next day the *Journal,* instead of being silently grateful for the warning, denounced the alleged discoveries as a hoax. Mr. Bennett, who by this time had the *Herald* once more in running order, not only cried "Hoax!" but named Locke as the author.

Probably Locke was glad that the suspense was over. He is said to have told a friend that he had not intended the story as a hoax, but as satire.

But while the *Sun's* rivals denounced the hoax, the *Sun* was not quick to admit that it had gulled not only its own readers but almost all the scientific world. On September 16, more than two weeks after the conclusion of the story, it printed a long editorial article on the subject of the authenticity of the discoveries, mentioning the widespread interest that had been displayed in them:

> Some persons of little faith but great good nature, who consider the "moon story," as it is vulgarly called, an adroit fiction of our own, are quite of the opinion that this was the amiable moral which the writer had in view. Other readers, however, construe the whole as an elaborate satire upon the monstrous fabrications of the political press of the coun-

> try and the various genera and species of its party editors. In the blue goat with the single horn, mentioned as it is in connection with the royal arms of England, many persons fancy they perceive the characteristics of a notorious foreigner who is the supervising editor of one of our largest morning papers.

The New York showmen of that day were keen for novelty, and the moon story helped them to it. Mr. Hannington, who ran the diorama in the City Saloon—which was not a barroom, but an amusement house—on Broadway opposite St. Paul's Church, put on "The Lunar Discoveries; a Brilliant Illustration of the Scientific Observation of the Surface of the Moon, to Which Will Be Added the Reported Lunar Observations of Sir John Herschel."

Locke had spoiled a promising tale for Poe—who tore up the second installment of *Hans Pfaall* when he "found that he could add very little to the minute and authentic account of Sir John Herschel"—but the poet took pleasure, in later years, in picking the *Sun's* moon story to bits.

"That the public were misled, even for an instant," Poe declared in his critical essay on Locke's writings, "merely proves the gross ignorance which, ten or twelve years ago, was so prevalent on astronomical topics."

And yet the hoax, Poe admitted, "was, upon the whole, the greatest hit in the way of sensation—of merely popular sensation—ever made by any similar fiction either in America or Europe."

"From the epoch of the hoax," he wrote, "the *Sun* shone with unmitigated splendor. Its success firmly established the 'penny system' throughout the country, and (through the *Sun*) consequently we are indebted to the genius of Mr. Locke for one of the most important steps ever yet taken in the pathway of human progress."

CHAPTER IV

DAY FINDS A RIVAL IN BENNETT

The Success of the "Sun" Leads to the Founding of the "Herald."—Enterprises of a Furious Young Journalism.—The Picturesque Webb and His Quarrels With Bennett.—Maria Monk.

THE usefulness of Richard Adams Locke as a *Sun* reporter did not end with the moon hoax. Far from expressing regret that its employee had gulled half the earth, the *Sun* continued to meet exposure with a calm and almost flippant front, insisting that it would never admit the nonexistence of the man-bats until official contradiction arrived from Edinburgh or the Cape of Good Hope. The paper realized the value, in public interest, of Locke's name, and was proud to announce, in November of 1835, that it had commissioned Locke to write another series of articles, telling the story of the "Life and Adventures of Manuel Fernandez, otherwise Richard C. Jackson, convicted of the murder of John Roberts, and to be executed at the Bellevue Prison, New York, on Thursday next, the 19th instant."

This was a big beat, for the young men of the *Courier and Enquirer*, and perhaps of the *Herald*, had been trying to get a yarn from the criminal, a Spaniard who had served in foreign wars, had been captured by savages in Africa, and had had many other adventures. Fernandez was convicted of killing another sailor for his attention to Fernandez' mistress, a Mrs. Schultz; and for about three weeks Locke spent several hours a day in the condemned man's cell. The "Life and Adventures," printed on the first page of the *Sun*, ran serially from November 14 to November 25, and was read with avidity.

It was ironical that the hero of the story, who had expressed to Locke an eagerness to have his career set before the public in its true light, was prevented from reading the later installments; for the law, taking no cognizance of the literary side of the matter, went about its business, and Fernandez was hanged in the Bellevue yard on the nineteenth, a morning when the *Sun's* narrative had wrecked the sailor off the coast of Wales.

"Give us one of your real Moscow fires," sighed the *Sun* in the first week of its existence.

The prayer was answered a little more than two years later, when about twenty blocks south of Wall Street, between Broad Street and the East River, were consumed. The fire started late in the evening of Wednesday, December 16, 1835, and all that the *Sun* printed about it the next morning was one triple-leaded paragraph:

> POSTSCRIPT—HALF PAST 1 O'CLOCK—A TREMENDOUS CONFLAGRATION is now raging in the lower part of the city. The Merchants' Exchange is in flames. Nearly all the blocks in the triangle bounded by William and Wall Streets and the East River are consumed! Several hundred buildings are already down, and the firemen have given out. God only knows when the fire will be arrested.

On Friday morning the *Sun* had two and a half columns about the fire, and gave an approximately correct estimate that seven hundred buildings had been burned, at a loss of twenty million dollars. The calamity provided an opportunity for the fine writing then indulged in, and the fire reporter did not overlook it; nor did he forget Moscow. Here are typical extracts:

> Where but thirty hours since was the rich and prosperous theater of a great and productive commerce, where enterprise and wealth energized with bold and commanding efforts, now sits despondency in sackcloth and a wide and dreary waste of desolation reigns.
>
> It seemed as if God were running in his anger and sweeping away with the besom of his wrath the proudest monuments of man. Destruction traveled and triumphed on every breeze, and billows of fire rolled over and buried in their burning bosoms the hopes and fortunes of thousands. Like the devouring elements when it fed on Moscow's palaces and towers, it was literally a "sea of fire," and the terrors of that night of woe and ruin rolling years will not be able to efface.
>
> The merchants of the First Ward, like Marius in the ruins of Carthage, sit with melancholy moans, gazing at the graves of their fortunes, and the mournful mementoes of the dreadful devastation that reigns.

On the afternoon of the following day the *Sun* got out an extra edition of 30,000 copies, its normal morning issue of 23,000 being too small to satisfy the popular demand. The presses ran without stopping for nearly twenty-four hours.

On Monday, the twenty-first, the *Sun* had the enterprise to print a map of the burned district. Copies of the

WHERE "THE SUN" WAS BORN
The arrow points to 222 William Street.

TWO OF "THE SUN'S" OLD HOMES
170 Nassau Street (Tammany Hall) and 156 Nassau Street, at the other end of the block.

special fire editions went all over the world. At least one of them ran up against poetic justice. When it reached Canton, China, six months after the fire, the English newspaper there classed the story of the conflagration with Locke's "Astronomical Discoveries," and begged its readers not to be alarmed by the new hoax.

The *Sun* had grown more and more prosperous. In the latter part of 1835 its four pages, each 11½ × 18 inches, were so taken up with advertising that it was not unusual to find reading-matter in only five of the twenty columns. Some days the publisher would apologize for leaving out advertisements, on other days, for having so little room for news. He promised relief, and it came on January 4, 1836, when the paper was enlarged. It remained a four-page *Sun,* but the pages were increased in size to 14 × 20 inches. In announcing the enlargement, the third in a year, the *Sun* remarked:

> We are now enabled to print considerably more than twenty-two thousand copies, on both sides, in less than eight hours. No establishment in this country has such facilities, and no daily newspaper in the world enjoys so extensive a circulation.

In the first enlarged edition Mr. Day made the boast that the *Sun* now had a circulation more than double that of all the sixpenny respectables combined. He had a word, too, about the penny papers that had sprung up in the *Sun's* wake:

> One after another they dropped and fell in quick succession as they had sprung up; and all, with but one exception worth regarding, have gone to the "receptacle of things lost upon earth." Many of

these departed ephemerals have struggled hard to keep within their nostrils the breath of life; and it is a singular fact that with scarcely an exception they have employed, as a means of bringing a knowledge of their being before the public, the most unlimited and reckless abuse of ourselves, the impeachment of our character, public and private; the implications, moral and political; in short, calumny in all its forms.

As to the last survivor of them worth note, which remains, we have only to say, the little world *we* opened has proved large enough for us both.

The exception to the general rule of early mortality was, of course, the *Herald*. In spite of this broad attitude toward his only successful competitor, Day could not keep from swapping verbal shots with Bennett. The *Sun* said:

Bennett, whose only chance of dying an upright man will be that of hanging perpendicularly upon a rope, falsely charges the proprietor of this paper with being an infidel, the natural effect of which calumny will be that every reader will believe him to be a good Christian.

Day had a dislike for Colonel Webb, of the *Courier and Enquirer,* almost as great as his enmity toward Bennett; so when Webb assaulted Bennett on January 19, 1836, it was rather a hard story to write. This is the *Sun's* account of the fray:

Low as he had fallen, both in public estimation and his own, we were astonished to learn last evening that Colonel Webb had stooped so far beneath anything of which we had ever conceived it possible for

> him to be guilty, as publicly, and before the eyes of hundreds who knew him, to descend to a public personal chastisement of that villainous libel on humanity of all kinds, the notorious vagabond Bennett. But so it is.
>
> As the story is told to us by an eye-witness, the colonel met the brawling coward in Wall Street, took him by the throat, and with a cowhide striped the human parody from head to foot. For the space of nearly twenty minutes, as we are told, did the right arm of the colonel ply his weapon with unremitted activity, at which time the bystanders, who evidently enjoyed the scene mightily, interceded in behalf of the suffering, supplicating wretch, and Webb suffered him to run.
>
> Had it been a dog, or any other decent animal, or had the colonel himself with a pair of good long tongs removed a polecat from his office, we know not that we would have been so much surprised; but that he could, by any possibility, have so far descended from himself as to come in public contact with the veriest reptile that ever defiled the paths of decency, we could not have believed.

Webb's quarrel with Bennett grew out of the *Herald's* financial articles. Bennett was the first newspaperman to see the news value of Wall Street. When he was a writer on the *Courier and Enquirer,* and one of Webb's most useful men, he made a study of stocks, not as a speculator, but as an investigator. He had a taste for money matters. In 1824, five years after his arrival in America from the land of his birth, Scotland, he tried to establish a commercial school in New York and to lecture on political economy. He could not make a go of it, and so returned to newspaper work as reporter, paragrapher, and poet.

In 1828 he became Washington correspondent of the *Enquirer,* and it was at his suggestion that Webb, in 1829, bought that paper and consolidated it with his own *Courier.* Bennett was a Tammany Society man, therefore a Jacksonian. He left Webb because of Webb's support of Nicholas Biddle, and started a Jackson organ, the *Pennsylvanian,* in Philadelphia. This was a failure, as the Jackson party declined to support it.

Meanwhile Bennett had seen the *Sun* rise, and he felt that there must be room for another penny paper in New York. With his knowledge of stocks he believed that he could make Wall Street news a telling feature. In his second issue of the *Herald,* May 7, 1835, he printed the first money-market report, and three days later he ran a table of sales on the stock exchange. At this time, and for three years afterward, Bennett visited Wall Street daily and wrote his own reports.

His flings at the United States Bank, of which Webb's friend Biddle was president, and his stories of alleged stock speculations by the colonel himself, were the cause of Webb's animosity toward his former associate. Bennett took Webb's assault calmly, and even wrote it up in the *Herald,* suggesting at the end that Webb's torn overcoat had suffered more damage than anything else.

Day's quarrel with Bennett, which never reached the physical stage, was the natural outcome of an intense rivalry among the most successful penny papers of that period—the *Sun,* the *Herald,* and the *Transcript.* Against the sixpenny respectables these three were one for all and all for one, but against one another they were as venomous as a young newspaper of that day felt that it had to be to show that it was alive.

Day's antagonism toward Webb was sporadic. Most of the time the young owner of the *Sun* treated the fiery editor of the *Courier and Enquirer* as flippantly as he could, knowing that Webb liked to be taken seriously. Day's constant *bête noire* was the commercial and foreign editor of Webb's paper, Mr. Hoskin, an Englishman.

On January 21, 1836, the *Sun* charged that Webb and Hoskin had rigged a "diabolical plot" against it. The sixpenny papers had formed a combination for the purpose of sharing the expense of running horse expresses from Philadelphia to New York, bringing the Washington news more quickly than the penny papers could get it by mail. The *Sun* and the *Transcript* then formed a combination of their own, and in this way saved themselves from being beaten on Jackson's annual message, sent to Congress in December, 1835.

In January, 1836, Jackson sent a special message to Congress. It was delivered on Monday, the eighteenth, and on Wednesday, the twentieth, the *Sun* published a column summary of it. Webb made the charge that his messenger from Washington had been lured into Day's offices, and that the *Sun* got its story by opening the package containing the message intended for the *Courier and Enquirer*. The *Sun* replied that it received the message legitimately, and that the whole thing was a scheme to discredit Mr. Day and his bookkeeper, Moses Y. Beach:

> The insinuation of Webb that we violated the sanctity of a seal we hurl back in proud defiance to his own brow.

Webb went to the police and to the grand jury, and for a few days it looked as if the hostile editors might reach for something of larger caliber than pens. Thus the *Sun* of January 22:

> We were informed yesterday at the police office, and subsequently by a gentleman from Wall Street, that Webb, of the *Courier and Enquirer,* had openly threatened to make a personal assault upon us. It was lucky for him that we did not hear this threat; but we can now only say that if such, or anything similar to it, be his intention, he will find each of the three editors of the *Sun* always provided with a brace of "mahogany stock" pistols, to accommodate him in any way he likes, or may not like.

The specification of "mahogany stock" referred to Colonel Webb's own supposed predilection for pistols of that description.

No sooner was this fierce clash with Webb over than the *Sun* found itself bombarded from many sides in the war over Maria Monk. This woman's *Awful Disclosures* had just been published in book form by Howe and Bates, of 68 Chatham Street, New York. They purported to be "a narrative of her sufferings during a residence of five years as a novice and two years as a black nun in the Hôtel Dieu Nunnery at Montreal." On January 18, 1836, the *Sun* began to publish these shocking stories, in somewhat condensed and expurgated form. It did not vouch for their truth, but declared that it printed them from an "imperative sense of duty." "We have no better means than are possessed by any reader," it cautiously added, "to decide upon their truth or falsehood."

The *Disclosures* ran in the *Sun* for ten days, during which time about one half of the book was printed. Maria Monk herself was in New York, and so cleverly had she devised the imposture that she was received in good society as a martyr. Such was the public interest that it was estimated by Cardinal Manning, in 1851, that between 200,000 and 250,000 copies of the volume were sold in America and England. The Know-Nothing Party used it for political capital, and anti-Catholic riots in several cities were the result of its publication.

Its partial appearance in the *Sun,* while it may have helped the circulation of the book, undoubtedly hastened the exposure of the fraud. The editor of the *Commercial Advertiser,* William Leete Stone, went to Montreal, visited the Hôtel Dieu, and minutely compared the details set down by the Monk woman in regard to the inmates of the nunnery and the plan of the building. The result of his investigation was to establish the fact that the *Awful Disclosures* were fiction, and he exposed the impostor, not only in his newspaper, but in his book, *Maria Monk and the Nunnery of the Hôtel Dieu.*

News matters of a genuine kind diverted the types from Maria Monk. There was the celebrated murder of Helen Jewett, a case in which Mr. Bennett played detective with some success, and the Alamo massacre. Crockett, Bowie, and the rest of that band of heroes met their death on March 6, 1836, but the details did not reach New York for more than a month; it was April 12 when the *Sun* gave a column to them.

Texas and the Seminole War kept the news columns full until May 10, when Colonel Webb again pounced upon James Gordon Bennett. Said the *Sun:*

> Upon calculating the number of public floggings which that miserable scribbler, Bennett, has received, we have pretty accurately ascertained that there is not a square inch of his body which has not been lacerated somewhere about fifteen times. In fact, he has become a common flogging property; and Webb has announced his intention to cowskin him every Monday morning until the Fourth of July, when he will offer him a holiday. We understand that Webb has offered to remit the flogging upon the condition that he will allow him to shoot him; but Bennett says:
>
> "No; skin for skin, behold, all that a man hath will he give for his life!"

The *Sun* beat the town on a great piece of news that spring. "Triumphant News from Texas! Santa Anna Captured!" the headlines ran.

This appeared on May 18, four weeks after Sam Houston had taken the Mexican president; but it was the first intimation New York had had of the victory at San Jacinto, where 750 Americans crying, "Remember the Alamo!" defeated Mexican forces which numbered 1,800.

During the investigation of the murder of Helen Jewett and the trial of Richard P. Robinson, the suspect, the *Sun* attacked Bennett for the manner in which the *Herald* handled the case. Bennett saw a good yellow story in the murder, for the house in which the murdered girl had lived could not be said to be questionable; there was no doubt about its character. Bennett's interviewing of the victim's associates did not please the *Sun*, which pictured the unfortunate women "mobbed by several hundred vagabonds of all sizes and ages—amongst whom the long, lank figure of the notorious Bennett was most conspicuous."

When it was not Bennett, it was Colonel Webb or one of his men. The *Sun* went savagely after the proprietor of the *Courier and Enquirer* because he led the hissing at the Park Theater against Mr. and Mrs. Joseph Wood, the English opera singers.

The fearlessness of the *Sun* did not stop with saucing its contemporaries. When Robinson was acquitted of the Jewett murder, after a trial which the *Sun* reported to the extent of nearly a page a day, the *Sun* editorially declared:

> Our opinion, calmly and dispassionately formed from the evidence, is that Richard P. Robinson is guilty of the willful and peculiarly atrocious murder of Helen Jewett. . . . Any good-looking young man, possessing or being able to raise among his friends the sum of fifteen hundred dollars to retain Messrs. Maxwell, Price, and Hoffman for his counsel, might murder any person he chose with perfect impunity.

On August 20, 1836, the *Sun* announced that its circulation averaged 27,000 copies daily, or 5,600 more than the combined sale of the eleven six-cent papers. Of the penny papers the *Sun* credited the *Herald* with 3,200 and the *Transcript* with 10,000, although both these rivals claimed at least twice as much. Columns were filled with the controversy which followed upon the publication of these figures. The *Sun* departed from a scholarly argument with the *Transcript* over the pronunciation of "elegiac," and denounced it as a "nestletripe," whatever that may have been.

There was a little room left for the news. Aaron Burr's

death got a stick; Marcy's nomination for governor of New York, an inch; Audubon's arrival in America, four lines. News that looks big now may not have seemed so imposing then, as this *Sun* paragraph of September 22, 1836, would show:

> Two more States are already spoken of for addition to the Union, under the names of Iowa and Wisconsin.

Richard Adams Locke left the *Sun* in the fall of 1836, and on October 6, in company with Joseph Price, started the *New Era,* a penny paper for which the *Sun* wished success. In less than a month, however, Locke and his former employer were quarreling about the price of meals at the Astor House. That famous hotel was opened in May, 1836, with all New York marveling at the wonders of its walnut furniture, so much nicer than the conventional mahogany! Before it was built, it was referred to as the Park Hotel. When it opened it was called Astor's Hotel, but in a few months it came to be known by the name which stuck to it until it was abandoned in 1913.

But to return to our meal. Said Mr. Locke's *New Era:*

> A paragraph is going the rounds of the papers abusing the Astor House. Nothing can be more groundless. Where the arrangements are complete, the charges, of course, must be corresponding. We suppose the report has been set afloat by some person who was kicked out for not paying his bill.

To this horrid insinuation Day replied:

> The report they speak of was set afloat by ourselves, after paying $1.25 for a breakfast for a lady and her infant a year and a half old, served just one hour and seven minutes after it was ordered, with coffee black as ink and without milk, and that, too, in a room so uncleanly as to be rather offensive.

Locke wanted to make the *New Era* another *Sun*, but he failed. His second hoax, "The Lost Manuscript of Mungo Park," which purported to tell hitherto unrelated adventures of the Scottish explorer, fell down. The public knew that the *New Era* was edited by the author of the moon story. When the *New Era* died, Locke went to the Brooklyn *Eagle*, just founded, and he succeeded Henry C. Murphy, the proprietor and first editor, when that famous lawyer and writer was running for mayor of Brooklyn. Locke afterward was a custom house employee. He died on Staten Island on February 16, 1871.

When the *Sun's* advertising business had increased until its income from that source was more than $200 a day, it bought two new presses of the Napier type from Robert Hoe, at a cost of $7,000. These enabled Mr. Day to run off 3,200 papers an hour on each press. On the second of January, 1837, the size of the *Sun* was slightly increased, about an inch being added to the length and width of each of its four pages.

In February, 1837, the price of flour rose from the normal of about $5.50 a barrel to double that amount. The *Sun* declared that the increase was not natural, but rather the result of a combination—a suspicion which seems to have been shared by a large number of citizens. The bread riots of February 13 and later were the result of an agitation for lower prices.

The *Journal of Commerce* denounced the *Sun* as an inciter of riots, and suggested that the grand jury should direct its attention toward Mr. Day. The *Sun* not only refused to recede from its stand, but suggested that the foreman of the grand jury, the famous Philip Hone, had himself incited a riot—the riot against the Abolitionists, July 11, 1834—which had a less worthy purpose than the *Sun's* stand on the matter of flour prices. The *Sun* was virtuously indignant, even more than it had been a short time before, when the *Transcript* charged the *Sun's* circulation man, Mr. Young, with biting two of the *Transcript's* carriers!

CHAPTER V

NEW YORK LIFE IN THE THIRTIES

A Sprightly City Which Daily Bought Thirty Thousand Copies of the "Sun."—The Rush to Start Penny Papers.—Day Sells the "Sun" to Moses Y. Beach for Forty Thousand Dollars.

NO dull city, that New York of Ben Day's time! Almost a dozen theaters of the first class were running. The Bowery, the first playhouse in America to have a stage lighted with gas, had already been twice burned and rebuilt. The Park, which saw the American début of Macready, Edwin Forrest, and James H. Hackett, was offering such actors as Charles Kean, Charles and Fanny Kemble, Charles Mathews, Sol Smith, Mr. and Mrs. Joseph Wood, and Master Joseph Burke, the Irish Roscius. Forrest, then talked of as a candidate for Congress, was the favorite of New York. On his appearance, said a *Sun* review of his acting in "King Lear," the audience uttered "the roar of seven thunders."

There was vaudeville to be enjoyed at Niblo's Garden, a circus at Vauxhall Garden. Drama held the boards at the Olympic and the National. The Franklin was one of the new theaters. It was in Chatham Street, between James and Oliver, and it was there that Barney Williams, the *Sun's* pioneer newsboy, made his first stage appearance, as a jig dancer, when he was fifteen years old.

Charlotte Cushman, Hackett, Forrest, and Sol Smith were the leading American actors of that day, although

Junius Brutus Booth had achieved some prominence. Edwin Booth, Joseph Jefferson, William J. Florence, and Maggie Mitchell were children.

There was gambling on Park Row—Chatham Row, it was called then—games in the Elysian Fields of Hoboken on Sundays, and duels there on week days; picnickings in the woods about where the Ritz-Carlton stands to-day; horse racing on the Boulevard, now upper Broadway, and rowing races on the Harlem. Those who liked thoroughbred racing went to the Union Course on Long Island, or to Saratoga.

Club life was young. Cooper, Halleck, Bryant, and other literary moguls had started the Bread and Cheese Club in 1824. The Hone Club, named for Mayor Hone, sprang up in 1836, and gave dinners for Daniel Webster, William H. Seward, and other great Whigs. In that same year the Union Club was founded—the oldest New York club that is still in existence.

The *Sun* found plenty to print.

"We write," it boasted, "more original editorial matter than any other paper in the city, great or small."

It poked with its paragraphs at the shinplaster, that small form of currency issued by private bankers. It made fun of phrenology, then one of the fads. It jeered at animal magnetism, another craze. It had the Papineau rebellion, the Patriot War, Indian uprisings, and the belated news from Europe. It printed extracts from the *Pickwick Papers*. Dickens was all the rage.

The *Sun's* comment on *Nicholas Nickleby*, when Dickens' fourth book reached New York in 1838, was that it was as well written as *Oliver Twist*, and "not so gloomy." Yet the grimness of the earlier novel had a fascination for the youth of that day. It was this book, read by candlelight after the store was closed, that so weakened the eyes of Charles A. Dana—still clerking in Buffalo—that he believed he would have to become a farmer.

The *Sun* did not mention, in its report of the Patriot War, that Dana was a member of the Home Guard in Buffalo, and had ideas of enlisting as a regular soldier. The *Sun* did not know of the youth's existence, nor is it likely that he read Mr. Day's paper.

A piece of "newspaper news" was printed in the *Sun* of June 1, 1837—a description of the first so-called endless paper roll in operation. Day still printed on small, flat sheets, but evidently he was impressed with the novelty. The touch about the rag mill, of course, was fiction:

> We have been shown a sheet of paper about a hundred feet in length and two feet wide, printed on both sides by a machine at one operation. This extraordinary invention enables a person to print off any length of paper required for any number of copies of a work or a public journal without a single stop, and without the assistance of any person except one to put in the rags at the extremity of the machine.
>
> This wonderful operation is effected by the placing of the types on stereotype plates on the surface of two cylinders, which are connected with the paper-making machinery. The paper, as it issues from the mill, enters in a properly moistened state between the rollers, which are evenly inked by an ingenious apparatus, and emerges in a printed form. The number of copies can be measured off by the yard or

mile. The work which we have seen from this press is *Robinson Crusoe,* and consists of one hundred and sixty duodecimo pages.

The Bible could be printed off and almost disseminated among the Indians in one continuous stream of living truth. The *Sun* would occupy a roll about seven feet in diameter, and our issue to Boston, Philadelphia, and other cities would be not far from a quarter of a mile long, each. The two cents postage on this would be but a trifle. The whole length of our paper would be about seventy-seven thousand feet, a papyrus which, it must be confessed, it would take Lord Brougham a longer time to unroll than the vitrified scrolls of Herculaneum and Pompeii.

All that is necessary for a man to do on going into a paper-mill is to take off his shirt, hand it to the devil who officiates at one extremity, and have it come out *Robinson Crusoe* at the other. We should like to exchange some of our old shirts in this way, as we cannot afford the expense, during these hard times, of getting them washed.

Mr. Thomas French, the inventor, is from Ithaca, and is now in this city. He has one roll about six inches in diameter which is six hundred feet long.

No display advertising was printed in the *Sun* of those years, but there was a variety of "liners." These were adorned with tiny cuts of ships, shoes, horses, cows, hats, dogs, clocks, and what not. For example:

Came to the premises of F. Reville, Gardener, on the 16th inst., a COW, which has since calved. The owner is requested to call, prove property, and pay expenses. Bloomingdale, between fifth and sixth mile-stones.

That is nearly five miles north of the City Hall, on the West Side—a region where now little grows except the rentals of palatial apartment houses. Here are two other advertisements characteristic of the time:

> A CARD—TO BUTCHERS—Mr. Stamler, having retired to private life, would be glad to see his friends, the Butchers, at his house, No. 5 Rivington Street, this afternoon, between the hours of 2 and 5 P.M., to partake of a collation.
>
> SIX CENTS REWARD!—Run away from the subscriber, on the 30th of May, Charles Eldridge, an indented apprentice to the Segar-Making business, about 16 years of age, 4 feet high, broken back. Had on, when he left, a round jacket and blue pantaloons. The above reward and no charges will be paid for his delivery to
>
> JOHN DIBBEN, No. 354 Bowery.

On June 15, 1837, the name of Benjamin H. Day, which had appeared at the masthead of the *Sun* since its beginning, disappeared. In its place was the legend: "Published daily by the proprietor." This gave rise to a variety of rumors, and about a week later, on June 23, the *Sun* said editorially:

> Several of our contemporaries are in a maze of wonder because we have taken our beautiful cognomen from the imprint of the *Sun*. Some of the loafers among them have even flattered themselves that our humble self in person had consequently disappeared. Not so, gentlemen—for though we may not be ambitious that our thirty thousand subscribers should daily pronounce our name while

> poring over advertisements on the first page, we nevertheless remain steadily at our post, and shall thus continue during the pleasure of a generous public, except, perchance, an absence of a few months on a trip to Europe, which we purpose to make this season.
>
> With regard to a certain report that we had lost twenty thousand dollars by shaving notes, we have nothing to say. Our private business transactions cannot in the least interest the public at large.

Day's name never went back. The reason for its disappearance was a libel suit brought by a lawyer named Andrew S. Garr. On May 3, 1837, the *Sun* printed a report of a case in the Court of Chancery, in which it was incidentally mentioned that Garr had once been indicted for conspiracy to defraud. The reporter neglected to add that Garr had been acquitted. At the end of the article was the quotation:

> When rogues get quarreling, the truth will out.

Garr sued Day for ten thousand dollars, and Day not only took his name from the top of the first column of the first page, but apparently made a wash sale of the newspaper.

The case was tried in February, 1838, and on the sixteenth of that month Garr got a verdict for three thousand dollars: "to be extracted," as the *Sun* said next morning

> from the right-hand breeches-pocket of the defendant, who about a year since ceased replenishing that fountain of the "needful" from the prolific source of the *Sun's* rays by virtue of a total, unconditional, and

unrevisionary sale of the same to its present proprietor.

The name of that "present proprietor" was not given; but on June 28, 1838, the following notice appeared at the top of the first page:

> Communications intended for the *Sun* must be addressed to Moses Y. Beach, 156 Nassau Street, corner of Spruce.

Day was really out of the *Sun* then, after having been its master for five years lacking sixty-seven days, and the paper passed into the actual ownership of Beach, who had married Day's sister, and who had acted as the bookkeeper of the *Sun* almost from its inception. There were those, including Edgar Allan Poe, who believed that Beach was the boss of the *Sun* even in the days of the moon hoax, but they were mistaken. The paper, as the *Sun* itself remarked on December 4, 1835, was "altogether ruled by Benjamin H. Day."

"I owned the whole concern," said Mr. Day in 1883, "till I sold it to Beach. And the silliest thing I ever did in my life was to sell that paper!"

And why did Day sell, for forty thousand dollars, a paper which had the largest circulation in the world—about thirty thousand copies? The answer is that it was not paying as well as it had paid.

There were a couple of years when his profits had been as high as twenty thousand dollars. The net return for the six months ending October 1, 1836, as announced by the *Sun* on April 19, 1837, was $12,981.88; but at the time when Day sold out, the *Sun* was about breaking even. The advertising, due to general dullness in business—for which the bank failures and the big fire were partly to blame—had fallen off. It was costing Day three hundred dollars a week more for operating expenses and materials than he got for the sales of newspapers, and this loss was barely made up by the advertising receipts. With what he had saved, and the forty thousand paid to him by Beach, he would have a comfortable fortune. He was only twenty-eight years old, and there might be other worlds to conquer.

From nothing at all except his own industry and common sense Day had built up an enterprise which the *Sun* itself thus described a few days before the change of ownership:

> Some idea of the business done in the little three-story building at the corner of Nassau and Spruce Streets occupied by the *Sun* for the publication of a penny paper may be formed from the fact that the annual outlay for material and wages exceeds ninety-three thousand dollars—very nearly two thousand a week, and more than three hundred a day for the six working days. On this outlay we circulate daily thirty thousand papers. Allowing the other nine morning papers an average of three thousand circulation—which may fall short in two or three cases, while it is a large estimate for all the rest—it will appear that the circulation of the *Sun* newspaper is daily more than all the others united.
>
> That this is not mere gasconade, but susceptible of proof, we refer the curious to the paper-makers who furnish the stock for this immense circulation; to the type-founders who give us a new dress three times a year, and to the Messrs. Hoe & Co., who built

THE EXTRA SUN.

ARRIVAL OF THE STEAM SHIP BRITISH QUEEN.

THE NEWS.

"THE SUN" ISSUED AN EXTRA ON JULY 28, 1839, WHEN A NEW STEAMSHIP ARRIVED

HOMES OF "THE SUN" AND "THE NEW YORK HERALD," NASSAU AND FULTON STREETS

our two double-cylinder Napier presses, which throw off copies of the *Sun* at the rate of four thousand per hour.

As for the influence of the paper among the people, the *Sun* dealt in no vain exaggeration when it said of itself, a year before Day's departure:

> Since the *Sun* began to shine upon the citizens of New York there has been a very great and decided change in the condition of the laboring classes and the mechanics. Now every individual, from the rich aristocrat who lolls in his carriage to the humble laborer who wields a broom in the streets, reads the *Sun;* nor can even a boy be found in New York City or the neighboring country who will not know in the course of the day what is promulgated in the *Sun* in the morning.
>
> Already can we perceive a change in the mass of the people. They think, talk, and act in concert. They understand their own interest, and feel that they have numbers and strength to pursue it with success.
>
> The *Sun* newspaper has probably done more to benefit the community by enlightening the minds of the common people than all the other papers together.

Day found New York journalism a pot of cold, stale water, and left it a boiling caldron, not so much by what he wrote as by the way in which he made his success. There were better newspapermen than Day before and during his time, plenty of them. They had knowledge and experience, they knew style, but they did not know the people.

The *Courier and Enquirer,* under Colonel Webb, belched broadsides of old-fashioned Democratic doctrine, and Webb hired the best men he could find to load the guns. He had Bennett, Noah, James K. Paulding, and, later, Charles King and Henry J. Raymond. These were all good writers, most of them good newspapermen; but so far as the general public was concerned, Colonel Webb might as well have put them in a cage.

The *Journal of Commerce* was a great sixpenny, but it was not for the people to read. From 1828 until the Civil War its editor was Gerard Hallock, an enterprising journalist who ran expensive horse expresses to Washington to get the proceedings of Congress, but would not admit that the public at large was more interested in a description of the murdered Helen Jewett's gowns than in a new currency bill. The clipper ships that lay off Sandy Hook to get the latest foreign news from the European vessels cost Hallock and Webb, who combined in this enterprise, twenty thousand dollars a year—probably more than they spent on all their local news.

In the solemn sanctum of the *Evening Post,* William Cullen Bryant and William Leggett wrote scholarly verse and free-trade editorials. They were live men, but their newspaper steed was slow. Leggett could urge Bryant to give a beating to Stone, the editor of the *Commercial Advertiser,* and he himself fought a duel with Blake, the treasurer of the Park Theater; but these great men had little steam when it came to making a popular newspaper.

Such were the men who ruled the staid, prosy, and expensive newspapers of New York when Day and his penny *Sun* popped up. Most of them are better known to fame than Day is, but not one of them did anything comparable to the young printer's achievement in making a popular, low-priced daily newspaper—and not only making it, but making it stick.

Bennett and his *Herald* were the first to profit by the example of Ben Day. It should have been easy for Bennett, yet he had already failed at the same undertaking. He was at work in the newspaper field of New York as early as 1824, nine years before Day started the *Sun*. He failed as proprietor of the Sunday *Courier* (1825), and he failed again with the Philadelphia *Pennsylvanian*. He had a wealth of experience as assistant to Webb and as the Washington correspondent of the *Enquirer*.

It was no doubt due to the success of the *Sun* that Bennett, after two failures, established the *Herald*. He saw the human note that Ben Day had struck, and he knew, as a comparatively old newspaperman—he was forty when he started the *Herald*—what mistakes Day was making in the neglect of certain news fields, such as Wall Street. But the value of the penny paper Day had already proved, and Day had established, ahead of everybody else, the newsboy system, by which the man in the street could get a paper whenever he liked without making a yearly investment.

Bennett may have written the constitution of popular journalism, but it was Day who wrote its declaration of independence. If it had not been for the untrained Day, fifteen years younger than Bennett, it is possible that there would have been no *Herald* to span nearly a century under the ownership of father and son; and the two James Gordon Bennetts not only owned but absolutely *were* the *Herald* from May 6, 1835, when the father started the paper, until May 14, 1918, when the son died.

Day's success with the *Sun* was responsible for the birth, not only of the *Herald*, but of a host of American penny papers, which were established at the rate of a dozen a year. Of the New York imitators the *Jeffersonian*, published by Childs and Devoe, and the *Man*, owned by George H. Evans, an Englishman who was the Henry George of his day, were not long for this world. The *Transcript*, started in 1834, flashed up for a time as a dangerous rival of the *Sun*. Three compositors, William J. Stanley, Willoughby Lynde, and Billings Hayward, owned it. Its editor was Asa Greene, erstwhile physician and bookseller and always humorist. He wrote *The Adventures of Dr. Dodimus Duckworth*, *The Perils of Pearl Street*, and *The Travels of Ex-Barber Fribbleton in America*—this last a travesty on the books of travel turned out by Englishmen who visited the States.

William H. Attree, a former compositor, wrote the *Transcript's* lively police-court stories, the *Sun's* rival having learned how popular was crime. The *Transcript* lasted five years, the earlier of them so prosperous that the proprietors thought they were going to be millionaires. But Reporter Attree went to Texas with the land boomers, and Lynde, who wrote the paragraphs, died. When the paper failed, in 1839, Hayward went to the *Herald*, where he worked as a compositor all the rest of his life.

The other penny papers that sprang up in New York to give battle—while the money lasted—to the *Sun*, the *Transcript*, and the *Herald*, were the *True Sun*, started by some of Day's discharged employees; the *Morning Star*, run by Major Noah, of the *Evening Star;* the *New Era*, already mentioned, which Richard Adams Locke started in 1836 in company with Jared D. Bell and Joseph

Price; the *Daily Whig*, of which Horace Greeley was Albany correspondent in 1838; the *Bee*, the *Serpent*, the *Light*, the *Express*, the *Union*, the *Rough Hewer*, the *News Times*, the *Examiner*, the *Morning Chronicle*, the *Evening Chronicle*, the *Daily Conservative*, the *Censor*, and the *Daily News*. All these bobbed up, in one city alone, in the five years during which Ben Day owned the *Sun*. Most of them were mushrooms in origin and morning-glories by nature.

Notable exceptions were two evenings papers, the *Express* and the *Daily News*. The *Express* was established in June, 1836, under the editorship of James Brooks and his brother Erastus, graduates of the *Advertiser*, of Portland, Maine. It was devoted to Whig politics and the shipping of New York. The *Daily News* took no considerable part in journalism until twenty-five years later, when Benjamin Wood bought it.

In other parts of the country the one-cent newspaper, properly conducted, met with the favor which the public had showered upon Ben Day. William M. Swain, who tried to dissuade Ben Day from the folly of starting the *Sun*, saw the wisdom of the penny paper, and saw, also, that the New York field was filled. He went to Philadelphia and established the *Public Ledger*, the first issue appearing on March 25, 1836. The *Ledger* was not the first penny sheet to be published in Philadelphia, the *Daily Transcript* having preceded it by a few days. These two newspapers soon consolidated, however.

Swain made three million dollars out of the *Ledger;* but when, during the Civil War, the cost of paper compelled nearly all the newspapers to advance prices, he tried to keep the *Ledger* at one cent, and lost a hundred thousand dollars within a year. Childs, who had been a newsdealer and book publisher, bought the paper from Swain in 1864, and raised its price to two cents.

When Swain went to Philadelphia he had two partners, Arunah S. Abell and Azariah H. Simmons, both printers, and, like Swain, former associates of Day. Simmons remained with Swain on the *Ledger* until his death in 1855, but Abell—the man who poked more fun than anybody else at Day for his penny *Sun* idea—went to Baltimore and there established a *Sun* of his own, the first copy coming out on May 17, 1837. It was a success from the start. How well it paid Abell to follow Ben Day's scheme may be judged by the fact that thirty years later Abell bought Guilford, a splendid estate near Baltimore, and paid $475,000 for it.

Other important newspapers started in the ten years that followed Day's founding of the *Sun* were the Detroit *Free Press*, the St. Louis *Republic*, the New Orleans *Picayune*, the Burlington *Hawkeye*, the Hartford *Times*, the New York *Tribune*, the Brooklyn *Eagle*, the Cincinnati *Enquirer*, and the Cleveland *Plain Dealer*.

In 1830 there were only 852 newspapers in the United States, which then had a population of 12,866,020, and these newspapers had a combined yearly circulation of 68,117,000 copies. Ten years later the population was 17,069,453, and there were 1,631 newspapers with a combined yearly circulation of 196,000,000 copies. In other words, while the population increased 32 per cent in a decade, the total sale of newspapers increased 187 per cent. The inexpensive paper had found its readers.

In his report on newspapers for the Census of 1880, S. N. D. North says that from 1830 to 1840—

By the sheer force of its superior circulation, the penny press exerted the most powerful newspaper influence that was felt in the United States, and during this interval its beneficial influence was the most apparent. It taught the higher-priced papers that political connection was properly subordinated to the other and higher function of the public journal—the function of gathering and presenting the news as it is, without reference to its political or other effect upon friend or foe.

The advent of the penny press concluded the transition period in American journalism, and had three effects which are easily traceable. It increased the circulation, decreased the price of daily newspapers, and changed the character of the reading-matter published.

Thus Ben Day's *Sun* remade American journalism—more by accident than design, as he himself remarked at a dinner to Robert Hoe in 1851.

It is evident that Day soon regretted the sale of the *Sun,* for in 1840 he established a penny paper called the *True Sun.* This he presently sold for a fair price, but his itch for journalism did not disappear. He started the *Tatler,* but it was not a success. In 1842, in conjunction with James Wilson, he founded the monthly magazine, *Brother Jonathan,* which reprinted English double-decker novels complete in one issue. This later became a weekly, and Day brought out illustrated editions semi-annually.

This was a new thing, at least in America, and Day may be called the originator of our illustrated periodicals as well as of our penny papers. His right-hand men in the editing of *Brother Jonathan* were Nathaniel P. Willis, the poet, and Horatio H. Weld, who was first a printer, next an editor, and at last a minister.

Day sold *Brother Jonathan* for a dollar a year. When the paper famine hit the publishing business in 1862, he suspended his publication and retired from business. He was well off, and he spent the remaining twenty-seven years of his life in ease at his New York home. He died on December 21, 1889. His son Benjamin was the inventor of the Ben Day process used in making engravings.

Day always watched the fortunes of the *Sun* with interest, but he did not believe that his immediate successors ran it just the right way. When the paper passed into the hands of Charles A. Dana, in 1868, Day—then not yet threescore—said:

"He'll make a newspaper of it!"

And it was then he added that the silliest thing he himself ever did was to sell the *Sun*.

CHAPTER VI

MOSES Y. BEACH'S ERA OF HUSTLE

The "Sun" Uses Albany Steamboats, Horse Expresses, Trotting Teams, Pigeons, and the Telegraph to Get News.—Poe's Famous Balloon Hoax and the Case of Mary Rogers.

THE second owner of the *Sun*, Moses Yale Beach, was, like Ben Day, a Yankee. He was born in the old Connecticut town of Wallingford on January 7, 1800. He had a little education in the common schools, but showed more interest in mechanics than in books. When he was fourteen he was bound out to a cabinetmaker in Hartford. His skill was so fine that he saw the needlessness of serving the customary seven years, and his industry so great that he was able, by doing extra work in odd times, to get together enough money to buy his freedom from his master. He set up a cabinet shop of his own at Northampton, Massachusetts.

When Beach was twenty, he made the acquaintance of Miss Nancy Day, of Springfield, the sister of Benjamin H. Day, founder of the *Sun*. He and Miss Day were married in 1821, and as the business at Northampton was not prospering, they settled down in Springfield.

The young man was a good cabinetmaker, but his mind ran to inventions rather than to chests and highboys. Steamboat navigation had not yet attained a commercial success, but Beach was a close student of the advance made by Robert Fulton and Henry Bell. First, however, he devoted his talents as an inventor to a motor in which the power came from explosions of gunpowder. He tried this on a boat which he intended to run on the Connecticut River between Springfield and Hartford. When it failed, he turned back to steam, and he undoubtedly would have made a success of this boat line if his money resources had been adequate.

Beach then invented a rag-cutting machine for use in papermills, and he might have had a fortune out of it if he had taken a patent in time, for the process is still used. As it was, the device enabled him to get an interest in a papermill at Saugerties, New York, where he removed in 1829. This mill was prosperous for some years, but in 1835 Beach found it more profitable to go to work for his young brother-in-law, Mr. Day, who had by this time brought the *Sun* to the point of assured success.

Beach was a great help to Day, not only as the manager of the *Sun's* finances, but as general supervisor of the mechanical department. In the three years of his association with Day he picked up a good working knowledge of the newspaper business. He recognized the features that had made the *Sun* successful—chiefly the presentation of news that interested the ordinary reader—and saw that the neglect of this policy was keeping the old-fashioned sixpenny papers at a standstill.

He did not underestimate other news. "Other news," in that day, meant the proceedings of Congress and the New York State Legislature, the condensed news of Europe, as received from a London correspondent or rewritten from the English journals, and such important items as might be clipped from the newspapers of the South and West.

Many of these American papers sent proof sheets of news articles to the *Sun* by mail.

When Beach bought the paper there was no express service. There had been, in fact, no express service in America except the one which Charles Davenport and N. S. Mason operated over the Boston and Taunton Railway. But in March, 1839, about a year after Beach got the *Sun*, William F. Harnden began an express service—later the Adams Express Company—between New York and Boston, using the boats from New York to Providence and the rail from Providence to Boston.

This was a big help to the New York papers, for with the aid of the express the English papers brought by ships landing at Boston were in the New York offices the next day. To a city which still lacked wire communication of any kind this was highly important, and there was hardly an issue of the *Sun* in the spring of 1839 that did not contain a paragraph laudatory of Mr. Harnden's enterprise.

The steamship, still a novelty, was the big thing in newspaperdom. While the *Sun* did not neglect the police-court reports and the animal stories so dear to its readers, the latest news from abroad usually had the place of honor on the second page. The first page remained the home of the advertisement and the haunt of the miscellaneous article.

On June 1, 1839, the *Sun* got out an extra on the arrival, at three o'clock that morning, of the *Great Western*, after a passage of thirteen days—the fastest trip up to that time—and 57,000 copies of the paper were sold. The *Sun's* own sailing vessels met the incoming steamships down the bay. The *Sun* had woodcuts made of all the leading ships, and these, with their curly waves, lit up a page wonderfully, if not beautifully. When the *British Queen* arrived on July 28, 1839, there was a half-page picture of her. She was the finest ship that had ever been built in Great Britain, with her total length of 275 feet—less than one-third as much as some of the modern giants—and her paddle wheels with a diameter of 31 feet. The *Sun* favored New York with a Sunday paper in honor of the event, and the Monday sale, with the same feature, was 49,000. Quoth the *Sun*:

> Who will wonder, after this, that the lazy lumbering *lazaroni* of Wall Street stick up their noses at us?

In January, 1840, when the packet ships *United States* and *England* arrived together, the *Sun* gave the story a front-page display, and actually used full-faced type for the subheads of the article.

In getting news from various parts of the United States, the *Sun* took a leaf from the book of Colonel Webb and other journalists who had used the horse express. In January, 1841, on the occasion of Governor William H. Seward's message to the Legislature, the *Sun* beat the town. The Legislature received the message at 11 A. M. on January 5:

> An express arriving exclusively for the *Sun* then started, it being one o'clock, and at six this morning reached our office, thus enabling us to repeat the triumph achieved by us last year over the whole combined press of New York, large and small. It is but just to say that our express was brought on by the horses of the Red Bird Line with unparalleled expedition, in spite of wind, hail, and rain.

Nowadays a governor's message is in the newspaper offices days before it is sent to the Legislature, and there, treated in the confidence that is never betrayed by a decent newspaper, it is prepared for printing, so that it may be on the street five minutes after it is delivered, if its importance warrants. In the old days the message, borne by relays of horse vehicles down the snow-covered post road from Albany to New York, was more important to the newspapers than the messages of this period appear to be. With newspapers, as with humans, that which is easy to get loses value.

In October, 1841, the *Sun* spent money freely to secure a quick report of the momentous trial of Alexander McLeod for the murder of Amos Durfee. War between the United States and Great Britain hinged on the outcome. During the rebellion in Upper Canada, in 1837, the American steamer *Caroline* was used by the insurgents to carry supplies down the Niagara River to a party of rebels on Navy Island. A party of loyal Canadians seized and destroyed the *Caroline* at Grand Island, and in the fight Durfee and eleven others were killed. The Canadian, McLeod, who boasted of being a participant, was arrested by the American authorities when he ventured across the American border in 1840.

The British government made a demand for his release, insisting that what McLeod had done was an act of war, performed under the orders of his commanding officer, Captain Drew. President Van Buren replied that the American government had several times asked the British government whether the destruction of the *Caroline* was an act of war, and had never received a reply; and further, that the Federal government had no power to prevent the State of New York from trying persons indicted within its jurisdiction.

The whole country realized the hostile attitude of the British ministry, and accepted its threat that war would be declared if McLeod were not released. The trial took place at Utica, New York, and the *Sun* printed from two to five columns a day about it. It ran a special train from Utica to Schenectady. There a famous driver, Otis Dimmick, waited with a fine team of horses to take the story to the Albany boat, the fastest means of transportation between the state capital and the metropolis. The *Sun* declared that one day Dimmick and his horses made the sixteen miles between Schenectady and Albany in forty-nine minutes.

And the end of it all was proof that McLeod, who had boasted of killing "a damned Yankee," had been asleep in Chippewa on the night of the *Caroline* affair, and was nothing worse than a braggart.

Beach was a man of great faith in railroads and all other forms of progress. When the Boston and Albany road was finished, the *Sun* related how a barrel of flour was growing in the field in Canandaigua on a Monday—the barrel in a tree and the flour in the wheat—and on Wednesday, transformed and ready for the baker, it was in Boston.

> Sperm candles manufactured by Mr. Penniman at Albany on Wednesday morning were burning at Faneuil Hall and at the Tremont, in Boston, on the evening of the same day.

The *Sun* had faith in Morse and his telegraph from the outset. The invention was born in Nassau Street, only a block or two from the *Sun's* office. Morse put the wire into practical use between Baltimore and Washington on May 24, 1844. That was a Friday. The *Sun* said nothing about it the next day, and had no Sunday paper; but on Monday it said editorially:

> MAGNETIC TELEGRAPH—The new invention is completed from Baltimore to Washington. The wire, perfectly secured against the weather by a covering of rope-yarn and tar, is conducted on the top of posts about twenty feet high and one hundred yards apart. The nominations of the convention this day are to be conveyed to Washington by this telegraph, where they will arrive in a few seconds. On Saturday morning the batteries were charged and the regular transmission of intelligence between Washington and Baltimore commenced. . . . At half past 11 A.M., the question being asked, what was the news at Washington, the answer was almost instantaneously returned: "Van Buren stock is rising." This is indeed the annihilation of space.

It is hardly necessary to say that the convention referred to was the Democratic national convention at Baltimore, that Van Buren's stock, high early in the proceedings, fell again, and that James K. Polk was the nominee.

But as New York was not fortunate enough to have the first commercial telegraph line, the *Sun* had to rely on its own efforts for speedy news from the convention. It ran special trains from Baltimore, "beating the United States mail train and locomotive an hour or two."

The *Sun* soon afterward expressed annoyance at a report that it was itself a part of a monopoly which was to control the telegraph, and that it had bought a telegraph line from New York to Springfield, Massachusetts. It insisted that there should be no monopoly, and that the use of the telegraph must be open to all. There was no suggestion that Morse intended to control his invention improperly, but the *Sun* was not quite satisfied with the government's lassitude. Morse had offered his rights to the government for $100,000, and Congress had sneered.

It was not until 1846 that the telegraph was extended to New York, and in the meantime the New York papers used such other means as they could for the collection of news. Besides trains, ships, horses, and the fleet foot of the reporter, there were pigeons. Beach went in for pigeons extensively. When the *Sun* moved from 156 Nassau Street, in the summer of 1842, it took a six-story building at the southwest corner of Nassau and Fulton Streets, securing about three times as much room as it had in the two-story building at Spruce Street. On the top of the new building Beach built a pigeon-house, which stood for half a century.

The strange, boxlike cote attracted not only the attention of Mr. Bennett, whose *Herald* was quartered just across the street, but of all the folk who came and went in that busy region. So many were the queries from friends and the quips from enemies concerning the pigeon house that the *Sun* (December 14, 1843), vouchsafed to explain:

> Why, we have had a school of carrier-pigeons in the upper apartments of the *Sun* office since we have occupied the building. Did our contemporaries believe that we ever could be at fault in furnishing the earliest news to our readers? Or did they in-

MOSES YALE BEACH
Owner of *The Sun*, 1838-1848.

dulge the hope that in newspaper enterprise they could ever catch us napping?

Carrier-pigeons have long been remarked for their sagacity and admired for their usefulness. They are, of all birds, the most invaluable, and as auxiliary to a newspaper cannot be too highly prized. Part of the flock in our possession were employed by the London *Morning Chronicle* in bringing intelligence from Dublin to London, and from Paris to London, crossing both channels; therefore they are not novices in the newspaper express.

If there was delay in the arrival of the Boston steamer, and the weather clear, we despatched our choice pigeon, Sam Patch, down the Sound, and he invariably came back with a slip of delicate tissue-paper tied under his wing, containing the news. We thus are apprised of the arrival of the steamer some two hours before any one else hears of her. Our men are at their cases; the steam is up in our press-room, and our extras are always out first.

We sometimes let one of our carriers fly to the Narrows, and in twenty minutes or so we know what is coming in, thirty miles from Sandy Hook Light. We despatch them as far as Albany, on any important mission; frequently to New Jersey, and in the summer-time they sometimes look in at Rockaway and let us know what is going on at the pavilion. We have a small sliding door in our observatory, on the top of the *Sun* office, through which the little aërials pass. By sending off one every little while, we ascertain the details of whatever is important or interesting at any given point.

They often fly at the rate of sixty miles an hour, easy! For example, a half-dozen will leave Washington at daylight this morning and arrive here about noon, beating the mail generally ten hours or so. They can come through from Albany in about two hours and a half, solar time. They fly exceedingly high, and keep so until they make the spires of the city, and then descend. We have not lost one by any accident, and believe ours is the only flock of value or importance in the country.

We give this brief detail of "them pigeons" because our prying friends and neighbors in the newspaper way have such a meager, guesswork account of them; and because we dislike any mystery or artifice in our business operations.

Speed and more speed was the newspaper demand of the hour, particularly among the penny papers. The *Sun* and the *Herald* had been battling for years, with competitors springing up about them, usually to die within the twelvemonth. Now the *Tribune* had come to remain in the fray, even if it had not as much money to spend on newsgathering as the *Sun* and the *Herald.*

Edgar Allan Poe saw the fever that raged among the rivals. He had just returned to New York from Philadelphia with his sick wife and his mother. He was a recognized genius, but his worldly wealth amounted to four dollars and fifty cents. He had written "The Narrative of A. Gordon Pym," "The Murders in the Rue Morgue," "The Gold Bug," and other immortal stories, but his livelihood had been precarious.

His fortunes were at their lowest when he arrived in New York on April 6, 1844. He and his family found rooms in Greenwich Street, near Cedar, now the thick of the business district. "The house is old and looks buggy," he wrote to a friend, but it was the best he could do with less than five dollars in his pocket.

He had to have more money. The newspapers seemed to be the most available place to get it, and the *Sun* the livest of them. Speed—that was what they wanted.

Poe wrote the "balloon hoax," and sold it to Mr. Beach. It appeared in the *Sun* of April 13, 1844.

Beneath a black-faced heading that was supplemented by a woodcut of three race horses flying under the whips of their jockeys and the subtitle "By Express," was the following introduction:

> ASTOUNDING INTELLIGENCE BY PRIVATE EXPRESS FROM CHARLESTON, VIA NORFOLK! — THE ATLANTIC OCEAN CROSSED IN THREE DAYS!!!—ARRIVAL AT SULLIVAN'S ISLAND OF A STEERING BALLOON INVENTED BY MR. MONCK MASON.
>
> We stop the press at a late hour to announce that by a private express from Charleston, South Carolina, we are just put in possession of full details of the most extraordinary adventure ever accomplished by man. *The Atlantic Ocean has actually been traversed in a balloon, and in the incredibly brief period of three days!* Eight persons have crossed in the machine, among others Sir Everard Bringhurst and Mr. Monck Mason. We have barely time now to announce this most novel and unexpected intelligence, but we hope by ten this morning to have ready an extra with a detailed account of the voyage.
>
> P. S.—The extra will be positively ready, and for sale at our counter, by ten o'clock this morning. It will embrace all the particulars yet known. We have also placed in the hands of an excellent artist a representation of the "Steering Balloon," which will accompany the particulars of the voyage.

The promised extra bore a head of studhorse type, six banks in all, and as many inches deep. It announced:

> Astounding News by Express, *via* Norfolk!—THE ATLANTIC CROSSED IN THREE DAYS!—SIGNAL TRIUMPH OF MR. MONCK MASON'S FLYING-MACHINE!!!—ARRIVAL AT SULLIVAN'S ISLAND, NEAR CHARLESTON, OF MR. MASON, MR. ROBERT HOLLAND, MR. HENSON, MR. HARRISON AINSWORTH, AND FOUR OTHERS IN THE STEERING BALLOON VICTORIA, AFTER A PASSAGE OF SEVENTY-FIVE HOURS FROM LAND TO LAND—FULL PARTICULARS OF THE VOYAGE!!!
>
> The great problem is at length solved. The air, as well as the earth and the ocean, has been subdued by science, and will become a common and convenient highway for mankind. The Atlantic has been actually crossed in a balloon! And this, too, without difficulty—without any great apparent danger—with thorough control of the machine—and in the inconceivably brief period of seventy-five hours from shore to shore!
>
> By the energy of an agent at Charleston, South Carolina, we are enabled to be the first to furnish the public with a detailed account of this most extraordinary voyage, which was performed between Saturday, the 6th instant, at 11 A.M. and 2 P.M. on Tuesday, the 9th instant, by Sir Everard Bringhurst, Mr. Osborne, a nephew of Lord Bentinck; Mr. Monck Mason, and Mr. Robert Holland, the well-known aëronauts; Mr. Harrison Ainsworth, author of "Jack Sheppard," *et cetera,* and Mr. Henson, the projector of the late unsuccessful flying-machine—

with two seamen from Woolwich—in all, eight persons.

The particulars furnished below may be relied on as authentic and accurate in every respect, as with a slight exception they are copied verbatim from the joint diaries of Mr. Monck Mason and Mr. Harrison Ainsworth, to whose politeness our agent is indebted for much verbal information respecting the balloon itself, its construction, and other matters of interest. The only alteration in the MS received has been made for the purpose of throwing the hurried account of our agent, Mr. Forsyth, into a connected and intelligible form.

The story that followed was about five thousand words in length. To summarize it, Monck Mason had applied the principle of the Archimedean screw to the propulsion of a dirigible balloon. The gas bag was an ellipsoid thirteen feet long, with a car suspended from it. The screw propeller, which was attached to the car, was operated by a spring. A rudder shaped like a battledore kept the airship on its course.

The voyagers, according to the story, started from Mr. Osborne's home near Penstruthal, in North Wales, intending to sail across the English Channel. The mechanism of the propeller broke, and the balloon, caught in a strong northeast wind, was carried across the Atlantic at the speed of sixty or more miles an hour. Mr. Mason kept a journal, to which, at the end of each day, Mr. Ainsworth added a postscript. The balloon landed safely on the coast of South Carolina, near Fort Moultrie.

The names of the supposed voyagers were well chosen by Poe to give verisimilitude to the hoax. Monck Mason and Robert Holland, or Hollond, were of the small party which actually sailed from Vauxhall Gardens, London, on the afternoon of November 7, 1836, in the balloon Nassau and landed at Weilburg, in Germany, five hundred miles away, eighteen hours later. Harrison Ainsworth, the novelist, was then one of the shining stars of English literary life. The others named by Poe were familiar figures of the period.

Poe adopted the plan, used so successfully by Locke in the moon hoax, of having real people do the thing that they would like to do; but there the resemblance of the two hoaxes ends, except for the technical bits that Poe was able to inject into his narrative. The moon hoax lasted for weeks; the balloon hoax for a day. Even the *Sun* did not attempt to bolster it, for it said the second day afterward:

> BALLOON—The mails from the South last Saturday night not having brought confirmation of the balloon from England, the particulars of which from our correspondent we detailed in our extra, we are inclined to believe that the intelligence is erroneous. The description of the balloon and the voyage was written with a minuteness and scientific ability calculated to obtain credit everywhere, and was read with great pleasure and satisfaction. We by no means think such a project impossible.

About a week later, when the *Sun* was still being pounded by its contemporaries, a few of which had been gulled into rewriting the story, another editorial article on the hoax appeared:

> BALLOON EXPRESS—We have been somewhat amused with the comments of the press upon the

balloon express. The more intelligent editors saw its object at once. On the other hand, many of our esteemed contemporaries—those who are too ignorant to appreciate the pleasant satire—have ascribed to us the worst and basest motives. We expected as much.

There was another story which Poe and the *Sun* shared —one that will outlive even the balloon hoax. Almost buried on the third page of the *Sun* of July 28, 1841, was this advertisement in agate type:

> Left her home on Sunday morning, July 25, a young lady; had on a white dress, black shawl, blue scarf, Leghorn hat, light-colored shoes, and parasol light colored; it is supposed some accident has befallen her. Whoever will give information respecting her at 126 Nassau shall be rewarded for their trouble.

The next day the *Sun* said in its news columns:

> The body of a young lady some eighteen or twenty years of age was found in the water at Hoboken. From the description of her dress, fears are entertained that it is the body of Miss Mary C. Rogers, who is advertised in yesterday's paper as having disappeared from her home, 126 Nassau Street, on Sunday last.

The fears were well grounded, for the dead girl was Mary Cecilia Rogers, the "beautiful cigar girl" who had been the magnet at John Anderson's tobacco shop at Broadway and Duane Street; the tragic figure of Poe's story, "The Mystery of Marie Roget," a tale which served to keep alive the features of that unsolved riddle of the Elysian Fields of Hoboken. To the *Sun,* which had then no Poe, no *Sherlock Holmes,* the murder was the text for a moral lesson:

> There can be no question that she had fallen a victim to the most imprudent and reprehensible practice, which has recently obtained to a considerable extent in this city, of placing behind the counters and at the windows of stores for the sale of articles purchased exclusively by males—especially of cigar-stores and drinking-houses—young and beautiful females for the purpose of thus attracting the attention, exciting the interest (or worse still), and thus inducing the visits and consequent custom, of the other sex—especially of the young and thoughtless.
>
> It was by being placed in such a situation, in one of the most public spots in the city, that this unfortunate girl was led into a train of acquaintances and associations which has eventually proved not only her ruin, but an untimely and violent death in the prime of youth and beauty. From being used as an instrument of cupidity—as a sort of "man-trap" to lure by her charms the gay and giddy into the path of the spendthrift and of constant dissipation—she has become the victim of the very passions and vices which her exposure to the public gaze for mercenary gain was so well calculated to engender and encourage.

The great social event of the town in 1842 was the visit of Charles Dickens. He had been expected for several years. In fact, as far back as October 13, 1838, the *Sun* remarked:

Boz is coming to America. We hope he will not make a fool of himself here, like a majority of his distinguished countrymen who preceded him.

The *Sun* got out an extra on the day when Dickens landed, but it was not in honor of Boz, but rather because of the arrival of the *Britannia* with a budget of foreign news. Buried in a mass of Continental paragraphs was this one:

> Among the passengers are Mr. Charles Dickens, the celebrated author, and his lady.

The ship-news man never even thought to ask Dickens how he liked America. But society was waiting for Boz, and he was tossed about on a lively sea of receptions and dinners. The *Sun* presently thought that the young author was being exploited overmuch:

> Mr. Dickens, we have no doubt, is a very respectable gentleman, and we know that he is a very clever and agreeable author. He has written several books that have put the reading world in most excellent good humor. In this way he has done much to promote the general happiness of mankind, and honestly deserves their gratitude.
>
> Having crossed the water for the purpose of traveling in America, where his works have been extensively read and admired, he is, of course, received and treated with marked civility, attention, and respect. We should be ashamed of our countrymen if it were otherwise. During his stay at Boston the citizens gave him a public dinner. At New Haven he received a similar token of kind regard. In this city a ball has been given him. All these attentions

were right and proper, and as far as we can learn they have been uniformly conducted in a gentlemanly and respectable manner, becoming alike to the characters of those who gave and him who received them.

But a few penny-catchers of the press are determined to make money out of Boz. The shop-windows are stuffed with lithograph likenesses of him, which resemble the original just about as much as he resembles a horse. His own wife would not recognize them in any other way than by the word "Boz" written under them.

Then a corps of sneaking reporters, most of them fresh from London, are pursuing him like a pack of hounds at his heels to catch every wink of his eye, every motion of his hands, and every word that he speaks, to be dished up with all conceivable embellishments by pen and pencil, and published in extras, pamphlets, and handbills. To make all this trash sell well in the market, the greatest possible hurrah must be made by the papers interested in the speculations, and therefore the whole American people are basely caricatured by them, and represented as one vast mob following Dickens from place to place, and striving even to touch the hem of his garment.

When Dickens sailed for home, in June, the *Sun* bade him *bon voyage* with but a paragraph. It was more than a year afterward that it came to him again; and meanwhile he had trodden on the toes of America:

The appearance of the current number of *The Life and Adventures of Martin Chuzzlewit* will not add to the happiness of retrospections. Where is that Boston committee, where the renowned getters-up of the City Hotel dinner and the ball at the Park

> Theater, with its *tableaux vivants,* its splendid decorations, and tickets at ten dollars each?
>
> The scene is passing now before our memory—the crammed theater, full up to its third tier, the dense crowd opening a passage for Mr. Dickens and the proud and happy committee while he passes up the center of the stage amid huzzas and the waving of handkerchiefs, while the band is playing "God Save the Queen" and "See, the Conquering Hero Comes." And *our* Irving, *our* Halleck, *our* Bryant passed around in the crowd, unnoticed and almost unknown. Shame! Let our cheeks crimson, as they ought.

The *Sun* itself was doing very nicely. On its tenth birthday, September 3, 1843, it announced that it employed eight editors and reporters, twenty compositors, sixteen pressmen, twelve folders and counters, and one hundred carriers. The circulation of the daily paper was thirty-eight thousand, of the *Weekly Sun* twelve thousand.

Mr. Beach owned the *Sun's* new home at Fulton and Nassau Streets and the building at 156 Nassau Street which he had recently vacated, and which was burned down in the fire of February 6, 1845. He had a London correspondent who ran a special horse express to carry the news from London to Bristol. A *Sun* reporter went to report Webster's speech on the great day when the Bunker Hill Monument was finished. He got down correctly at least the last sentence: "Thank God, I—I also—am an American!"

With a circulation by far the largest in the world, the *Sun* was obliged to buy a new dress of type every three months, for the day of the curved stereotype plate was still far off. Early in 1846 two new presses, each capable of six thousand *Suns* an hour, were put in at a cost of twelve thousand dollars.

The size of the paper grew constantly, although Beach stuck to a four-page sheet because of the limitations of the presses. Instead of adding pages, he added columns. From Day's little three-column *Sun* the paper had grown, by April of 1840, to a width of seven columns. Of the total of twenty-eight columns in an issue, twenty-one and a half were devoted to advertising, three to mixed news and editorials, two and a half to the court reports, and one column to reprint.

With the page seven columns wide, Beach thought that the two words—*The Sun*—looked lonely, and to fill out the heading he changed it to read *The New York Sun*. This continued from April 13 to September 29, 1840, when the proprietor saw how much more economical it would be to cut out "New York" and push the first and seventh columns of the first page up to the top of the paper. Then it was *The Sun* once more in headline as well as body.

Three years after that the *Sun* became an eight-column paper, and there were no more sneers at the blanket sheets, for the *Sun* itself was getting pretty wide.

It was in the reign of Moses Y. Beach as owner of the *Sun*, that Horace Greeley came to stay in New York journalism. He had been fairly successful as editor of the *New Yorker*, and his management of the campaign paper called the *Log Cabin*, issued in 1840 in the interest of General Harrison, was masterly. With the prestige thus obtained, he was able, on April 10, 1841, to start the *Tribune*.

In the first number he announced his intention of excluding the police reports which had been so valuable to "our leading penny papers"—meaning the *Sun* and the *Herald*—and of making the *Tribune* "worthy of the hearty approval of the virtuous and refined." It was a week before the *Sun* mentioned its former friend, and then it was only to say:

> A word to Horace Greeley—if he wishes us to write him or any of his sickly brood of newspapers into notice, he must first go to school and learn a little decency. He must further retract the dirty, malignant, and wholesale falsehood which he procured to be published in the Albany *Evening Journal* a year ago last winter, with the hope of injuring the *Sun*. He must then deal in something besides misstatements of facts. Until he does all this we shall feel very indifferent to any thrust that he can make at us with his dagger of lath.

Soon afterward the *Sun* rubbed it in by quoting the Albany *Evening Journal*:

> Galvanize a large New England squash, and it would make as capable an editor as Horace.

Beach soon recognized Greeley as a considerable rival in the morning field, and there was a long tussle between the *Sun* and the *Tribune*. It did not content itself with words, and there were street battles between the boys who sold the two papers. Stung by one of Beach's articles, Greeley called the *Sun* "the slimy and venomous instrument of Locofocoism, Jesuitical and deadly in politics and groveling in morals." The term Locofoco had then lost its original application to the Equal Rights section of the Democratic party and was applied—particularly by the Whigs—to any sort of Democrat.

Moses Y. Beach had no such young journalists about him as Dana or Raymond, but he had two sons who seemed well adapted to take up the ownership of the *Sun*. He took them in as partners on October 22, 1845, under the title of "M. Y. Beach & Sons." The elder son, Moses Sperry Beach, was then twenty-three years old, and had already been well acquainted with the newspaper business, particularly with the mechanical side of it. Before his father took him as a partner young Moses had joined with George Roberts in the publication of the Boston *Daily Times*, but he was glad to drop this and devote himself to the valuable property at Fulton and Nassau Streets.

If a genius for invention is inheritable, both the Beach boys were richly endowed by their father. Moses S. invented devices for the feeding of rolls of paper, instead of sheets, to flat presses; for wetting newsprint paper prior to printing; for cutting the sheets after printing; and for adapting newspaper presses to print both sides of the sheet at the same time.

Alfred Ely Beach was only nineteen when he became partner in the *Sun*. After leaving the academy at Monson, Massachusetts, where he had been schooled, he worked with his father in the *Sun* office, and learned every detail of the business. The inventive vein was even deeper in him than in his brother. When he was twenty he formed a partnership with his old schoolmate, Orson D. Munn, of Monson, and they bought the *Scientific*

American from Rufus Porter and combined its publishing business with that of soliciting patents.

Alfred Beach retained his interest in the *Sun* for several years, but he is best remembered for his inventions and for his connection with scientific literature.

CHAPTER VII

"THE SUN" IN THE MEXICAN WAR

Moses Y. Beach as an Emissary of President Polk.—The Associated Press Founded in the Office of the "Sun."—Ben Day's Brother-in-Law Retires with a Small Fortune.

THE Beaches, father and sons, owned the *Sun* throughout the Mexican War, a period notable for the advance of newspaper enterprise; and Moses Yale Beach proved more than once that he was the peer of Bennett in the matter of getting news.

Shortly before war was declared—April 24, 1846—the telegraph line was built from Philadelphia to Fort Lee, New Jersey, opposite New York. June found a line opened from New York to Boston; September, a line from New York to Albany. The ports and the capitals of the nation were no longer dependent on horse expresses, or even upon the railroads, for brief news of importance. Morse had subdued space.

For a little time after the Mexican War began there was a gap in the telegraph between Washington and New York, the line between Baltimore and Philadelphia not having been completed; but with the aid of special trains the *Sun* was able to present the news a few hours after it left Washington. It was, of course, not exactly fresh news, for the actual hostilities in Mexico were not heard of at Washington until May 11, more than two weeks after their accomplishment.

The good news from the battlefields of Palo Alto and Resaca de la Palma was eighteen days in reaching New York. All Mexican news came by steamer to New Orleans or Mobile, and was forwarded from those ports, by the railroad or other means, to the nearest telegraph-station. Moses Y. Beach was instrumental in whipping up the service from the South, for he established a special railroad news service between Mobile and Montgomery, a district of Alabama where there had been much delay.

On September 11, 1846, the *Sun* uttered halleluiahs over the spread of the telegraph. The line to Buffalo had been opened on the previous day. The invention had been in everyday use only two years, but more than twelve hundred miles of lines had been built, as follows:

New York to Boston	265
New York to Albany and Buffalo	507
New York to Philadelphia, Baltimore and Washington	240
Philadelphia to Harrisburg	105
Boston to Lowell	26
Boston toward Portland	55
Ithaca to Auburn	40
Troy to Saratoga	31
TOTAL	1,269

England had then only 175 miles of telegraph. "This," gloated the *Sun*, "is American enterprise!"

The *Sun* did not have a special correspondent in Mexico, and most of its big stories during the war, including the account of the storming of Monterey, were those sent to the New Orleans *Picayune* by George W. Kendall, who is supposed to have put in the mouth of

General Taylor the words, "A little more grape, Captain Bragg!"

Moses Yale Beach himself started for Mexico as a special agent of President Polk, with power to talk peace, but the negotiations between Beach and the Mexican government were broken off by a false report of General Taylor's defeat by Santa Anna, and Mr. Beach returned to his paper.

The more facilities for news-getting the papers enjoyed, the more they printed—and the more it cost them. Each had been doing its bit on its own hook. The *Sun* and the *Courier and Enquirer* had spent extravagant sums on their horse expresses from Washington. The *Sun* and the *Herald* may have profited by hiring express trains to race from Boston to New York with the latest news brought by the steamships, but the outflow of money was immense. The news boats—clipper ships, steam vessels and rowboats—which went down to Sandy Hook to meet incoming steamers cost the *Sun*, the *Herald*, the *Courier and Enquirer*, and the *Journal of Commerce* a pretty penny.

With the coming of the Mexican War there were special trains to be run in the South. And now the telegraph, with its expensive tolls, was magnetizing money out of every newspaper's till. Not only that, but there was only one wire, and the correspondent who got to it first usually hogged it, paying tolls to have a chapter from the Bible, or whatever was the reporter's favorite book, put on the wire until his story should be ready to start.

It was all wrong, and at last, through pain in the pocket, the newspapers came to realize it. At a conference held

Alfred Ely Beach
Part owner of *The Sun*, 1845-1852.

in the office of the *Sun,* toward the close of the Mexican War, steps were taken to lessen the waste of money, men, and time.

At this meeting, presided over by Gerard Hallock, the veteran editor of the *Journal of Commerce,* there were represented the *Sun,* the *Herald,* the *Tribune*—the three most militant morning papers—the *Courier and Enquirer,* the *Express,* and Mr. Hallock's own paper. The conference formed the Harbor Association, by which one fleet of newsboats would do the work for which half a dozen had been used, and the New York Associated Press, designed for coöperation in the gathering of news in centers like Washington, Albany, Boston, Philadelphia, and New Orleans. Thus in the office where some of the bitterest invective against newspaper rivals had been penned, there began an era of good feeling.

As an example of the change in the personal relations of the newspaper editors and proprietors, the guests present at a dinner given by Moses Y. Beach in December, 1848, when he retired from business and turned the *Sun* over to his sons Moses and Alfred, were the venerable Major Noah, then retired from newspaper life; Gerard Hallock, Horace Greeley, Henry J. Raymond, of the *Courier and Enquirer,* and James Brooks, of the *Express.* All praised Beach and his fourteen years of labor on the *Sun,* but there was never a word about Benjamin H. Day. Evidently that gentleman's reëntry into the newspaper field as the proprietor of the *True Sun* had put him out of tune with his brother-in-law. Richard Adams Locke, author of the moon hoax, was there, however—the only relic of the first régime.

What the *Sun* thought of itself then is indicated in an

editorial printed on December 4, when the Beach brothers relieved their father, who was in bad health:

> We ask those under whose eyes the *Sun* does not shine from day to day—our *Sun*, we mean; this large and well-printed one-cent newspaper—to look it over and say whether it is not one of the wonders of the age. Does it not contain the elements of all that is valuable in a diurnal sheet? Where is more effort or enterprise expended for so small a return?
>
> Of this effort and enterprise we feel proud; and a circulation of over fifty thousand copies of our sheet every day among at least five times that number of readers, together with the largest cash advertising patronage on this continent, convinces us that our pride is widely shared.

The *Sun* that Ben Day had turned over to Moses Y. Beach was no longer recognizable. Fifteen years had wrought many changes from the time when the young Yankee printer launched his venture on the tide of chance. The steamship, the railroad, and the telegraph had made over American journalism. The police-court items, the little local scandals, the animal stories—all the trifles upon which Day had made his way to prosperity—were now being shoved aside to make room for the quick, hot news that came in from many quarters, The *Sun* still strove for the patronage of the People, with a capital P, but it had educated them away from the elementary.

The elder Beach was enterprising but never rash. He made the *Sun* a better business proposition than ever it was under Day. Ben Day carried a journalistic sword at his belt; Beach, a pen over his ear. Perhaps Day could not have brought the *Sun* up to a circulation of fifty thousand and a money value of a quarter of a million dollars; but, on the other hand, it is unlikely that Beach could ever have started the *Sun*.

Once it was started, and once he had seen how it was run, the task of keeping it going was fairly easy for him. He was a good publisher. Not content with getting out the *Sun* proper, he established the *Weekly Sun*, issued on Saturdays, and intended for country circulation, at one dollar a year. In 1848, he got out the *American Sun*, at twelve shillings a year, which was shipped abroad for the use of Europeans who cared to read of our rude American doings. Another venture of Beach's was the *Illustrated Sun and Monthly Literary Journal*, a sixteen-page magazine full of woodcuts.

Mr. Beach had for sale at the *Sun* office all the latest novels in cheap editions. He wrote a little book himself —*The Wealth of New York: A Table of the Wealth of the Wealthy Citizens of New York City Who Are Estimated to Be Worth One Hundred Thousand Dollars or Over, with Brief Biographical Notices*. It sold for twenty-five cents.

Perhaps Beach was the father of the newspaper syndicate. In December, 1841, when the *Sun* received President Tyler's message to Congress by special messenger, he had extra editions of one sheet printed for twenty other newspapers, using the same type for the body of the issue, and changing only the title head. In this way such papers as the *Vermont Chronicle*, the Albany *Advertiser*, the Troy *Whig*, the Salem *Gazette*, and the Boston *Times* were able to give the whole text of the message to their readers without the considerable delay and expense of setting it in type.

Here is Dana's own estimate of the second proprietor of the *Sun:*

> Moses Y. Beach was a business man and a newspaper manager rather than what we now understand as a journalist—that is to say, one who is both a writer and a practical conductor and director of a newspaper. Mr. Beach was a man noted for enterprise in the collection of news. In the latter days when he owned and managed the *Sun* in New York, the telegraph was only established between Washington and Boston, though toward the end of his career it was extended, if I am not mistaken, as far towards the South as Montgomery in Alabama. The news from Europe was then brought to Halifax by steamers, just as the news from Mexico was brought to New Orleans. Mr. Beach's energy found a successful field in establishing expresses brought by messengers on horseback from Halifax to Boston and from New Orleans to Montgomery, thus bringing the news of Europe and the news of the Mexican War to New York much earlier than they could have arrived by the ordinary public conveyance. With him were associated, sooner or later, two or three of the other New York papers; but the energy with which he carried through the undertaking made him a conspicuous and distinguished figure in the journalism of the city. The final result was the organization of the New York Associated Press, which has now become a world-embracing establishment for the collection of news of every description, which it furnishes to its members in this city and to other newspapers in every part of the country. Under the stimulus of Mr. Beach's energetic intellect, aided by the cheapness of its price, the *Sun* became in his hands

an important and profitable establishment. Yet he is scarcely to be classed among the prominent journalists of his day.

Through conservatism, good business sense, and steady work, Moses Y. Beach amassed from the *Sun* what was then a handsome fortune, and when he retired he was only forty-eight. His last years were spent at the town of his birth, Wallingford, where he died on July 19, 1868, six months after the *Sun* had passed out of the hands of a Beach and into the hands of a Dana.

Beach Brothers, as the new ownership of the *Sun* was entitled, made but one important change in the appearance and character of the paper during the next few years. Up to the coming of the telegraph the *Sun* had devoted its first page to advertising, with a spice of reading matter that usually was in the form of reprint. But when telegraphic news came to be common but costly, newspapers began to see the importance of attracting the casual reader by means of display on the front page. The Beaches presently used one or two columns of the latest telegraph matter on the first page; sometimes the whole page would be so occupied.

In 1850, from July to December, they issued an *Evening Sun*, which carried no advertising.

On April 6, 1852, Alfred Ely Beach, more concerned with scientific matters than with the routine of daily publication, withdrew from the *Sun*, which passed into the sole possession of Moses S. Beach, then only thirty years old. It was reported that when the partnership was dissolved the division was based on a total valuation of $250,000 for the paper, which, less than nineteen years before, Ben Day had started with an old hand press and a hatful of type. Horace Greeley, telling a committee of the British Parliament about American newspapers, named that sum as the amount for which the *Sun* was valued in the sale by brother to brother. "It was very cheap," he added.

CHAPTER VIII

"THE SUN" DURING THE CIVIL WAR

One of the Few Entirely Loyal Newspapers of New York.—Its Brief Ownership by a Religious Coterie.—It Returns to the Possession of M. S. Beach, Who Sells It to Dana.

IN 1852, when Moses Sperry Beach came into the sole ownership of the *Sun,* it was supposed that the slavery question had been settled forever, or at least with as much finality as was possible in determining such a problem. The Missouri Compromise, devised by Henry Clay, had acted as a legislative mandragora which lulled the United States and soothed the spasms of the extreme Abolitionists. Even Abraham Lincoln, now passing forty years, was losing that interest in politics which he had once exhibited and was devoting himself almost entirely to his law practice in Springfield, Illinois.

The *Sun* had plenty of news to fill its four wide pages, and its daily circulation was above fifty thousand. The Erie Railroad had stretched itself from Piermont, on the Hudson River, to Dunkirk, on the shore of Lake Erie. The Hudson River Railroad was built from New York to Albany. The steamship *Pacific,* of the Collins Line, had broken the record by crossing the Atlantic in nine days and nineteen hours. The glorious yacht, *America,* had beaten the British *Titania* by eight miles in a race of eighty miles.

Kossuth, come as the envoy plenipotentiary of a

Hungary ambitious for freedom, was New York's hero. Lola Montez, the champion heartbreaker of her century, danced hither and yon. The volunteer firemen of New York ran with their engines and broke one another's heads. Messrs. Heenan, Morrissey, and Yankee Sullivan furnished, at frequent intervals, inspiration to American youth. The cholera attacked New York regularly, and as regularly did the *Sun* print its prescription for cholera medicine, which George W. Busteed, a druggist, had given to Moses Yale Beach in 1849. The elder Beach, enjoying himself in Europe with his son, Joseph Beach, sent articles on French and German life to his son Moses Sperry Beach's paper.

Literature was still advancing in New England. Persons of refinement were reading Hawthorne's *Scarlet Letter* and *The House of Seven Gables*, Ik Marvel's *Reveries of a Bachelor*, Irving's *Mahomet*, and Parkman's *Conspiracy of Pontiac*. Marion Harland had written *Alone*. Down in Kentucky young Mary Jane Holmes was at work on her first novel, *Tempest and Sunshine*. But brows both high and low were bent over the installments in the *National Era* of the most fascinating story of the period, Harriet Beecher Stowe's *Uncle Tom's Cabin*.

The writing of news had not gone far ahead in quality. Most of the reporters still wrote in a groove a century old. Every chicken thief who was shot, "clapped his hand to his heart, cried out that he was a dead man, and presently expired." But the editorial articles were well written. On the *Sun* John Vance, a brilliant Irishman, was turning out most of the leaders and getting twenty dollars a week. In the *Tribune* office Greeley pounded rum and slavery, while his chief assistant, Charles A. Dana, did such valuable work on foreign and domestic political articles that his salary grew to the huge figure of fifty dollars a week.

Bennett was working harder than any other newspaper-owner, and was doing big things for the *Herald*. Southern interests and scandal were his long suits. "We call the *Herald* a very bad paper," said Greeley to a Parliamentary committee which was inquiring about American newspapers. He meant that it was naughty; but naughtiness and all, its circulation was only half as big as the *Sun's*.

Henry J. Raymond was busy with his new venture, the *Times*, launched by him and George Jones, the banker. With Raymond were associated editorially Alexander C. Wilson and James W. Simonton. William Cullen Bryant, nearing sixty, still bent "the good gray head that all men knew" over his editor's desk in the office of the *Evening Post*. With him, as partner and managing editor, was that other great American, John Bigelow.

J. Watson Webb, fiery as ever in spirit, still ran the *Courier and Enquirer*, "the Austrian organ in Wall Street," as Raymond called it because of Webb's hostile attitude toward Kossuth. Webb had been minister to Austria, a post for which Raymond was afterward to be nominated but not confirmed. The newspapers and the people were all pretty well satisfied with themselves. And then Stephen A. Douglas put his foot in it, and Kansas began to bleed.

Douglas had been one of the *Sun's* great men, for the *Sun* listed heavily toward the Democratic party nationally; but it did not disguise its dislike of the Little Giant's unhappily successful effort to organize the Territories of Kansas and Nebraska on the principle of squatter sovereignty. After the peace and quiet that had followed the Missouri Compromise, this attempt to bring slavery across the line of thirty-six degrees and thirty minutes by means of a local option scheme looked to the *Sun* very much like kicking a sleeping dragon in the face.

After Douglas had been successful in putting his bill through Congress, the *Sun* still rejected its principles. Commenting on the announcements of certain Missourians that they would take their slaves into the new territory, the *Sun* said:

> They may certainly take their slaves with them into the new Territory, but when they get them there they will have no law for holding the slaves. Slavery is a creation of local law, and until a Legislature of Kansas or Nebraska enacts a law recognizing slavery, all slaves taken into the Territory will be entitled to their freedom.

It was at this time that the germs of secession began to show themselves on the culture-plates of the Continent. The *Sun* was hot at the suggestion of a division of the Union:

> It can only excite contempt when any irate member of Congress or fanatical newspaper treats the dissolution of the Union as an event which may easily be brought about. There is moral treason in this habit of continually depreciating the value of the Union.

The *Sun* saw that Douglas' repeal of the Missouri Compromise was a smashing blow delivered by a Northern

Democrat to the Democracy of the North; but the sectional hatred was not revealed in all its intensity until 1856, when Representative Preston S. Brooks, of South Carolina, made his murderous attack on Senator Charles Sumner, of Massachusetts, in the Senate Chamber. This and its immediate consequences were well covered by the *Sun*, not only through its Associated Press despatches, but also in special correspondence from its Washington representative, "Hermit." It had a report nearly a column long of Sumner's speech, "The Crime against Kansas," which caused Brooks to assault the great opponent of slavery.

That year was also the year of the first national convention of the Republican party, conceived by the Abolitionists, the Free Soilers, and the Know-Nothings, and born in 1854. The *Sun* had a special reporter at Philadelphia to tell of the nomination of John C. Frémont, but the paper supported Buchanan. Its readers were of a class naturally Democratic, and although the paper was not a party organ, and had no liking for slavery or secession, the new party was too new, perhaps too much colored with Know-Nothingism, to warrant a change of policy.

On the subject of the Dred Scott decision, written by Chief Justice Taney and handed down two days after Buchanan's inauguration, the *Sun* was blunt:

> We believe that the State of New York can confer citizenship on men of whatever race, and that its citizens are entitled, by the Constitution, to be treated in Missouri as citizens of New York State. To treat them otherwise is to discredit our State sovereignty.

John Brown's raid at Harpers Ferry was found worthy of a column in the *Sun*, but space was cramped that morning, for four columns had to be given to a report of the New York firemen's parade. The firemen read the *Sun*.

But Mr. Beach sent a special man to report Brown's trial at Charlestown, Virginia. The editorial columns echoed the sense of the correspondence—that the old man was not having a fair show. Besides, the *Sun* believed that Brown was insane and belonged in a madhouse rather than on the gallows. It printed a five-thousand-word sermon by Henry Ward Beecher on Brown's raid. Beecher and the Beaches were very friendly, and there is still in Beecher's famous Plymouth Church, Brooklyn, a pulpit made of wood brought from the Mount of Olives by Moses S. Beach.

When John Brown was hanged, December 2, 1859, the *Sun* remarked:

> The chivalry of the Old Dominion will breathe easier now. . . . But, while Brown cannot be regarded as a common murderer, it is only the wild extravagance of fanatical zeal that will attempt to elevate him to the rank of a martyr.

In the Illinois campaign of 1858 the *Sun* was slow to recognize Abraham Lincoln's prowess as a speaker, although Lincoln was then recognized as the leading exponent of Whig doctrine in his state. Referring to the debates between Lincoln and Douglas in their struggle for the senatorship, the *Sun* said:

> An extraordinary interest is attached by the leading men of all parties to the campaign which Senator Douglas is conducting in the State of Illinois. His

rival for the Senatorial nomination, Mr. Lincoln, being no match for the Little Giant in campaign oratory, Senator Trumbull has taken the stump on the Republican side.

Two years later, when Lincoln was nominated for president, the *Sun* saw him in a somewhat different light:

> Mr. Lincoln is an active State politician and a good stump orator. As to the chances of his election, that is a matter upon which we need not at present speculate.

But the time for the *Sun* to speculate came only three days later (May 22, 1860), when it frankly stated:

> It is now admitted that Mr. Lincoln's nomination is a strong one. . . . He is, emphatically, a man of the people. . . . That he would, if elected, make a good President, we do not entertain a doubt. His chances of election are certainly good. The people are tired of being ruled by professional politicians.

That was written before the Democratic national convention. The *Sun* wanted the Democrats to nominate Sam Houston. It saw that Douglas had estranged the antislavery Democrats of the North. When Douglas was nominated, the *Sun* remarked:

> Of the six candidates in the field—Lincoln, Bell, Houston, Douglas, Breckinridge, and Gerrit Smith—Lincoln has unquestionably the best chance of an election by the people.

The *Sun* had no illusions as to the candidacy of John C. Breckinridge, the vice-president under Buchanan, when he was nominated for president by the Democrats of the South, who refused to flock to the colors of Douglas:

> The secessionists do not expect that Breckinridge will be elected. Should Lincoln and Hamlin be elected by the votes of the free States, then the design of the conspirators is to come out openly for a disruption of the Union and the erection of a Southern confederacy.

"The Union cannot be dissolved," the *Sun* declared on August 4, "whosoever shall be elected President!"

And on the morning of election day the *Sun*, which had taken little part except to criticize the conduct of the Democratic campaign, said prophetically: "History turns a leaf to-day." Its comment on the morning after the election was characteristic of its attitude during the canvass: "Mr. Lincoln appears to have been elected, and yet the country is safe."

In a paragraph of political gossip printed a week later the *Sun* said that Horace Greeley could have the collectorship of the port of New York if he resigned his claims to a seat in the cabinet, and that—

> For the postmastership Charles A. Dana of the *Tribune*, Daniel Ullman, Thomas B. Stillman, and Armor J. Williamson are named. Either Mr. Dana or Mr. Williamson would fill the office creditably.

That was probably the first time that Charles A. Dana got his name into the *Sun*.

Although unqualifiedly opposed to secession, the *Sun* did not believe that military coercion was the best way to prevent it. It saw the temper of South Carolina and other southern states, but thought that it saw, too, a diplomatic way of curing the disorder. South Carolina, it said, had a greater capacity for indignation than any other political body in the world. Here was the way to stop its wrath:

> Open the door of the Union for a free and inglorious egress, and you dry up the machine in an instant.

This was somewhat on a plane with Horace Greeley's advice in the *Tribune*—"Let the erring sisters go in peace." The *Sun*, however, was more Machiavellian:

> Our proposition is that the Constitution be so amended as to permit any State, within a limited period, and upon her surrrender of her share in the Federal property, to retire from the confederacy [the Union] in peace. It is a plan to emasculate Secession by depriving it of its present stimulating illegality. Does any one suppose that even South Carolina would withdraw from the Union if her withdrawal were normal?

This was printed on December 8, 1860, some weeks before the fate of the Crittenden Compromise, beaten by southern votes, showed beyond doubt that the South actually preferred disunion.

With mingled grief and indignation the *Sun* watched the southern states march out of the Union. It poured its wrath on the head of the Mayor of New York, Fernando Wood, when that peculiar statesman suggested, on January 7, 1861, that New York City should also secede. "Why may not New York disrupt the bonds which bind her to a venal and corrupt master?" Wood had inquired.

The *Sun* had more faith in Lincoln than most of its Democratic contemporaries exhibited. Of his inaugural speech it said:

> There is a manly sincerity, geniality, and strength to be felt in the whole address.

The day after the fall of Fort Sumter the *Sun* found a moment to turn on the South-loving *Herald:*

> We state only what the proprietor of the *Herald* undoubtedly believes when we say that if the national ensign had not been hung out yesterday from its windows, as a concession to the gathering crowd, the issue of that paper for another day would have been more than doubtful.

Shortly afterward the *Sun* charged that the *Herald* had had in its office a full set of Confederate colors, "ready to fling to the breeze of treason which it and the mayor hoped to raise in this city." Later in the same year the *Sun* accused the *Daily News* and the *Staats-Zeitung* of disloyalty, and intimated that the *Journal of Commerce* and the *Express* were not what they should be.

The *Sun* took the setback of Bull Run with better grace than most of the papers—far better than Horace Greeley, who yelled for a truce. It seemed to see that this was only the beginning of a long conflict, which must be fought to the end, regardless of disappointments. On August 15, 1861, it declared:

Let there be but one war. Better it should cost millions of lives than that we should live in hourly dread of wars, contiguous to a people who could make foreign alliances and land armies upon our shores to destroy our liberties.

On the subject of the war's cost it said:

No more talk of carrying on the war economically! The only economy is to make short and swift work of it, and the people are ready to bear the expense, if it were five hundred millions of dollars, to-day.

This was printed when the war was very young; when no man dreamed that it would cost the Federal government six times five hundred millions.

The *Sun's* editorial articles were not without criticism of the conduct of the war. It was one of the many papers that demanded the resignation of Seward at a time when the secretary of state was generally blamed for what seemed to be the dillydallying of the government. Lincoln himself was still regarded as a politician as well as a statesman—a view which was reflected in the *Sun's* comment on the preliminary proclamation of emancipation, September 22, 1862:

As the greatest and most momentous act of our nation, from its foundation to the present time, we would rather have seen this step disconnected from all lesser considerations and from party influences.

The inference in this was that Lincoln had deliberately made his great stroke on the eve of the Republican state convention in New York.

The *Tribune* declared that the proclamation was "the beginning of the end of the rebellion." "The wisdom of the step is unquestionable," said the *Times;* "its necessity indisputable." The businesslike *Herald* remarked that it inaugurated "an overwhelming revolution in the system of labor." The *World* said that it regretted the proclamation and doubted the president's power to free the slaves. "We regard it with profound regret," said the *Journal of Commerce.* "It is usurpation of power!" shouted the *Staats-Zeitung.*

Such was the general tone of the New York morning newspapers during the war. Only three—the *Sun,* the *Tribune,* and the *Times*—could be described as out-and-out loyalists. The *Sun* was for backing up Lincoln whenever it believed him right, and that was most of the time; yet it was free in its criticism of various phases of the conduct of the war.

Like most of the Democrats of New York, the *Sun* was an admirer of General McClellan, and it believed that his removal from the command of the army was due to politics. But when the election of 1864 came around, the *Sun* refused to join its party contemporaries in wild abuse of Lincoln and Johnson. On the morning after the Republican nominations, it said:

> It is no time to quarrel with those men who honestly wish to crush the rebellion on the ground that they have nominated a rail-splitter and a tailor. It would be more consistent with true democracy if these men were honored for rising from an humble sphere.

The *Sun* supported McClellan, praising him for his repudiation of the plank in the Democratic platform which declared the war a failure; but in the last days of the campaign it was frank in its predictions that Lincoln would be elected. On the morning after election it had this to say:

> The reëlection of Abraham Lincoln announces to the world how firmly we have resolved to be a free and united people.

After the assassination of President Lincoln the *Sun* said:

> In the death of Mr. Lincoln the Southern people have lost one of the best friends they had at the North. He would have treated them with more gentleness than any other statesman. From him they would have obtained concessions it is now almost impossible for our rulers and people to grant.

The methods of gathering war news, early in the conflict, were haphazard. The first reports to reach New York from southern fields were usually the government bulletins, but they were not as trustworthy as the official bulletins of the European war.

On the morning after the first battle of Bull Run, the *Sun's* readers were treated to joyous headlines:

> A GREAT BATTLE—SEVENTY THOUSAND REBELS IN IT—OUR ARMY VICTORIOUS—GREAT LOSS OF LIFE—TWELVE HOURS' FIGHTING—RETREAT OF THE REBELS—UNITED STATES FORCES PRESSING FORWARD.

But on the following morning the tune changed:

RETREAT OF OUR TROOPS—OUR ARMY SCATTERED—ONLY TWENTY-TWO THOUSAND UNION TROOPS ENGAGED—ENEMY NINETY THOUSAND STRONG—OUR CANNON LEFT BEHIND.

As a matter of fact, only about eighteen thousand troops were engaged on each side.

The *Sun* had no famous correspondents at the front. It sent three reporters to Virginia in 1861, and these sent mail stories and some telegraph matter, which was of value in supplementing the official bulletins, the Associated Press service, the specials from "Nemo" and "Hermit," the *Sun* correspondents in Washington, and the matter rewritten from the Philadelphia and western newspapers.

The *Sun* was still a local paper, with a constituency hungry for news of the men of the New York regiments. To the *Sun* readers the doings of General Meagher, of the Irish Brigade, or Colonel Michael Corcoran, of the Sixty-Ninth Regiment, were more important than the strategic details of a large campaign.

The *Sun*, like all other northern papers, was frequently deceived by false reports of Union victories. Federal troops were in Fredericksburg—on the front page—weeks before they were in it in reality; in Richmond, years too soon. But there was no doubt about Gettysburg, although the North did not get the news until July 5. The *Sun* came out on Monday, the sixth, with these headlines:

VICTORY!—INVASION COMES TO GRIEF—LEE UTTERLY ROUTED—HIS DISASTROUS RETREAT—ALL FEDERAL PRISONERS RE-

CAPTURED—EIGHTEEN THOUSAND PRISONERS CAPTURED—MEANS OF ESCAPE DESTROYED.

On April 10, 1865, the headlines were sprinkled with American flags and cuts of Columbia, and the types carried the welcome news for which the North had waited for four long years:

OUR NATION REDEEMED—SURRENDER OF LEE AND HIS WHOLE ARMY—THE TERMS—OFFICERS AND MEN PAROLED AND TOLD TO GO HOME—THE COUNTRY WILD WITH JOY, ETC., ETC., ETC.

It was not until May, 1862, that the *Sun* abandoned the ancient custom of giving a large part of the first page to advertising. This reform came late, perhaps because Moses S. Beach was out of the *Sun* in the early months of the war.

On August 6, 1860, the control of the paper had passed from Mr. Beach to Archibald M. Morrison, a rich young man of religious fervor, who was prompted by other religious enthusiasts to get the *Sun* and use it for evangelical purposes. Mr. Morrison gave Mr. Beach $100,000 for the good will of the paper, and agreed to pay a rental for the material. Mr. Beach retained the ownership of the building, of the presses, and, indeed, of every piece of type.

The new proprietors of the *Sun* held a prayer meeting at noon every day in the editorial rooms. They also injected a bit of religion into the columns by printing on the first page reports of prayer meetings in the Sailors' Home and of the doings of missionaries in Syria and elsewhere. In spite of the new spirit that pervaded the office, however, it was still possible for the unregenerate old subscriber to find some little space devoted to the fistic clashes of Heenan and Morrissey.

The new management made a sort of department paper of the *Sun*, the front page being divided with the headings "Financial," "Religious," "Criminal," "Calamities," "Foreign Items," "Business Items," and "Miscellaneous." It was not a bad newspaper, and it was quite possible that some business men would prefer it to the Beach kind of sheet; but it is certain that the advertisers were not attracted and that some readers were repelled. One of the latter climbed the stairs of the building at Fulton and Nassau Streets early one morning and nailed to the door of the editorial rooms a placard which read: "Be ye not righteous overmuch!"

During the Morrison régime the *Sun* refused to accept advertisements on Sunday. Of course, the printers worked on Sunday night, getting out Monday's paper, but that was something else. The *Sun* went so far (July 23, 1861) as to urge that the Union generals should be forbidden to attack the enemy on Sundays. "Our troops must have rest, and need the Sabbath," it said.

William C. Church, one of the rising young newspapermen of New York, was induced to become the publisher under the *Sun's* new management. He was only twenty-four years old, but he had had a good deal of newspaper experience in assisting his father, the Reverend Pharcellus Church, to edit and publish the New York *Chronicle*. After a few weeks in the *Sun* office, however, Mr. Church saw that the paper, though daily treated with evangelical serum, was not likely to be a howling success; and on

Moses Sperry Beach
Owner of *The Sun*, 1852-1868.

December 10, 1860, four months after he took hold as publisher, it was announced that Mr. Church had "withdrawn from the publication of the *Sun* for the purpose of spending some months in European travel and correspondence for the paper."

Mr. Church wrote a few letters from Europe, but when the Civil War started he hurried home and went with the joint military and naval expedition headed by General T. W. Sherman and Admiral S. F. Dupont. He was present at the capture of Port Royal, and wrote for the *Evening Post* the first account of it that appeared in the North. Later he acted as a war correspondent of the *Times*, writing under the pseudonym "Pierrepont." In October, 1862, he was appointed a captain of volunteers, and toward the close of the war he received the brevets of major and lieutenant colonel.

During the war Mr. Church and his brother, Francis Pharcellus Church, established the *Army and Navy Journal*, and in 1866 they founded that brilliant magazine, the *Galaxy*—later merged with the *Atlantic Monthly*—which printed the early works of Henry James. Colonel Church owned the *Army and Navy Journal*, and was its active editor, until his death, May 23, 1917, at the age of eighty-one. He was the biographer and literary executor of John Ericsson, the inventor, and he wrote also a biography of General Grant.

At the end of 1861, what with the expense of getting war news, and perhaps with the reluctance of the readers to absorb piety, the *Sun's* cash drawer began to warp from lack of weight, and Mr. Beach, who had never relinquished his rights to all the physical part of the paper, took it back. This is the way he announced his resumption of control on New Year's morning, 1862:

> Once more I write myself editor and sole proprietor of the New York *Sun*. My day-dream of rural enjoyment is broken, and I am again prisoner to pen and types. For months I sought to avoid the surrender, but only to find resistance without avail. . . . But I congratulate myself on my surroundings. Never was prisoner more royally treated.
>
> What, then, to the readers of the *Sun?* Nothing save the announcement that I am henceforth its publisher and manager. They require no other prospectus, program, or platform.
>
> MOSES S. BEACH

John Vance, who is said to have worked twelve years without a vacation, left the *Sun* about that time because Mr. Beach refused to name him as editor-in-chief. Vance was a good writer, but he and Beach were often at odds over the *Sun's* policies. It probably was Vance's influence that kept the paper in line for Douglas in the presidential campaign of 1860—a campaign in which the *Sun* was run for two months by Beach and for three months by the Morrisonites.

On Beach's return to the *Sun* he set out to recover its lost advertising and to restore some of the livelier news features that had been suppressed by the Morrison group. Early in the summer of 1862 he began to shift advertising from the front page, to make room for the big war headlines that had been run on the second page. He also used maps and woodcuts of cities, ships, and generals. The *Sun's* pictures of the *Monitor* and the *Merrimac* were printed in one column by deftly standing the gallant ironclads on their sterns.

It was in this summer that Beach reduced expenses and speeded up the issue of the paper by adopting the stereotyping process, one of the greatest advances in newspaper history:

> About a week ago we commenced printing the *Sun* by a new process—that of stereotyping and printing with two presses. We are much gratified to-day in being able to say that the process has proved eminently successful. From this time forth we may expect to present a clean face to our many readers every day. We have completed one stereotype within seventeen minutes and a quarter, and two within nineteen minutes and a half.

That was rapid work for 1862, but the stereotypers of the present day will take a form from the composing room, make the papier-mâché impression, pour in the molten metal, and have the curved plate ready for the press in four and one-half minutes.

The new process saved Beach a lot of money as well as much precious time. Before its coming, when the paper was printed directly from the face of the type, the *Sun* had to buy a full new set of type six or eight times a year, at an annual cost of six thousand dollars.

The war played havoc with newspaper finances. The price of newsprint paper rose to twenty-four cents a pound. All the morning papers except the *Sun* raised their prices to three or four cents in 1862. The *Sun* stayed at its old penny.

On January 1, 1863, in order to meet advancing costs

and still sell the *Sun* for one cent, Beach found it necessary to "remove one column from each side of the page" —a more or less ingenuous way of saying that the *Sun* was reduced from seven columns to five. The columns were shortened, too, and the whole paper was set in agate type. The *Sun* then looked much as it had appeared twenty years before.

With these economies Beach was able to keep the price at one cent until August 1, 1864, when the *Sun* slyly said:

> We shall require the one cent for the *Sun* to be paid in gold, or we will receive as an equivalent two cents in currency.
>
> Apologies or explanations are needless. An inflated currency has raised the price of white paper nearly threefold.

Of course nobody had one cent in gold, so the *Sun* readers grinned and paid two cents in copper.

From that day on the price of the *Sun* was two cents until July 1, 1916, when Frank A. Munsey bought the *Sun*, combined his one-cent newspaper, the New York *Press*, with it, and reduced the price to one cent. On January 26, 1918, by reason of heavy expenses incidental to the War, the *Sun*, with all the other large papers of New York, increased its price to two cents a copy. When the *Sun* became an evening paper its price was raised to three cents.

The *Sun* was constantly profitable in the decade before the Civil War. The average annual profits from 1850 to 1860 were $22,770. The high-water mark in that period was reached in 1853, when the advertising receipts were $89,964 and the net profits $42,906. Its circulation in September, 1860, was 59,000 copies daily, of which 45,000 were sold on the island of Manhattan.

One of the secrets of the *Sun's* popularity in the years when it had no such news guidance as Bennett gave to the *Herald,* no such spirited editorials as Greeley put into the *Tribune,* no such political prestige as Raymond brought to the *Times,* was Moses S. Beach's belief that his public wanted light fiction. The appetite created by Scott and increased by Dickens was keen in America. True, the penny *Sun's* literary standards were not of Himalayan height. Hawthorne was too spiritual for its readers, Poe too brief. The young mechanic had to have something he could understand without knitting his brows. For him, *The Grocer's Apprentice; A Tale of the Great Plague,* and *Dick Egan; or, the San Francisco Bandits,* written for the *Sun* by H. Warren Trowbridge.

In the days before the Civil War, wives snatched the *Sun* from husbands to read *Maggie Miller; or, Old Hagar's Secret,* "written expressly for the *Sun*" by Mary J. Holmes, already famous through *Lena Rivers* and *Dora Deane.*

Horatio Alger, Jr., wrote several of his best tales for Mr. Beach, who printed them serially in the *Sun* and the *Weekly Sun.* To the New York youth of 1859, who dreamed not that in three years he would be clay on the slope at Fredericksburg, it was the middle of a perfect day to pick up the *Sun,* read a thrilling news story about Blondin cooking an omelet while crossing the Niagara gorge on a tight rope, and then, turning to the last page, to plunge into *The Discarded Son; or, the Cousin's Plot,* by the author of *The Secret Drawer, The Cooper's Ward, The Gipsy Nurse,* and *Madeline the Temptress*—for all these were written expressly for the *Sun* by young Mr. Alger. He was only twenty-five then, with the years ahead when, a Unitarian minister, he should see fiction material in the New York street boy and write the epics of *Ragged Dick* and *Tattered Tom.*

What did the women readers of the *Sun* care about the discovery of oil in Pennsylvania or the wonderful trotting campaign of Flora Temple, when they could devour daily two columns of *Love and Pride?* The *Sun* might condense A. T. Stewart's purchase of two city blocks into a paragraph, but there must be no short measure of *Gerald Vane's Lost One,* by Walter Savage North.

When the religious folk held the reins of the *Sun* they tried to compromise by printing *Great Expectations* as a serial, but the wise Mr. Beach, on getting the paper back, quickly flung to his hungry readers *Hunted Down,* by Ann S. Stephens.

One column of foreign news, one of city paragraphs, one of editorial articles, one of jokes and miscellany, one of fiction, and nineteen of advertising—that was about the make-up of Beach's *Sun* before the Civil War; that was the prescription which enabled the *Sun* to sell nearly 60,000 copies in a city of 800,000 people. It was a fairly well condensed paper. In February, 1857, when it printed one day two and a half columns about the mysterious murder of Dr. Harvey Burdell, the rich dentist of Bond Street, it broke its record for length in a police story.

It was in Moses S. Beach's time that the Atlantic cable, second only to the telegraph proper as an aid to newspapers, was laid. On August 6, 1858, when Cyrus W. Field telegraphed to the Associated Press from Newfoundland that the ends of the cables had reached both shores of the sea, the *Sun* said that it was "the greatest triumph of the age." Eleven days later the *Sun* contained this article:

> We received last night and publish to-day what purports to be the message of Queen Victoria, congratulating the President of the United States on the successful completion of the Atlantic telegraph. We are assured that the message is genuine, and that it came through the Atlantic cable. It is not surprising, however, that the President, on receiving it, doubted its genuineness, as among the hundreds who crowded our office last evening the doubters largely preponderated.
>
> The message, accepting it as the queen's, is, in style and tone, utterly unworthy of the great event which it was designed to celebrate.
>
> The message is so shabbily like royalty that we cannot believe it to be a fabrication.

Perhaps that was written by John Vance, the Irish exile. And perhaps the editorial article which appeared the following day was written by Beach himself:

> Victoria's message . . . in its complete form, as it appears in our columns to-day, is friendly and courteous, though rather commonplace in expression and style.

New York had a great celebration over the laying of the cable that week. The *Sun's* building bore a sign illuminated by gaslight:

S. F. B. MORSE AND CYRUS W. FIELD, WIRE-PULLERS OF THE NINETEENTH CENTURY.

The first piece of news to come by cable was printed in the *Sun* of August 27, 1858, and ran:

> A treaty of peace has been concluded with China, by which England and France obtain all their demands, including the establishment of embassies at Peking and indemnification for the expenses of the war.

It will be remembered that this first cable was not a success, and that permanent under-sea telegraph service did not come until 1866; but the results produced in 1858 convinced the world that Field and his associates were right, and that perseverance and money would bring perfect results.

After the war, when paper became cheaper, Beach preferred to enlarge the *Sun* rather than reduce its price to one cent. He never printed more than four pages, but the lost columns were restored, with interest, so that there were eight to a page. Even at two cents a copy it was still the cheapest of the morning papers; still the beloved of the working classes and the desired of the politicians. Just after the war ended, the *Sun* declared that it was read by half a million people.

On January 25, 1868, when the *Sun* had been in the possession of the Beaches for about thirty of its thirty-five years. a new editor and manager, speaking for a new ownership of the *Sun,* made this announcement at the head of the editorial column:

THE SUN

The Oldest Cheap Paper in New York

Notice is hereby given that the *Sun* newspaper, with its presses, types, and fixtures, has become the property of an association represented by the undersigned, and including among its prominent stockholders Mr. M. S. Beach, recently the exclusive owner of the whole property. It will henceforth be published in the building known for the last half-century as Tammany Hall, on the corner of Nassau and Frankfort Streets. Its price will remain as heretofore at two cents a copy, or six dollars per annum to mail subscribers. It will be printed in handsome style on a folio sheet, as at present; but it will contain more news and other reading matter than it has hitherto given.

In changing its proprietorship, the *Sun* will not in any respect change its principles or general line of conduct. It will continue to be an independent newspaper, wearing the livery of no party, and discussing public questions and the acts of public men on their merits alone. It will be guided, as it has been hitherto, by uncompromising loyalty to the Union, and will resist every attempt to weaken the bonds that unite the American people into one nation.

The *Sun* will support General Grant as its candidate for the Presidency. It will advocate retrenchment and economy in the public expenditures, and the reduction of the present crushing burdens of taxation. It will advocate the speedy restoration of the South, as needful to revive business and secure fair wages for labor.

The *Sun* will always have all the news, foreign, domestic, political, social, literary, scientific, and commercial. It will use enterprise and money freely to make the best possible newspaper, as well as the cheapest.

It will study condensation, clearness, point, and will endeavor to present its daily photograph of the whole world's doings in the most luminous and lively manner.

It will not take as long to read the *Sun* as to read the London *Times* or *Webster's Dictionary,* but when you have read it you will know about all that has happened in both hemispheres. The *Sun* will also publish a semi-weekly edition at two dollars a year, containing the most interesting articles from the daily, and also a condensed summary of the news prepared expressly for this edition.

The *Weekly Sun* will continue to be issued at one dollar a year. It will be prepared with great care, and will also contain all the news in a condensed and readable form. Both the weekly and semi-weekly will have accurate reports of the general, household, and cattle markets. They will also have an agricultural department, and will report the proceedings of the Farmers' Club. This department will be edited by Andrew S. Fuller, Esq., whose name will guarantee the quality of his contributions.

We shall endeavor to make the *Sun* worthy the confidence of the people in every part of the country. Its circulation is now more than fifty thousand copies daily. We mean that it shall soon be doubled; and in this, the aid of all persons who want such a newspaper as we propose to make will be cordially welcomed.

CHARLES A. DANA,
Editor and Manager.

NEW YORK, January 25, 1868.

Beneath this announcement was a farewell message from Moses Sperry Beach to the readers whom he had served for twenty years:

> With unreserved confidence in the ability of those who are to continue this work of my life, I lay aside an armor which in these latter years has been too loosely borne.

So Moses S. Beach retired from journalism at forty-five. With the $175,000 paid to him for the *Sun,* and the profits he had made in his many years of ownership, he was rich enough to realize his dream of quiet rural life—a realization that lasted until his death in 1892.

But who was this Dana who was taking up at forty-eight the burden that a younger man was almost wearily laying down?

It is very likely that he was not well known to the readers of the *Sun.* The newspaper world knew him as one who had been the backbone of Greeley's *Tribune* in the turbulent period before the Civil War and for a year after the war was on. The army world knew him as the man who had been chosen by Lincoln and Stanton for important and confidential missions. Students knew him as one of the editors of the *New American Encyclopedia.* By many a fireside his name was familiar as the compiler of the *Household Book of Poetry.* Highbrows remembered him as one of the group of geniuses in the Brook Farm colony.

In none of these categories were many of the men who ran with the fire engines, voted for John Kelly, and bought the *Sun.* But the *Sun* was the *Sun;* it was their paper, and they would have none other; and they would see what this Dana would do with it.

CHAPTER IX

THE REIGN OF DANA

A New Era in Journalism Begun.—An Editor Whose Only Rule was "Be Interesting." His Views on News.—Mitchell's Picture of Him.—His Great Contemporaries.

THE life of Dana until his forty-eighth year, when he acquired the *Sun*, was so full that the present space does not permit a full record of it. It is detailed in James Harrison Wilson's *Life of Charles A. Dana.* Dana's own *Recollections of the Civil War* is also useful.

Dana was born in Hinsdale, New Hampshire, on August 8, 1819. He was the son of Anderson Dana, who was sixth in descent from Richard Dana, the colonial settler. His mother was Ann Denison, who died when Charles was nine years old. Three years later he went to work for his uncle, William Dana, in the general store of Staats and Dana, Buffalo. When he was eighteen years old his employers failed and, with $200 he had saved, he went to Harvard. In 1840 he was obliged, through lack of money, to leave college and teach school. In 1841 he entered Brook Farm, the famous idealistic community settlement at Roxbury, Massachusetts, and remained there five years, working on the farm by day and writing at night for magazines. He was married in 1846 to Miss Eunice Macdaniel, also a Brook Farmer. In 1847 he became city editor of the New York *Tribune* under Horace Greeley. Later he was managing editor and, in Greeley's absence, editor. In 1862 he and Greeley disagreed over war policies and Dana resigned. Secretary of War Stanton appointed Dana second assistant secretary. Lincoln sent Dana to investigate the report that General Grant was drinking too hard. Dana was with Grant at Vicksburg. Later in the war he acted as the confidential agent of Lincoln at the front. After the war Dana was for a short time the editor of the Chicago *Republican,* a newspaper which failed for lack of capital. He returned to New York and interested a group of prominent Republicans, including Roscoe Conkling, William M. Evarts, Salem H. Wells, and A. B. Cornell, in the purchase of the *Sun.*

Why Dana and his friends did not start a new paper is explained in the following letter, written by Dana to General Wilson:

> Just as we were about commencing our own paper, the purchase of the *Sun* was proposed to me and accepted. It had a circulation of from fifty to sixty thousand a day, and all among the mechanics and small merchants of this city. We pay a large sum for it—$175,000—but it gives us at once a large and profitable business.
>
> If you have a thousand dollars at leisure, you had better invest it in the stock of our company, which is increased to $350,000 in order to pay for the new acquisition. Of this sum about $220,000 is invested in the Tammany Hall real estate, which is sure to be productive, independent of the business of the paper.

The "Tammany Hall real estate" was the building at the corner of Nassau and Frankfort Streets, where

Tammany kept its headquarters from 1811, when it moved from Martling's Long Room, at Nassau and Spruce Streets, to 1867, when Dana and his friends bought the building with the expectation of starting a new paper. If Moses S. Beach had attracted Dana's attention to the *Sun* in time, he might have sold him, as well as the paper, his own building at Nassau and Fulton Streets. But the Tammany Hall building was a better-placed home for the *Sun* than its old quarters. It faced City Hall Park and was a part of Printing-House Square.

Dana changed the appearance of the *Sun* overnight. He kept it as a folio, for he always believed in a four-page paper, even when he was printing ten pages, but he reduced the number of columns on a page from eight to seven, widening each column a little. The principal headlines, which had been irregular in size and two to the page, were made smaller and more uniform, and four appeared at the top of the front page. The editorial articles, which had been printed in minion, now appeared a size larger, in brevier.

Dana changed the title head of the *Sun* from roman, which it had been from the beginning, to Old English, as it stands to-day. He also changed the accompanying emblem. It had been a variation of the seal of the State of New York, with the sun rising in splendor behind mountains; on the right, Liberty with her Phrygian cap held on a staff, gazing at an outbound vessel; on the left, Justice with scales and sword, so facing that if not blindfolded she would see a locomotive and a train of cars crossing a bridge. These classic figures were kept, but the eagle—the state crest—which brooded

CHARLES A. DANA
Editor of *The Sun*, 1868-1897.

above the sunburst in Beach's time, was removed, so that the rays went skyward without hindrance. Dana liked "It Shines for All," the *Sun's* old motto, but he took it from the scroll in the emblem and replaced there the state motto, "Excelsior."

The *Sun* under its new master, rose auspiciously—master, not masters, for in spite of the number of his financial associates, Dana was absolute. As General Wilson wrote in his biography:

> From this time forth it may be truthfully said that Dana was the *Sun,* and the *Sun* Dana. He was the sole arbiter of its policy, and it was his constant practice to supervise every editorial contribution that came in while he was on duty.

Dana was a man whose natural intellectual gifts had been augmented by his travels, his experience on the *Tribune,* his exploits in the war, and his association with the big men of his time. Add to all this his solid financial backing and his acquirement of a paper with a large circulation, and the combination seemed an assurance of success. Yet, had Dana lacked the peculiarly human qualities that were his, the indefinable newspaper instinct that knows when a tomcat on the steps of the City Hall is more important than a crisis in the Balkans, the *Sun* would have set.

Only genius could enable a lofty-minded Republican, with a Republican aristocracy behind him, to take over the *Sun* and make a hundred thousand mechanics and tradesmen, nearly all Democrats, like their paper better than ever before. And that is what Dana did; except that he added to the *Sun's* former readers a new army of admirers.

When Dana came into control of the *Sun,* the city of New York, which then included only Manhattan and the Bronx, had less than a million population, yet it supported, or was asked to support, more newspapers than it has to-day. That was the day of the great personal editor. Bennett had his *Herald,* with James Gordon Bennett, Jr., as his chief helper. Horace Greeley was known throughout America as the editor of the *Tribune.* Henry J. Raymond was at the head of the *Times.* Manton Marble was the intellectual chief of the highly intellectual *World.*

The greatest Republican politician of that day, Thurlow Weed, was the editor of the *Commercial Advertiser.* Weed was seventy-one years old, but not the Nestor of New York editors, for William Cullen Bryant was three years his senior and still the active editor of the *Evening Post.* The *Evening Express,* later to be incorporated with the *Mail,* was ruled by the brothers Brooks, James as editor-in-chief and Erastus as manager. David M. Stone ran the *Journal of Commerce.* Ben Wood owned the only penny paper in town—the *Evening News.* Marcus M. Pomeroy, better known as Brick Pomeroy, had just started his sensational sheet, the *Democrat,* on the strength of the reputation he had won in the West as editor of the La Crosse *Democrat.* Later he changed the title of the *Democrat* to *Pomeroy's Advance Thought.*

These were the men who assailed or defended the methods of the reconstruction of the South; who stood up for President Johnson, or cried for his impeachment; who supported the presidential ambitions of Grant, then the looming figure in national politics, or decried the elevation of one whose fame had been exclusively military; who hammered at the wicked gates of Tammany Hall, or tried to excuse its methods.

Dana did not try to turn the general journalism of that day out of certain deep grooves into which it had sunk. He had his own ideas of what news was, how it should be written, how displayed; but they were ideas, not theories. He was not perturbed because the *Sun* had not handled a big story just the way the *Herald* or the *Tribune* dished it up; nor was it of the slightest consequence to him what Mr. Bennett or Mr. Greeley thought of the way the *Sun* used the story.

Dana made no rules. Other newspapers have printed commandments for their writers, but the *Sun* has never wasted a penny's worth of paper on rules. If there ever was a rule in the office, it was "Be interesting," and it was not only an unwritten rule, but generally an unspoken one.

Dana's realization that journalism was a profession which could be neither guided nor governed by set rules was expressed in a speech made by him before the Wisconsin Editorial Association at Milwaukee, in 1888:

> There is no system of maxims or professional rules that I know of that is laid down for the guidance of the journalist. The physician has his system of ethics and that sublime oath of Hippocrates which human wisdom has never transcended. The lawyer also has his code of ethics and the rules of the courts and the rules of practice which he is instructed in; but I have never met with a system of maxims that seemed to me to be perfectly adapted to the general direction of a newspaperman. I have written down a few prin-

ciples which occurred to me, which, with your permission, gentlemen, I will read for the benefit of the young newspapermen here to-night:

> Get the news, get all the news, get nothing but the news.
>
> Copy nothing from another publication without perfect credit.
>
> Never print an interview without the knowledge and consent of the party interviewed.
>
> Never print a paid advertisement as news-matter. Let every advertisement appear as an advertisement; no sailing under false colors.
>
> Never attack the weak or the defenseless, either by argument, by invective, or by ridicule, unless there is some absolute public necessity for so doing.
>
> Fight for your opinions, but do not believe that they contain the whole truth or the only truth.
>
> Support your party, if you have one; but do not think all the good men are in it and all the bad ones outside of it.
>
> Above all, know and believe that humanity is advancing; that there is progress in human life and human affairs; and that, as sure as God lives, the future will be greater and better than the present or the past.

In a lecture delivered at Cornell University in 1894—three years before his death—Mr. Dana uttered more maxims "of value to a newspaper-maker":

> Never be in a hurry.
>
> Hold fast to the Constitution.
>
> Stand by the Stars and Stripes. Above all, stand for liberty, whatever happens.
>
> A word that is not spoken never does any mischief.

All the goodness of a good egg cannot make up for the badness of a bad one.

If you find you have been wrong, don't fear to say so.

These maxims did not convey the mysterious prescription with which Dana revived American journalism from that trance in which it had forgotten that everybody is human and that the English language is alive and fluid.

If there had been rules by which a living newspaper could be made from men and ink and wood pulp, Dana would have known them; but there were none, nor are there now. E. P. Mitchell, who knew Dana better than any other man knew him, said in an address at the Pulitzer School of Journalism a few years ago:

> Mr. Dana used to lecture on journalism sometimes, when he was invited, but in the bottom of my heart I don't believe he had any theories of journalism other than common sense and free play for individual talent when discovered and available. And I do remember distinctly that when he sent Mr. Joseph Pulitzer, then fresh from St. Louis, on to Washington to report in semi-editorial correspondence the critical stage of the electoral controversy of 1876 Mr. Dana did not think it necessary to instruct that correspondent to assimilate his style to the *Sun's* methods and traditions. Never was a job of momentous journalistic importance better done in the absence of plain sailing directions; but that, perhaps, was due partly to the fact that Mr. Pulitzer was somewhat of an individualist himself.
>
> For the ancient common law of journalism, as derived from England, and perhaps before that from

away back in Bœotia, Mr. Dana didn't care one comic supplement. If anybody had asked Mr. Dana to compile a set of specific directions for running a newspaper, his reply, I am sure, would have been something like this:

"Heaven bless you, young man, there aren't any rules! Go ahead and write when you have something to say, not when you think you ought to say something. I'll edit out the nonsense. And, by the way, unless there happens to have been born into your noodle a little bit of the native aptitude, you ought to go and be a lawyer or a farmer or a banker or a great statesman."

Make rules for news? How is it possible to make a rule for something the value of which lies in the fact that it is the narrative of what never had happened, in exactly the same way, before? John Bogart, a city editor of the *Sun* who absorbed the Dana idea of news and the handling thereof, once said to a young reporter:

"When a dog bites a man, that is not news, because it happens so often. But if a man bites a dog, that is news."

Here is Mr. Dana's own definition of news:

The first thing which an editor must look for is news. If the newspaper has not the news it may have everything else, yet it will be comparatively unsuccessful; and by news I mean everything that occurs, everything which is of human interest, and which is of sufficient interest to arrest and absorb the attention of the public or of any considerable part of it.

There is a great disposition in some quarters to say that the newspapers ought to limit the amount of news that they print; that certain kinds of news ought not to be published. I do not know how that is. I am not prepared to maintain any abstract proposition in that line; but I have always felt that whatever the divine Providence permitted to occur I was not too proud to report.

A belief has been accepted in some quarters that the *Sun* of Dana's time preferred college men for its staff. This was in a way false, but it is true that a great many of the *Sun's* young men came from the colleges. Mr. Dana's views on the matter of educational equipment were quite plainly expressed by himself:

> If I could have my way, every young man who is going to be a newspaperman, and who is not absolutely rebellious against it, should learn Greek and Latin after the good old fashion. I had rather take a young fellow who knows the "Ajax" of Sophocles, and has read Tacitus, and can scan every ode of Horace—I would rather take him to report a prize-fight or a spelling-match, for instance, than to take one who has never had those advantages.
>
> At the same time, the cultivated man is not in every case the best reporter. One of the best I ever knew was a man who could not spell four words correctly to save his life, and his verb did not always agree with the subject in person and number; but he always got the fact so exactly, and he saw the picturesque, the interesting, the important aspect of it so vividly, that it was worth another man's while, who possessed the knowledge of grammar and spelling, to go over the report and write it out.
>
> Now, that was a man who had genius; he had a talent the most indubitable, and he got handsomely paid in spite of his lack of grammar, because after

his work had been done over by a scholar it was really beautiful. But any man who is sincere and earnest and not always thinking about himself can be a good reporter. He can learn to ascertain the truth; he can acquire the habit of seeing.

When he looks at a fire, what is the most important thing about that fire? Here, let us say, are five houses burning; which is the greatest? Whose store is that which is burning? And who has met with the greatest loss? Has any individual perished in the conflagration? Are there any very interesting circumstances about the fire? How did it occur? Was it like Chicago, where a cow kicked over a spirit-lamp and burned up the city?

All these things the reporter has to judge about. He is the eye of the paper, and he is there to see which is the vital fact in the story, and to produce it, tell it, write it out.

Dana saw the usefulness to a reporter of certain qualities which are acquired neither at school nor in the office:

In the first place, he must know the truth when he hears it and sees it. There are a great many men who are born without that faculty, unfortunately. But there are some men that a lie cannot deceive; and that is a very precious gift for a reporter, as well as for anybody else. The man who has it is sure to live long and prosper; especially if he is able to tell the truth which he sees, to state the fact or the discovery that he has been sent out after, in a clear and vivid and interesting manner.

The invariable law of the newspaper is to be interesting. Suppose you tell all the truths of science in a way that bores the reader; what is the good?

> The truths don't stay in the mind, and nobody thinks any the better of you because you have told the truth tediously. The reporter must give his story in such a way that you know he feels its qualities and events and is interested in them.

Even as he advised young men to read everything from Shakespeare and Milton down, Dana repeatedly warned them against the imitation, unconscious or otherwise, of another's style:

> Do not take any model. Every man has his own natural style, and the thing to do is to develop it into simplicity and clearness. Do not, for instance, labor after such a style as Matthew Arnold's—one of the most beautiful styles that has ever been seen in any literature. It is no use to try to get another man's style or to imitate the wit or the mannerisms of another writer. The late Mr. Carlyle, for example, did, in my judgment, a considerable mischief in his day, because he led everybody to write after the style of his "French Revolution," and it became pretty tedious.

Dana wanted good English always, but a constant spice of variety in the treatment of a subject, and in the style itself; therefore he chose a variety of men.

If he believed that the best report of a ship launching could be written by a longshoreman, he would have hired the hard-handed toiler and assigned him to the job. He wanted men who would look at the world with open eyes and find the new things that were going on.

To Dana life was not a mere procession of elections, legislatures, theatrical performances, murders, and lectures. Life was everything—a new kind of apple, a crying child on the curb, a policeman's epigram, the exact weight of a candidate for president, the latest style in whiskers, the origin of a new slang expression, the idiosyncrasies of the City Hall clock, a strange four-master in the harbor, the headdresses of Syrian girls, a new president or a new football coach at Yale, a vendetta in Mulberry Bend—everything was fish to the great net of Dana's mind.

With a word or an epigram he destroyed traditions that had fettered the profession since the days of the hand press.

One day he held up a string of proofs—a long obituary of Bismarck, or Blaine, or some other celebrity who had just passed away.

"Mr. Lord," he said to his managing editor, "isn't that a lot of space to give to a dead man?"

Yet the next day the same Dana came from his office to the city editor's desk to inquire who had written a certain story two inches long, and, upon learning, went over to the reporter who was the author.

"Very good, young man, very good," he said, pointing to the item. "I wish I could write like that!"

Names of writers meant nothing to Dana. A dull article from a celebrity he returned to its envelope with the note "Respectfully declined," and without a thought of the author's surprise, or possibly rage. But over a poem from an up-state unknown he might spend half an hour if the verses contained the germ of an idea new to him.

One clergyman who had come into literary prominence offered to write some articles for the *Sun*. Dana told him he might try. The clergyman evidently had a notion that the *Sun's* cleverness was a worldly, reckless devilishness, and he adapted the style of his first article to what he supposed was the tone of the paper. Dana read it, smiled, wrote across the first page "This is too damned wicked," and mailed it back to the author.

He was a patient man. A clerk in the New York post office copied by hand Edward Everett Hale's story, *The Man without a Country,* and offered it to the *Sun*—as original matter—for a hundred dollars. It was suggested to Mr. Dana that the poor fool should be exposed.

"No," said Dana, "mark it 'Respectfully declined,' and send it back to him. He has been honest enough to enclose postage stamps."

Surroundings were nothing to Dana. To him an office was a place to work, to convert ideas into readable form. What would works of art be in such a place to a man who took more interest in the crowds that went to and fro on Park Row beneath his window? Let the room itself be described by Mr. Mitchell, who set down this picture of it after he had spent hours in it with Mr. Dana almost daily for twenty years:

> In the middle of the small room a desk-table of black walnut of the Fulton Street style and the period of the first administration of Grant; a shabby little round table at the window, where Mr. Dana sits when the day is dark; one leather-covered chair, which does duty at either post, and two wooden chairs, both rickety, for visitors on errands of business or ceremony; on the desk a revolving case with a few dozen books of reference; an ink-pot and pen, not much used except in correcting manuscript and proofs, for Mr. Dana talks off to a stenographer his editorial

articles and his correspondence, sometimes spending on the revision of the former twice as much time as was required for the dictation; a window-seat filled with exchanges, marked here and there in blue pencil for the editor's eyes; a big pair of shears, and two or three extra pairs of spectacles in cache against an emergency—these few items constitute what is practically the whole objective equipment of the editor of the *Sun*. The shears are probably the newest article of furniture in the list. They replaced, three or four years ago, another pair of unknown antiquity, besought and obtained by Eugene Field, and now occupying, alongside of Mr. Gladstone's ax, the place of honor in that poet's celebrated collection of edged instruments.

For the non-essentials, the little trapezoid-shaped room contains a third table containing a file of the newspaper for a few weeks back, and a heap of new books which have passed review; an iron umbrella-rack; on the floor a cheap Turkish rug; and a lounge covered with horsehide, upon which Mr. Dana descends for a five minutes' nap perhaps five times a year.

The adornments of the room are mostly accidental and insignificant. Ages ago somebody presented to Mr. Dana, with symbolic intent, a large stuffed owl. The bird of wisdom remains by inertia on top of the revolving bookcase, just as it would have remained there if it had been a stuffed cat or a statuette of "Folly." Unnoticed and probably long ago forgotten by the proprietor, the owl solemnly boxes the compass as Mr. Dana swings the case, reaching in quick succession for his Bible, his Portuguese dictionary, his compendium of botanical terms, or his copy of the Democratic national platform of 1892. On the mantelpiece is an ugly, feather-haired little totem figure from Alaska, which likewise keeps its place solely by possession. It stands between a photograph of Chester A. Arthur, whom Mr. Dana liked and admired as a man of the world, and the japanned calendar-case which has shown him the time of year for the last quarter of a century. A dingy chromolithograph of Prince von Bismarck stands shoulder to shoulder with George, the Count Joannes.

The same mingling of sentiment and pure accident marks the rest of Mr. Dana's picture-gallery. There is a large and excellent photograph of Horace Greeley, who is held in half-affectionate, half-humorous remembrance by his old associate in the management of the *Tribune*. Another is of the late Justice Blatchford, of the United States Supreme Court; it is the strong face of the fearless judge whose decision from the Federal bench in New York twenty years ago blocked the attempt to drag Mr. Dana before a servile little court in Washington to be tried without a jury on the charge of criminal libel, at the time when the *Sun* was demolishing the District Ring.

Over the mantel is Abraham Lincoln. There are pictures of the four Harper brothers and of the Appletons. Andrew Jackson is there twice, once in black and white, once in vivid colors. An inexpensive Thomas Jefferson faces the livelier Jackson. A framed diploma certifies that Mr. Dana was one of several gentlemen who presented to the State a portrait in oils of Samuel J. Tilden. On different sides of the room are William T. Coleman, the organizer of the San Francisco Vigilantes, and a crude colored print of the Haifa colony at the foot of Mount Carmel in Syria. Strangest of all in this singular collection is a photograph of a tall, dark, lank, and superior-looking New England mill-girl, issued as an advertisement by some Connecticut concern engaged in the manufacture of spool-cotton.

For a good many years the most available wall-space in Mr. Dana's office was occupied by a huge pasteboard chart, showing elaborately, in deadly parallel columns, the differences in the laws of the several States of the Union respecting divorce. It was put there, and it remained there, serving no earthly purpose except to illustrate the editor's indifference as to his immediate surroundings, until it disappeared as mysteriously as it had come.

Such were Mr. Dana's surroundings, with nothing to indicate, as Mr. Mitchell remarked, that the occupant "knew Manet from Monet, or old Persian luster from Gubbio."

Dana was interested in everything, read everything, saw almost everybody. His own office was almost as free as the great main office of the *Sun*, where sat everybody from the managing editor down to the office boy.

The belief was once common, among those ignorant of editorial methods and the limitations of human powers, that Mr. Dana wrote every word that appeared on the editorial page of the *Sun*. It is likely that this flattering myth came to his ears and caused him more than one chuckle. Dana wrote pieces for the *Sun*, many of them, but he never essayed the superhuman task of filling the whole page with his own self. Nobody knew better than he what a bore a man becomes who flows opinion constantly, whether by voice or by pen.

That another man's work should be mistaken for his own, or his own for another man's, was to Dana nothing at all, except perhaps a source of amusement. The anonymity of the writers on the *Sun* was so complete that the public knew their work only as a whole; but whenever anything particularly biting or humorous appeared, the same public instantly decided that Dana must have written it.

No king, no clown, to rule this town!

That line, born in the *Sun's* editorial page, will live as long as Shakespeare. In eight words it embodied the protest of New York against the arrogance and stupidity of machine political rule. Ten thousand times, at least, it has been credited to Dana, but as a matter of fact it was written by W. O. Bartlett.

Four years after he became the master of the *Sun*, and a quarter of a century before death took him from it, Dana found himself the Nestor of metropolitan journalism. Of the three other great New York editors of Dana's time—three who had founded their own papers and lived with those papers until the wing of Azrael shut out the roar of the presses—Raymond had been the first, and the youngest, to go; for his end came when he was only forty-nine, eighteen years after the establishment of his *Times*.

Bennett, the inscrutable monarch of the *Herald*, died in 1872, three years after Raymond, but Bennett, who did not establish the *Herald* until he was forty, had owned it, and had given every waking hour to its welfare, for thirty-seven years. The year of Bennett's death saw the passing of the unfortunate Greeley, broken in body and mind from his fatuous chase of public office, within three weeks of his defeat for the presidency. As the sprightly young editor of the Louisville *Courier-Journal,* Colonel Henry Watterson, who was always interested in New York and its newspapers, wrote in his paper in January, 1873:

> Mr. Bryant being no longer actively engaged in newspaper work, Mr. Dana is left alone to tell the tale of old-time journalism in New York. He, of all his fellow creditors of the great metropolis, has passed the period of middle age; though—years apart—he is as blithe and nimble as the youngest of them, and has performed, with the *Sun,* a feat in modern newspaper practice that entitles him to the stag-horns laid down at his death by James Gordon Bennett. Mr. Dana is no less a writer and scholar than an editor; as witness his sketch of Mr. Greeley, which for thorough character-drawing is unsurpassed. In a word, Mr. Dana at fifty-three is as vigorous, sinewy, and live as a young buck of thirty-five or forty.
>
> His professional associates were boys when he was managing editor of the *Tribune.* Manton Marble was at college at Rochester, and Whitelaw Reid was going to school in Ohio. Young Bennett and Bundy were wearing short jackets.
>
> They were rough-and-tumble days, sure enough, even for New York. There was no Central Park. Madison Square was "out of town." Franconi's Circus, surnamed a "hippodrome," sprawled its ugly wooden towers, minarets, and sideshows over the ground now occupied by the Fifth Avenue Hotel. *Miss Flora McFlimsy* of the opposite square had not come into being; nay, Madison Square itself existed in a city ordinance merely, and, like the original of

Mr. Praed's Darnell Park, was a wretched waste of common, where the boys skated and played shinny.

The elder Harpers stood in the shoes now worn by their sons, who were off at boarding-school. George Ripley was as larky as John Hay is. Delmonico's, downtown, was the only Delmonico's. The warfare between the newspapers constituted the most exciting topic of the time. Bennett was "Jack Ketch," Raymond was the "little villain," and Greeley was by turns an "incendiary," a "white-livered poltroon," and a "free-lover." Parke Godwin and Charles A. Dana were managing editors respectively; both scholars and both, as writers, superior to all the rest, except Greeley, who, as a newspaper writer, never had a superior.

The situation is changed completely. Bennett, Greeley, and Raymond are dead. Dana and Godwin, both about of an age, stand at the head of New York journalism, while Reid, Marble, and Jennings, all young men, wear the purple of a new era.

Will it be an era of reforms? There are signs that it will be. Marble is a recruit. Reid is essentially a man of the world. Jennings is an Englishman. One would think that these three, led by two ripe scholars and gentlemen like Godwin and Dana, would alter the character of the old partisan warfare in one respect at least, and that if they have need to be personal, they will be wittily so, and not brutally and dirtily personal; the which will be an advance.

There will never be an end to the personality of journalism. But there is already an end of the efficacy of filth. In this, as in other things, there are fashions. What ill thing, for example, can be said personally injurious of Reid, Marble, Jennings, Bundy, and the rest, all hard-working, painstaking men, without vices or peculiarities, who do not invite attack?

"There will never be an end to the personality of journalism." It is curious to note in passing that Henry Watterson, who retired from the active editorship of the *Courier-Journal* on August 7, 1918, after fifty years' service, was the last of the men who, according to the measure of forty years ago, were "personal journalists." "Dana says," "Greeley says," "Raymond says"—such oral credits are no longer given by the readers of the really big and reputable newspapers of New York to the men who write opinions. "Henry Watterson says" was the last of the phrases of that style.

Dana believed in personal journalism and thought it would not pass away. A few days after the death of Horace Greeley, the editor of the *Sun* printed his views on the subject:

> A great deal of twaddle is uttered by some country newspapers just now over what they call personal journalism. They say that now that Mr. Bennett, Mr. Raymond, and Mr. Greeley are dead, the day for personal journalism is gone by, and that impersonal journalism will take its place. That appears to be a sort of journalism in which nobody will ask who is the editor of a paper or the writer of any class of article, and nobody will care.
>
> Whenever in the newspaper profession a man rises up who is original, strong, and bold enough to make his opinions a matter of consequence to the public, there will be personal journalism; and whenever newspapers are conducted only by commonplace individuals whose views are of no interest to the world

and of no consequence to anybody, there will be nothing but impersonal journalism.

And this is the essence of the whole question.

For all that, Dana must have felt lonely, for at that moment, at any rate, the new chiefs of the *Sun's* rivals did not measure up to the heights of their predecessors. To Dana, the trio that had passed were men worthy of his steel, and worthy, each in his own way, of admiration.

Bennett was followed in the possession of the *Herald* by his son and namesake. Whitelaw Reid took Greeley's place at the head of the *Tribune*. In a "Survey of Metropolitan Journalism" which appeared in the editorial columns of the *Sun* on September 3, 1875—the *Sun's* forty-second birthday—Dana wrote:

> The *Times* is a very respectable paper, and more than that, a journal of which the Republican party has reason to be proud. It is not a servile organ, but a loyal partisan. We prefer for our own part to keep aloof from the party politicians. They are disagreeable fellows to have hanging about a newspaper office, and their advice we do not regard as valuable. But we do not decry party newspapers. They have their field, and must always exist. The *Times* is a creditable example of such a newspaper. It would be better, however, if Mr. Jennings himself wrote the whole editorial page.
>
> The mistake of the *Times* was in lapsing into the dulness of respectable conservatism after its Ring fight. It should have kept on and made a crusade against frauds of all sorts.
>
> The *Herald* has improved since young Mr. Bennett's return. We are attracted toward this son of his father. He has a passion for manly sports, and

that we like. If the shabby writers who make jest of his walking-matches had an income of three or four hundred thousand dollars a year, perhaps they would drive in carriages instead of walking and dawdle away their time on beds of ease or the gorgeous sofas of the Lotos Club. Mr. Bennett does otherwise. He strides up Broadway with the step of an athlete, dons his navy blue and commands his yacht, shoots pigeons, and prefers the open air of Newport to the confinement of the *Herald* office.

The *World* is a journal which pleases us on many accounts . . . but occasionally there is a bit of prurient wit in its columns that might better be omitted. The *World* is also too often written in too fantastic language. Its young men seem to vie with each other in tormenting the language. They will do better when they learn that there is more force in simple Anglo-Saxon than in all the words they can manufacture. We advise them to read the Bible and Common Prayer Book. Those books will do their souls good, anyway, and they may also learn to write less affectedly.

The *Sun* was as frank in discussing its own theories and ambitions as it was in criticizing its contemporaries for dullness and poor writing. Dana's dream, never to be realized, was a newspaper without advertisements. He believed that by getting all the news, condensing it into the smallest readable space, and adding such literary matter as the readers' tastes demanded, a four-page paper might be produced with a reasonable profit from the sales, after paper and ink, men and machinery, had been paid for.

For the first twenty years of the Dana régime the week-

The Sun.

THE FIRST NUMBER OF "THE SUN" UNDER DANA
The Old English title head has been used ever since.

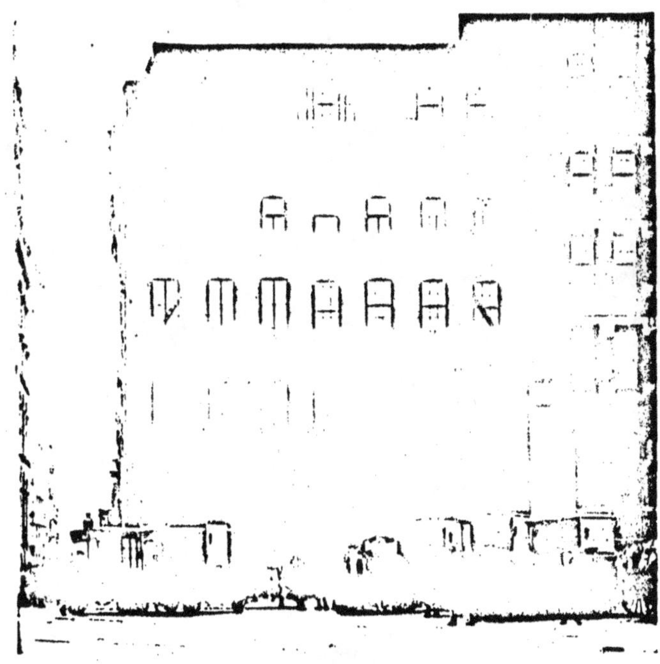

170 NASSAU STREET
Home of *The Sun* from 1868 to 1915.

day *Sun* never appeared in more than four pages, except in emergencies. In the end, of course, the scheme was beaten by the very excellence of its originator's qualities. The *Sun*, by its popularity, drew more and more advertising. Through his own genius Dana destroyed his own dream, but not without having almost proved that it was possible of realization.

Dana believed that most of the newspapers of his day —particularly in the seventies—were tiring out not only the reader but the writer. Commenting on a decline in the newspaper business in the summer of 1875, the *Sun* said:

> Some of our big contemporaries have been overdoing the thing. They seem to think that to secure circulation it is necessary to overload the stomachs of their readers.
>
> The American newspaper-reader demands of an editor that he shall not give him news and discussions in heavy chunks, but so condensed and clarified that he shall be relieved of the necessity of wading through a treatise to get at a fact, or spending time on a dilated essay to get a bite at an argument.
>
> Six or seven dreary columns are filled with leading articles, no matter whether there are subjects to discuss of public interest, or brains at hand to treat them. Our big contemporaries exhaust their young men and drive them too hard. The stock of ideas is not limitless, even in a New York newspaper office.
>
> Another thing has been bad. Men with actual capacity of certain sorts for acceptable writing have been frightened off from doing natural and vigorous work by certain newspaper critics and doctrinaires who are in distress if the literary proprieties are seemingly violated, and if the temper and blood of

> the writer actually show in his work. They measure our journalistic production by an English standard, which lays it down as its first and most imperative rule that editorial writing shall be free from the characteristics of the writer. This is ruinous to good writing, and damaging to the sincerity of writers. . . . If we choose to glow or cry out in indignation, we do so, and we are not a bit frightened at the sound of our own voice.

Dana himself had that peculiar faculty, as indescribable as instinct, of knowing, when he saw an article in the paper, just how much work the author of it had put in—particularly in cases where the labor had been in leaving out, rather than in writing. As a result of this intuition he never drove his men. He would accept three lines or three columns for a day's work, and his admiration might go out more heartily to the three lines. As for the appearance of characteristics in men's writing, that was as necessary, in Dana's opinion, as it was wicked in the judgment of the ancient editors.

CHAPTER X

"THE SUN" AND "HUMAN INTEREST"

Something about Everything, for Everybody.—A Wonderful Four-Page Paper.—Interviews with Commodore Vanderbilt and Inventor Edison.

FROM the beginning of Dana's reign the *Sun* fed a little bit of everything to its readers. The Moody and Sankey revivals, Mr. Keely's motor, which didn't work, and young Edison's multiple telegraph, which did; the baseball games of the days when Spalding pitched for Boston and Anson and Reach were at first and second base, respectively, for the Philadelphia Athletics; the presentation of a cup to John Cable Heenan, the prize-fighter, as the handsomest and best-dressed man at the ball of the Shandley Association; an interview with Joaquin Miller on Longfellow; the wiggles of the sea serpent off Swampscott; a ghost-story from Long Island, with a beautiful spook lashed to the rigging of a spectral bark; the arrival of New York's first Chinese laundry-man; Father Tom Burke's lectures on Ireland; the lectures of Tyndall on newly discovered phenomena of light; the billiard matches between Cyrille Dion and Maurice Daly; a tar-and-feathers party in Brooklyn—the *Sun* skimmed the pan of life and served the cream for two cents.

The familiar three-story headline, which was first used by the *Sun* on the day of Grant's inauguration, and which stayed the same until long after Mr. Dana's death, attracted readers with the magic of the head writers' art. "The Skull in the Chimney," "Shaved by a Lady Barber," "A Man Hanged by Women," "Burned Alive for $5,000," "The Murder in the Well," "Death Leap in a Theater," "An Aged Sinner Hanged," "The Duel in the Bedroom," "Horrors of a Madhouse," "A Life for a Love-Letter"—none could glance at the compelling titles of the *Sun* stories without remaining to read. They are still fascinating in an age when lady barbers would attract no attention.

A typical *Sun* of 1874 might contain, in its four pages, six columns about the Beecher-Tilton case; four columns of editorial articles; a letter from Eli Perkins (Melville DeLancey Landon) at Saratoga, declaring that the spa was standing still commercially because of its lack of good drinking water; a column, also from Saratoga, describing the defeat of Preakness by Springbok; the latest in the strange case of Charley Ross; a column headed "Life in the Metropolis—Dashes Here and There by the Sun's Reporters"; a column of "Sunbeams," a column about trout fishing, two columns of general news, and five columns of advertisements.

Instead of Eli Perkins's letter, there might be a critique by Leopold Damrosch, from Baireuth, of Wagner's "Götterdämmerung," just presented; or a dissection, by "Monsieur X," of E. H. Sothern's *Dundreary*.

In the "Sunbeams" column were crowded the vagrant wit and wisdom of the world. The items concerned everything from great men in European chancelleries to organ grinders in Nassau Street:

The mules are all dying in Arkansas.

A printer in Texas has named his first-born Brevier Fullfaced Jones.

Real estate is looking up at New Orleans.

Translations from Hawthorne are becoming popular in France.

Venison costs six cents a pound in St. Paul.

Queen Victoria says every third woman in Cork is a beauty.

Goldwin Smith is coming to the United States.

The Pope denounces short dresses.

The same terseness is seen in the "Footlight Flashes," begun in 1876:

Clara Morris takes her lap-dog out for a daily drive.

Miss Claxton is meeting with indifferent success in "Conscience."

Not less than $30,000 was spent last evening in the theaters of New York.

John T. Raymond drew excellent houses as *Colonel Sellers* at the Brooklyn Theater.

For the term of their appearance in "King Lear," Lawrence Barrett will receive $1,200 a week; E. E. Sheridan, $1,000; Frederick B. Warde, $500.

The interview, invented by the elder Bennett, was becoming more and more popular. The *Sun* used it, not only as the vehicle of acquired information, but sometimes as the envelope of humor. Take, for example, this bit, printed in 1875, but as fresh in style and spirit as if it were the product of to-day:

INTERVIEWING VANDERBILT

ANOTHER REPORTER COMES AWAY FREIGHTED WITH VALUABLE INFORMATION

Commodore Vanderbilt was eighty-one years old yesterday. He spent the day in his Fourth Avenue offices, taking his usual drive in the afternoon. A *Sun* reporter visited him in the evening to inquire about a favorable time for selling a few thousands of New York Central.

"This," said the commodore, slowly and solemnly, as he entered the drawing-room, "is my birthday."

"Indeed!" said the reporter. "Do you think the preferred stock——"

"To-day," the commodore interrupted, "I am eighty-one years old. I am stronger——"

"Is there any prospect of an immediate rise?"

"I have never gone into the late-supper business," the commodore answered, apparently not catching the drift of the question; "and I have always been a very temperate man. But how did you find out that this was my birthday?"

"You hinted at the fact yourself," the reporter replied. "Will the Erie troubles——"

"The Erie troubles will not prevent me from beginning my eighty-second year with a young heart and a clear conscience."

"And with the prospect of seeing a good many more birthday anniversaries?" the reporter asked.

"That, my dear boy," said the commodore, "is one of those things that no fellow can tell about."

"Do you think that this is a good time to sell?"

"No, it's never a good time to sell after banking hours."

"Good evening!"

"Good evening! Drop in again."

The great robber boss, William M. Tweed, was a source of news from his rise in the late sixties to his death in 1878. As early as March, 1870, the *Sun* gave its readers an intimate idea of Tweed's private extravagances under the heading:

> BILL TWEED'S BIG BARN—DEMOCRATIC EXTRAVAGANCE VERSUS THAT OF THE WHITE HOUSE—GRANT'S BILLIARD SALOON, CALIGULA'S STABLE, AND LEONARD JEROME'S PRIVATE THEATER ECLIPSED—MARTIN VAN BUREN'S GOLD SPOONS NOWHERE—BELMONT'S FOUR-IN-HAND OVERSHADOWED—A PICTURE FOR RURAL DEMOCRATS.

Beneath this head was a column story beginning:

> The Hon. William M. Tweed resides at 41 West Thirty-sixth Street. The Hon. William M. Tweed's horses reside in East Fortieth Street, between Madison and Park Avenues.

That was the *Sun's* characteristic way of starting a story.

Boss Tweed was, in a way, responsible for the appearance of a *Sun* more than four pages in size. Up to December, 1875, there was no issue of the *Sun* on Sundays. In November of that year it was announced that beginning on December 5 there would be a Sunday *Sun*, to be sold at three cents, one cent more than the week-day price, but nothing was said, or thought, of an increase in size.

On Saturday, December 4, Tweed, with the connivance of his keepers, escaped from his house in Madison Avenue. This made a four-column story on which Mr. Dana had not counted. Also, the advertisers had taken advantage of the new Sunday issue, and there were more than two pages of advertisements. There was nothing for it but to make an eight-page paper, for which Dana, who then believed that all the news could be told in a folio, apologized as follows:

> We confess ourselves surprised at the extraordinary pressure of advertisements upon our pages this morning; and disappointed in being compelled to present the *Sun* to our readers in a different form from that to which they are accustomed. We trust, however, that they will find it no less interesting than usual; and, still more, that they will feel that although the appearance may be somewhat different, it is yet the same friendly and faithful *Sun*.

But the Sunday issue of the *Sun* never went back to four pages, for the eight-page paper had been made so attractive with special stories, reprint, and short fiction that both readers and advertisers were pleased. It was ten years, however, before the week-day *Sun* increased its size. Even during the Beecher trial (January, 1875) when the *Sun's* reporter, Franklin Fyles, could not condense the day's proceedings within a page of seven columns, the *Sun* still gave all the rest of the day's news.

The *Sun* omitted the weary introductions that had been the fashion in newspapers—leading paragraphs which told over again what was in the headlines and were merely a prelude to a third and detailed telling. The *Sun* reporter began at the beginning, thus:

> The Hon. John Kelly, wearing a small bouquet in the lapel of his coat, stepped out of his coach in front of Cardinal McCloskey's residence in Madison Avenue just before eight o'clock yesterday morning. A few minutes later three other coaches arrived, and their occupants entered the house. Many of the neighbors knew that a niece of the cardinal was to be married to Mr. Kelly, and they strained their eyes through plate-glass windows in the hope that they might see the bride and the groom. Cardinal McCloskey, having been apprized of the arrival of the wedding-party, went to the chapel in the other part of the house, and at about a quarter past eight, the time fixed for the mass *pro sponsis*, the marriage ceremony was begun.

In the longer and more important stories, the rule was adhered to as closely as possible. Prolixity, fine writing, and hysteria were taboo. Mark the calmness with which the *Sun* reporter began his story of the most sensational crime of the late seventies:

> Two little mounds of red-colored earth around a small hole in the ground, and a few feet of down-trodden grass, were all that marked the last resting-place of Alexander T. Stewart yesterday morning. In the dead of the night robbers had dug into the earth above the vault, removed one of the stones that covered it, and stolen the body of the dead millionaire.

The human lights of life were caught by the *Sun* men and transferred to every page of every issue. In 1878 a *Sun* reporter was sent to Menlo Park, New Jersey, to see how a young inventor there, who had just announced the possibility of an incandescent electric light, worked:

> Here Mr. Edison dropped his cigar-stump from his mouth, and, turning to Griffin, asked for some chewing-tobacco. The private secretary drew open his drawer and passed out a yellow cake as large as a dinner-plate. The professor tore away a chew, saying:
>
> "I am partly indebted to the *Sun* for this tobacco. It printed an article saying that I chewed poor tobacco. That was so. The Lorillards saw the article and sent me down a box of the best plug that ever went into a man's mouth. All the workmen have used it, and Grif says there is a marked moral improvement in the men. It seems, however, to have the opposite effect on Grif. You see that he has salted away the last cake for his own use."

Nearly fifty years later *Sun* reporters still went to see Mr. Edison borrow white magic from nature and chewing tobacco from his employees, and to describe both interesting processes.

In 1882 the *Sun* made the calculation that the average effect of certain sorts of news in increase of circulation was about as follows:

Presidential elections	82,000
State and city elections	42,000
Last days of walking-matches	25,000
October state elections in Presidential years	21,000
Great fires	10,000
Notable disasters	9,000
Hangings in or near New York	8,000

The *Sun* expressed a curiosity to know—

> Who are the eighty or ninety thousand people, not regular readers of the *Sun*, that buy the paper after

a Presidential election? Where do they live? Do they read the papers only after exciting events?

On its fiftieth birthday—September 3, 1883—the *Sun* printed a table showing the high-tide marks of its circulation:

Nov. 8, 1876—Presidential election	222,390
Sept. 20, 1881—Garfield's death.............	212,525
Nov. 3, 1880—Presidential election	206,974
July 13, 1871—Orange riots	192,224
Sept. 21, 1881—Second day after Garfield's death	180,215
Nov. 3, 1875—State and city elections	177,588
July 3, 1881—Garfield shot	176,093

In the same article, a page review written by Mr. Mitchell, the reasons for the *Sun's* success were succinctly given:

> No waste of words, no nonsense, plain, outspoken expressions of honest opinion, the abolishment of the conventional measures of news importance, the substitution of the absolute standard of real interest to human beings, bright and enjoyable writing, wit, philosophical good humor, intolerance of humbug, hard hitting from the shoulder on proper occasions—do we not see all these qualities now in our esteemed contemporaries on every side of us, and in every part of the land?

CHAPTER XI

DANA AND POLITICS

High fight against the Whisky Ring, Crédit Mobilier, "Addition, Division, and Silence."—The "Sun's" Opposition to President Cleveland.

THE first ten years of Dana's service on the *Sun* were marked by the uprooting of many public evils. To use the mild phrasing of the historian John Fiske, "Villains sometimes succeeded in imposing upon President Grant, who was an honest, simple-hearted soldier without much knowledge of the ways of the world." To say it more concretely, hardly a department of the national government but was alive with fraud. The *Sun*, which had supported Grant in the election of 1868, turned against his administration in its first months, and for years it continued to keep before the public the revelations of corruption—which were easily made, so bold were the scoundrels, so coarse their manners of theft.

Among the scandals which the *Sun* either brought to light or was most vigorous in assailing, these were the principal:

The Crédit Mobilier Scandal.—This involved the names of many senators and representatives who were accused of accepting stock in the Crédit Mobilier of America, the fiscal company organized to build the Union Pacific Railroad, as a reward for using their influence and votes in favor of the great enterprise.

The Navy Department Scandal.—In this the *Sun* accused George M. Robeson, Secretary of the Navy, of having permitted double payment to contractors and of violating the law in making large purchases without competitive bidding. Mr. Dana appeared as a witness in the congressional investigation of Robeson, who, in the end, while not convicted of personal corruption, was censured for the laxity of his official methods.

The Whisky Ring.—This evil combination cheated the government out of millions of dollars. It was made up of distillers, wholesale liquor dealers, and employees of the internal revenue office, these conspiring together to avoid the payment of the liquor tax. The first attack on the corrupt alliance was made in the *Sun* of February 3, 1872, in an article by "Sappho," one of the *Sun's* Washington correspondents. Other great newspapers took up the fight, but the *Sun* was the chief aggressor. As a result of the exposure, 238 men were indicted and many of them, including the chief clerk of the Treasury Department, were sent to prison.

"Addition, Division, and Silence."—On March 20, 1867, W. H. Kemble, state treasurer of Pennsylvania and one of the Republican bosses, wrote the following letter to Titian J. Coffey, a lawyer and claim-agent in Washington:

> MY DEAR TITIAN:
>
> Allow me to introduce to you my particular friend, Mr. George O. Evans. He has a claim of some magnitude that he wishes you to help him in. Put him through as you would me. He understands addition, division, and silence.
>
> W. H. KEMBLE

When this letter fell into the hands of the *Sun*, which had already made war on the ring formed for the collection of war claims, it saw in Kemble's last four words the sententious platform of widespread fraud. It printed the letter, and kept on printing it, with that iteration which Dana knew was of value in a crusade. In a few months the whole country was familiar with the phrase so suggestive of plunder.

Kemble was a politician with a thick skin, but he at last became so enraged at the repetition of "addition, division, and silence," whether uttered by street urchins or printed all over America as the watchword of corruption—"honest graft," he would have called it, if that phrase had then been common—that he sued out a writ of criminal libel against Mr. Dana and had him arrested as he was passing through Philadelphia. The only result of this was to make the phrase more common than before.

Kemble was afterward convicted of trying to bribe Pennsylvania legislators and was sent to prison for a year.

The Post-Trader Scandal.—William W. Belknap, Grant's Secretary of War, was charged with receiving from Caleb P. Marsh fifteen hundred dollars in consideration for the appointment of John S. Evans to maintain a trading establishment at Fort Sill, in the Indian Territory. The scandal came to the surface through the remark of Mrs. Belknap that Mrs. Evans would have no place in society, "as she is only a post-trader's wife," and the retort of Mrs. Evans, upon hearing of this, that "a post-trader's wife is as good as the wife of an official who takes money for the appointment of a post-trader."

The *Sun* laid the story of bribery wide open, and the

Senate proceeded to impeach the Secretary of War. He escaped punishment by resigning his office, twenty-five senators voting "not guilty" on the ground that Belknap's resignation technically removed him from the Senate's jurisdiction. Thirty-five senators voted "guilty," but a two-thirds vote was necessary to punish.

The Salary Grab.—This was the act of Congress of March 3, 1873, which raised the president's salary from $25,000 to $50,000, and the salaries of senators and representatives from $5,000 to $7,500. Its evil lay not in the increases, but in the retroactive clause which provided that each congressman should receive $5,000 as extra pay for the two-year term then ending. The assaults of the *Sun* and other newspapers so aroused public indignation that Congress was obliged to repeal the act in January, 1874, and many members returned their share of the spoil to the Treasury.

The Boss Shepherd Scandal.—The *Sun* printed an article from Washington accusing Alexander Shepherd, vice president of the Board of Public Works of the District of Columbia, and Henry D. Cooke, governor of the District, with having a financial interest in the Metropolitan Paving Company, which had many street contracts in the national capital. Shepherd and Cooke laid a complaint of criminal libel against Mr. Dana, and an assistant district attorney of the District of Columbia came to New York and procured from United States Commissioner Davenport a warrant for the editor's arrest.

It was the intent of the prosecution to hale Dana to a Washington police court, where he would be tried without a jury. Dana had gone willingly, even eagerly, to Washington when summoned in the Robeson case, but the Shepherd strategy was so manifestly an attempt to railroad him that an appeal was taken to the Federal court for the southern district of New York. The historic decision of the district judge—Samuel Blatchford, subsequently promoted to the United States Supreme Court—may be summed up in one of its paragraphs:

> The Constitution says that all trials shall be by jury, and the accused is entitled, not to be first convicted by a court and then to be convicted by a jury, but to be convicted or acquitted *in the first instance* by a jury.

As the *Sun* said of this decision, important to the freedom of the individual as well as to that of the press:

> Those who sought to murder liberty, where they looked for a second Jeffreys, found a second Mansfield.

The Safe Burglary Conspiracy.—Columbus Alexander, a reputable citizen of Washington, was active in the movement to smash the Washington contractors' ring. He sought to bring certain contractors' books into court and exposed the false set that was produced. The ringsters hired a man to go to Mr. Alexander with a story that he could bring him the genuine books. Then the gang, which included men in the secret-service departments of the government, placed some of the genuine books in the safe of the district attorney's office and employed three professional burglars to blow open the safe.

The books, taken from the safe, were carried to Alexander's home by the man who had approached him. Close behind came police, who were prepared to arrest Alexander as soon as he received the "stolen property."

He was to be accused of hiring the burglars to crack the district attorney's safe. But the hour was early in the morning, Alexander was sleeping the deep sleep of the just, and the criminal rang his doorbell and beat upon the door panels in vain.

The ringsters then "arrested" the "thief," and caused him to sign a false confession, accusing Alexander; but the failure of their theatricals had broken the hireling's nerve as well as their own, and the conspiracy collapsed. Two of the hired criminals turned state's evidence at the trial, but the powerful politicians of the ring were able to bring about a disagreement of the jury.

These were the greatest of the scandals which the *Sun* exposed in its news columns and denounced on its editorial page. It was the cry of the ringsters, and even of some honest men, that the *Sun's* assaults on the evils that marred Grant's administration were the result of Dana's personal dislike of the President. More specifically it was declared that Dana was a disappointed office-seeker, and that the place of collector of customs at the port of New York was the office he sought.

We have it on the unimpeachable testimony of General James Harrison Wilson, the biographer of Dana, and, with Dana, a biographer of Grant, that General Rawlins, Grant's most intimate friend, told Dana's associates, and particularly General Wilson, that Dana was to be appointed collector. There is no evidence that Dana ever asked Grant, or any other man, for public office. One place, that of appraiser of merchandise at the port of New York, was offered him, and he refused it. The *Sun* said editorially, replying to an insinuation made by the *Commercial Advertiser* that if Dana had been made collector his paper would not denounce the administration:

> The idea that the editor of the *Sun,* which shines for all, could consent to become collector of the port of New York is extravagant and inadmissible. It would be stepping down and out with a vengeance.
>
> And yet we do not mean that the collector of New York need be other than an upright man. Moses H. Grinnell was such, and Tom Murphy, though a politician, a crony of Boss Grant, and one of the donors of Boss Grant's cottage, certainly never took a dollar of money from the Federal Treasury to which he was not entitled. General Arthur, the present collector, is a gentleman in every sense of the word.
>
> The office of collector is respectable enough, but it is not one that the editor of the *Sun* could desire to take without deserving to have his conduct investigated by a proceeding *de lunatico.*

Dana and the *Sun* lost friends because of the assaults on Grantism. The warfare was bitter and personal. In the case of Belknap, for instance, the *Sun* was attacking a man whom Dana, having known him as a good soldier, had recommended for appointment as secretary of war. But it must be recalled that at the very height of his antagonism to Grant, the President, Dana never receded from his opinion that Grant, the general, was the Union's greatest soldier. And the *Sun* was quick to applaud him as President when, as in currency matters, he took a course which Dana considered right.

The friends of Grant, nevertheless, turned against Dana and his paper. Some of them, stockholders in the Sun

Printing and Publishing Association, quit the concern when they found themselves unable to turn Dana from his purpose. All their pleadings were vain.

"A few years from now," Dana would reply, "I shall be willing to accept whatever judgment the nation passes on my course of action; but now I must do as I think right."

So far as the material prosperity of the *Sun* was concerned, the desertion of Grant's friends hurt it not a whit. For every reader lost, four or five were won. Men may stop reading a paper because it disgusts them; they rarely quit it because it is wounding them.

"I don't read the *Sun*," said Henry Ward Beecher during his trial, "and don't allow anybody to read it to me. What's the good of a man sticking pins into himself?"

The *Sun* made this reply to Beecher's assertion:

> Everybody reads the *Sun*—the good, that they may be stimulated to do better; the bad, in fear and trembling lest their wickedness shall meet its deserts.

In Beecher's case, as in Grant's, the *Sun* believed that it was doing a public service in laying open wrongful conditions. In answer to one who criticized its brutal candor about the Plymouth Church scandal the *Sun* said:

> The exposure of the moral nastiness in Brooklyn is a salutary thing. If, when the exposure of the scandal took place, the people had been indifferent—as indifferent as Beecher assumed to be—and had received no shock to their sense of purity and propriety, then the Jeremiahs might well have bewailed

> the turpitude of society and prophesied evil things for the country. Then, indeed, the poison would have been in the whole social atmosphere. . . .
>
> The Plymouth pastor, if a guiltless man, brought all this trouble on himself by his cowardly course in dealing with the accusations against him. . . .
>
> If he is not a bold man, strong in the truth and in purity, what business has he to preach the religion of the Apostles to his fellow men—he who distributed Sharp's rifles to the Kansas combatants with slavery, who denounced sin and bore his head high as a man of freedom of thought and action? To have kept himself consistent, he should not have dallied with Tilton and Moulton in secret, but if entrenched in innocence he should have dragged out their slanders and torn to pieces their plans from the pulpit where he had preached courage under difficulties, divine faith under sorrow, and bold encounter with sin. This would soon have expelled the poison lurking in the social atmosphere, but Beecher did not do it.

Perhaps Beecher's thanks were not due to Dana, but Grant's surely were. It is impossible that scandals like those of the Whisky Ring could have lain hidden forever. If they had not been exposed when they were, they would have come to the top later, perhaps after Grant went out of office, and when his cry, "Let no guilty man escape!" would have been in vain.

The *Sun's* fights against the scandals of the Grant period were no more bitter than its attacks on the frauds attending the presidential election of 1876, although Dana had no cause for personal animosity toward Hayes. The *Sun's* chief Washington correspondent, A. M. Gibson, who handled many of the Grant scandals, wrote most of the news stories about the theft of the presidency by Mr. Hayes's managers. He also published in book form an official history of the fraud.

Joseph Pulitzer, then newly come from the West, was assigned by Dana to cover the proceedings of the Electoral Commission in semi-editorial style. Pulitzer was later, in 1878, a European correspondent of the *Sun.*

An adequate history of the *Sun's* political activities during Dana's time would fill volumes. Rather than the editor of an organ of the opposition, Dana was usually an opposition party in himself; not merely for the sake of opposition, but because the parties in power from 1869 to 1897 usually happened to have practices or principles with which he, as the editor of the *Sun,* was in disagreement. His attacks on the Grant administration for the thievery that spotted it, and on the Hayes administration because of the circumstances under which Mr. Hayes came to the presidential chair, were bitter and without relent. His opposition to Grover Cleveland, an intellectual rather than a personal war, began before Mr. Cleveland was a national figure. In September, 1882, when the hitherto obscure Buffalonian was nominated for governor of New York, the *Sun* said:

> It is usually not a wise thing in politics, any more than in war, to take a private from the ranks and at one bound to promote him to be commander-in-chief; yet that is what has been done in the case of Grover Cleveland.

In the presidential campaign of 1884 the *Sun* would not support Cleveland and could not support Blaine, whose conduct in Congress the *Sun* haa frequently condemned; so it advocated the hopeless cause of General Benjamin F. Butler, who had been elected governor of Massachusetts in 1882, the year when Cleveland was chosen governor of New York. Dana was not an admirer of Butler's spectacular army career, or of his general political leanings, but he admired him for his attitude in the Hayes-Tilden scandal, and he believed that Butler, if elected president, would shake things up in Washington. The *Sun* supported him "as a man to be immensely preferred to either of the others and as a protest against such nominations." Dana personally announced that sooner than support Blaine he would quit work and burn his pen.

In 1885, opposing Cleveland's free-trade policy, the *Sun* vigorously supported Samuel J. Randall, of Pennsylvania, a protectionist Democrat, for speaker of the House, as against John G. Carlisle, of Kentucky, a free-trader; but Randall was beaten. The *Sun* ridiculed Cleveland's theories of civil-service reform, although it believed that real reforms were needed. For all of its opposition to Cleveland, whom it dubbed the "stuffed prophet," the *Sun* preferred him to General Harrison in the campaign of 1888. It feared a return to power of the influences which it had combated during the administrations of Grant and Hayes. Four years afterward, however, the *Sun* was strongly against the third nomination of Cleveland.

In Mr. Cleveland's second term the *Sun* supported his course when Dana believed it to be American. While at first it considered the President too mild and conciliatory in matters of foreign policy, it praised him and his Secretary of State, Richard Olney, for their stand against

Great Britain in the Venezuela boundary dispute; praised them just as heartily as it had condemned Mr. Cleveland's earlier action in the Hawaiian matter, when the President withdrew the treaty of annexation which his predecessor had sent to the Senate.

The *Sun's* most deadly weapon, ridicule, was constantly in play in the years of the Hawaiian complications. It found vulnerable spots in Mr. Cleveland's reëstablishment of the deposed Queen Liliuokalani and in the President's sending of a commissioner—"Paramount" Blount, as the *Sun* called him—without the advice and consent of the Senate. The *Sun* had the satisfaction of a complete victory in the Hawaiian matter.

On the other hand, the *Sun* applauded Mr. Cleveland's attitude on the money question and his brave stand against the mob in the Chicago railway strikes of 1894, when the President used troops to prevent the obstruction of the mails by Eugene V. Debs and his followers.

Dana was seventy-seven years old when William J. Bryan—whom the *Sun* had already immortalized as the Boy Orator of the Platte—was nominated for the presidency in 1896, but the veteran editor went at the task of exposing the free-silver fallacy with the same blithe vigor that he had shown twenty years before. His opinion, printed in the *Sun* of August 6, 1896, is a good example of Dana's clear style:

> The Chicago platform invites us to establish a currency which will enable a man to pay his debts with half as much property as he would have to use in order to pay them now. This proposition is dishonest. I do not say that all the advocates of the free coinage of silver are dishonest. Thousands of

> them—millions, if there be so many—are doubtless honest in intention. But I am unable to reconcile with any ideal of integrity a change in the law which will permit a man who has borrowed a hundred dollars to pay his debt with a hundred dollars each one of which is worth only half as much as each dollar he received from the lender.

Dana's opinions on political questions were more eagerly sought than those of any other editor after Greeley's death, and the *Sun's* political news was complete; yet with Dana, and with the *Sun*, politics was, after all, only one small part of life. The whole world, with its facts and fancies, not the political problems of one continent, was the real field to be covered.

Dana's curiosity was all embracing. After the *Sun's* financial success was assured he went abroad frequently, and saw not only western Europe, but Russia and the Levant. Of these he wrote in his *Eastern Journeys*. He knew a dozen languages. He conversed with the Pope about Dante and with Russian peasants about Tolstoy. His knowledge of Spanish, acquired early in life, made easy his travels in Mexico and Cuba. Everywhere he went he talked of freedom with its friends, and encouraged them. He knew Kossuth, Mazzini, Garibaldi, Clémenceau, Marti, and Parnell.

With Dana there was no slow decay of body or mind. He died at his country home, Dosoris, on October 17, 1897, in the thirtieth year of his reign over the *Sun*.

A few years before, on observing an obituary paragraph which Mr. Dana had written about some noted man, John Swinton asked his new chief how much space he (Swinton) would get when his time came.

"For you, John, two sticks," said Mr. Dana. Turning to Mr. Mitchell, then his chief editorial writer, he added: "For me, two lines."

On the morning after Mr. Dana's death every newspaper but one in New York printed columns about the career of the dean of American journalism. The *Sun* printed only ten words, and these were carried at the head of the first editorial column, without a heading:

> CHARLES ANDERSON DANA, editor of the *Sun,* died yesterday afternoon.

Mr. Swinton perhaps believed that Mr. Dana was joking when he said "two lines," but Mr. Mitchell knew that his chief was in earnest. The order was characteristic of Dana. It was not false modesty. Perhaps it was a certain fine vanity that told him what was true—that he and his work were known throughout the land. He had made the paper so great that the withdrawal from it of one man's hand was negligible.

CHAPTER XII

DANA'S SUCCESSORS

The Administrations of His Son Paul, William M. Laffan, Edward P. Mitchell and William C. Reick.—Mr. Lord Retires from the Managing Editorship.

SHORTLY after the death of his father, Paul Dana, who was then forty-five years old, and who had been on the *Sun* editorial staff for seventeen years, was made editor by vote of the trustees of the Sun Printing and Publishing Association. In the following year (1898) the younger Dana bought from Thomas Hitchcock, who was one of Charles A. Dana's associates both in a financial and in a literary way, enough shares to give him the control of the paper.

Paul Dana continued in control of the property for several years and held his father's title of editor until 1903. William Mackay Laffan, who had been associated with the elder Dana since 1877, next obtained the business control. His proprietorship was announced on February 22, 1902, and it continued until his death in 1909.

Laffan, who was born in Dublin, Ireland, and had a light and delightful brogue, was educated at Trinity College and at St. Cecilia's School of Medicine. When he was twenty he went to San Francisco, where, beginning as a reporter, he became city editor of the *Chronicle* and managing editor of the *Bulletin*. In 1870 he went to Baltimore, to be a reporter on the *Daily Bulletin*, and of this newspaper he became editor and part owner. Eventually he became the full owner of both the *Daily Bulletin* and the *Sunday Bulletin*, and in this capacity he endeared himself to the citizens of Baltimore by his fight against political rings.

He left newspaper work for a short time to become general passenger agent of the Long Island Railroad; but in 1877, on Mr. Dana's invitation, he went on the *Sun* as a general writer. Himself an artist who modeled in clay, painted in oils and water colors, and etched, his judgment made him valuable to the paper as an art critic.

Like Mr. Dana, he was interested in Chinese porcelains, and he made a deeper study of them than did his employer. When a catalogue was needed for the Chinese porcelains in the Morgan collection in the Metropolitan Museum of Art, Mr. Laffan, who was an active trustee of the museum, was called upon to edit the work. He also edited a book on Oriental porcelain. He was the author of *American Wood Engravers*, published in 1883. For these things he is remembered in the world of art. The men of the stage remember him as one of the most distinguished dramatic critics that New York has seen. Even to-day, in the comparison of the styles of critics old and new, Laffan's reviews are recalled as standards.

In the business world of journalism Laffan is thought of chiefly as the publisher of the *Sun* from 1884 on, and as the live spirit of the *Evening Sun* for many of its years. As the actual director of the *Sun*—although his editorial powers were almost entirely delegated to Edward P. Mitchell—Mr. Laffan was a picturesque and powerful figure.

A New York newspaper once remarked of Laffan that

"he never drove any man to drink, but he drove many a man to the dictionary." That was a commentary on the unusual words which Laffan, whose vocabulary was wide, would occasionally use in an editorial article. His articles were never involved, however. They were not frequent, they were generally short, never without important purpose, and they drove home.

There was a keen humor in the big Irish head. Laffan was opposed to the amendment to the New York state constitution which provided for an expenditure of more than a hundred million in improving the Erie Canal. Under his direction a *Sun* reporter, John H. O'Brien, wrote a series of articles intended to shatter public faith in the huge investment. The amendment, however, was approved by a great majority.

"Mr. O'Brien," said Mr. Laffan to the reporter, a few days after the election, "I think it would be a very graceful thing on your part to give a little dinner to all those gentlemen who voted against the canal project."

Upon Mr. Laffan's death, in November, 1909, the trustees of the Sun Printing and Publishing Association asked Mr. Mitchell, who had been made editor of the *Sun* on July 20, 1903, to take up the administrative burden as well as the editorial. This Mr. Mitchell did for a little more than two years, although his personal inclinations were toward the literary construction and supervision of the paper rather than toward the business detail incident to the presidency of so large a corporation. The double load was lightened in December, 1911, when control of the *Sun* was gained through stock purchase by William C. Reick, who became the president of the company, Mr. Mitchell being permitted to return to the editorial func-

William M. Laffan
Owner of *The Sun*, 1902-1909.

tions which engrossed him, either as Mr. Dana's aid or as editor-in-chief, for more than forty-five years.

Mr. Reick, who was born in Philadelphia in 1864, entered newspaper work in that city when he was nineteen years old. A few years later he removed to Newark, New Jersey, where he became the correspondent of the New York *Herald*. He attracted the attention of Mr. Bennett, the owner of the *Herald*, and in 1888 he was made editor of the *Herald's* London and Paris editions. A year later he returned to America to become city editor of the *Herald*, the highest title then given on that newspaper. In 1903 he was elected president of the New York Herald Company, and he remained in that position until 1906, when he left the *Herald* to become associated with Adolph Ochs in the publication of the New York *Times* and with George W. Ochs in the publication of the Philadelphia *Public Ledger*.

When Mr. Reick assumed the control of the *Sun* properties, he devoted much care to the improvement of the *Evening Sun*, putting it under the managing editorship of George M. Smith, who had served for many years as news editor of the *Sun* under Chester S. Lord.

Among the events of the Reick régime were the retirement of Chester S. Lord from the managing editorship and of George B. Mallon from the city editorship, and the removal of the newspaper from its old home at Nassau and Frankfort Streets to the American Tract Society Building, one block farther south, at Nassau and Spruce Streets.

It was during Mr. Reick's control of the *Sun* that Frank A. Munsey, in the summer of 1912, bought the New York *Press*, a one-cent Republican morning daily holding an Associated Press membership. The *Sun* had lacked the Associated Press service since the fateful night when Mr. Dana bolted from that organization and started the Laffan News Bureau. Mr. Munsey bought the *Sun* from Mr. Reick on June 30, 1916, and four days later, on July 3, the *Press*, with its Associated Press service, its best men, and some of its popular features, was absorbed by the *Sun*.

CHAPTER XIII

FRANK A. MUNSEY

Remarkable Career of the Publisher Who Found His First Complete Newspaper Success in the "Sun."—The Great Amalgamator.

FRANK ANDREW MUNSEY, like Ben Day, Moses Yale Beach, Charles A. Dana, and Edward P. Mitchell, was a New Englander. On his father's side he was descended from William Munsey, who settled at Durham, New Hampshire, in 1686. His mother, Mary Jane Merritt Hopkins, had in her family tree eight Mayflower names, including Brewster, Mullins, Alden, and Warren.

Mr. Munsey was born on the farm of his father, Andrew Munsey, near Mercer, Maine, in the Sandy River country, on August 21, 1854. When he was an infant his parents removed to Gardiner and later to Bowdoin. In 1861 his father went to war with the Twentieth Maine Infantry, not to return for three years. In that period the boy, seven years old when his father left and ten when he returned, faced with his mother and sister the work and worry of a New England farm and showed the qualities of determination and tirelessness which distinguished his whole life.

When Frank was fourteen years old the family moved to Lisbon Falls, on the Androscoggin. In hours free from school he clerked in the post office and there learned telegraphy. This led to his employment in the Western

Union office at Augusta, the state capital. He was promoted to be manager of the office and in this position met men of an outer and greater world of which he had read and dreamed. The telegraph office became to him, as he wrote many years afterward, "as a cage to a tiger yearning for the boundless freedom of the jungle."

He wanted "a future in a big world." He would willingly have given ten years of his life without pay, he said, to gain a foothold in some leading industry. In Augusta, which had many publishing houses, he learned a little about the magazine business—"just enough to be dangerous." With $500 he had saved he bought manuscripts and, in 1882, when he was twenty-six years old, he went to New York with forty dollars in his pocket to start a juvenile magazine to be called the *Golden Argosy*. In 1922 he made his famous epigram: "Forty dollars, forty years, forty millions." He rented an office, bought a table and two chairs for $8, and set to work. An acquaintance in Maine who had promised to invest $2,500 in the enterprise failed to make good. Munsey took his plan to a magazine publisher and turned it over to him on condition that he be hired as manager and editor. The *Golden Argosy* saw the light, but at the end of five months the publisher failed, owing Munsey $1,000, and gave him the good will of the magazine in lieu of cash. With $300, borrowed from a Maine friend, Munsey began anew. It was "such a struggle," to use his own words, "as no man is justified in undertaking."

He was "everything from editor and publisher down to office boy." He worked eighteen hours a day, using his nights to write the serials—*Afloat in a Great City, Under*

Fire, and *The Boy Broker*—which kept his magazine alive. Denying himself everything except food (he lived in a boarding house at $8 a week) he poured back every dollar of his receipts into advertising and promotion and, after five years of incessant struggle, this indomitable Yankee found himself a pecuniary success. By 1894, his magazines—he had changed the *Golden Argosy* into an adult monthly, the *Argosy*, and had founded *Munsey's*—were earning $70,000 a year. In 1905 the net receipts passed the million-dollar mark.

Mr. Munsey's first newspaper venture was the New York *Continent*, a respectable tabloid daily. It was not a success, and, realizing that the day of the tabloid had not come, he discontinued it. In 1901 he bought the Washington *Times* for $200,000 and the New York *Daily News* for $400,000 and in 1902 the Boston *Journal* for $500,000. The *Daily News* was a loser and he sold it in 1904. In 1908 he bought the Baltimore *News* for $1,500,000 and started the Philadelphia *Evening Times*. A chain of 500 newspapers was his dream.

"Such economics would be effected," he wrote in the Baltimore *News*, "that the highest salaries would be mere details of business, and the product of the combined genius of the men in control would be the most uplifting force the world has ever known."

But the dream never approached realization. The Boston *Journal* was sold in 1913; the Philadelphia *Evening Times* was discontinued in 1914. Mr. Munsey had not lost his interest in newspapers, but he decided that New York was particularly his field. He could afford to give daily journalism his personal attention, for his other great interests—magazines, stores, banking, etc.—were in the capable hands of his general manager, William T. Dewart. In the summer of 1912 Mr. Munsey bought for $1,000,000 the New York *Press* so that he could support the candidacy of Theodore Roosevelt for president. He retained Ervin Wardman as the editor, enlarged the paper, and, in four years, increased the circulation from 90,000 to 135,000. In 1915 he sold the Washington *Times* to Arthur Brisbane and the Baltimore *News* to Stuart Olivier. In 1917 he regained the *News*. In 1921 he bought the Baltimore *American* and the Baltimore *Star* for $1,500,000 and combined the *News* and the *Star* under the title of the *News*. He sold his Baltimore papers to William Randolph Hearst on April 1, 1923, for $3,000,000.

On June 30, 1916, Mr. Munsey purchased the *Sun* and the *Evening Sun* from William C. Reick for $2,468,000. He merged the *Press*, which had an Associated Press franchise, with the *Sun*, the name of the *Press* vanishing. Mr. Munsey liked the *Press*, but he wisely remarked that "fifty years might not have given it the prestige it will get in a single day through amalgamation with the *Sun*." He reduced the price of the *Sun* from two cents to one cent. Edward P. Mitchell was retained as editor of the *Sun* with all his staff, Mr. Wardman becoming publisher. Keats Speed, who had been managing editor of the *Press* since 1913, was appointed managing editor of the *Sun*. Kenneth Lord, son of Chester S. Lord, and city editor of the *Sun* since 1912, remained at his post until 1922.

In October, 1917, Mr. Munsey bought, for $2,210,000, the Stewart Building at 280 Broadway, at the corner of Chambers Street, and on November 30, 1919, the *Sun* moved there, leaving the rented quarters at 150 Nassau

Street which it had occupied since 1911. The editorial, news, and composing rooms fill almost the entire second floor, with the counting room on the ground floor, and the basement and sub-basement are occupied by the presses and the stereotyping machinery. The executive offices are on the seventh floor. There the president is assisted by an executive board which includes Richard H. Titherington, Clarman T. Dixon, Fred A. Walker, Gilbert T. Hodges and Robert H. Davis, all veterans of the Munsey-Dewart organization.

On January 14, 1920, Mr. Munsey surprised New York by announcing his purchase of the New York *Herald*, which had been under trustee management since the death of James Gordon Bennett on May 14, 1918.

The New York *Telegram*, an evening newspaper, and the European edition of the New York *Herald* were included in the sale and the total price was $4,000,000. Ten days later Mr. Munsey created a fresh sensation by amalgamating the *Sun* and the *Herald* under the title *The Sun and New York Herald*. Less than a year later, on October 1, 1920, he separated the *Sun* from the *Herald*, continuing the latter in the morning field and making the *Sun* an evening paper to take the place of the *Evening Sun*. Mr. Munsey was actively the editor of the *Herald* from 1920 until March 17, 1924, when he sold it for $5,000,000 to Ogden M. Reid, owner of the New York *Tribune*, the Paris *Herald* being included in the transaction. He had wished to buy the *Tribune* and amalgamate it with the *Herald*, believing that New York could not support two newspapers, no matter how excellent they might be, that were so generally alike. As the Reid family would not sell the *Tribune* to him, he sold the *Herald* to them. He then found himself, for the first time in many years, owner of only two newspapers—the *Sun* and the New York *Telegram,* the latter being combined, in January, 1924, with the *Evening Mail,* which Mr. Munsey purchased from Henry L. Stoddard for $2,000,000. What was more to his liking, he now became owner, for the first time, of a newspaper that was successful from every point of view. By combining the *Sun* with the *Globe,* which he bought on May 27, 1923, for $2,000,000, he had secured for the *Sun* an afternoon franchise of the Associated Press. The *Sun,* already successful, grew steadily stronger in circulation and advertising.

Mr. Munsey was sometimes criticized for "putting newspapers out of business." His own view of it was that through mergers carefully considered he put newspapers on a sound basis.

"There is no business," he said in 1908, "that cries so loud for organization and combination as that of newspaper publishing. The waste under existing conditions is frightful and the results miserably less than they could be made. For one thing, the number of newspapers is at least 60 per cent greater than we need."

To reform what he considered an extravagant business he spent money without stint. When he reëntered the New York field in 1912, the standard daily newspapers of the city were as follows:

MORNING PAPERS

New York Times *The Sun*
New York Herald *The World*
New York Press *New York Tribune*
New York American

EVENING PAPERS

Evening Sun	*Evening Mail*
Evening Post	*New York Telegram*
The Globe	*Evening Journal*
Evening World	

When he died thirteen years later the list had been reduced to the following:

MORNING PAPERS

Herald Tribune	*New York Times*
The World	*New York American*

EVENING PAPERS

The Sun	*New York Telegram*
Evening Post	*Evening Journal*
Evening World	

Mr. Munsey alone had cut the number of morning papers from seven to four and the number of evening papers from seven to five. The survivors were far better off than they had been before he entered on his campaign. It is unlikely that those who criticized his mergers would to-day be willing to undo his work. What may have appeared to be merciless to some is now regarded as merciful. Mr. Munsey's restless way in journalism was well analyzed in an editorial article on him, written by Mr. Mitchell, the day of Mr. Munsey's death:

> This patient, persistent and even nigh ruthless adherence to the essentials of the course laid out, combined with utter indifference to what he regarded as negligible details and carelessness as to whether the end be reached by steam or sail, sometimes gave rise to the impression that Mr. Munsey felt a fierce enjoyment in change, for the mere sake of change.

That theory does not stand the test of a more intimate knowledge of his idiosyncrasies. His hand was fearlessly swift at business surgery, but at least from his point of view the surgery was always constructive surgery, the destruction always for reparation. If a shop of any kind proved after sufficient experience an impossible unit in the complex system of his activities, he closed it and tried something else. If an edifice did not suit his architectural taste or meet his needs in respect to utility, he altered it or unhesitatingly tore it down and put up another in its place. If the form or content of one of his magazines seemed to him to have surpassed its productive usefulness, he departed without compunction from tradition and precedent and adopted another form or another policy as to contents. If a newspaper he had acquired at huge expense failed to fit easily into his general scheme, or had already fulfilled the immediate purpose for which he bought it, or had fallen short of his experimental hopes concerning it, he calmly proceeded to pronounce its obituary eulogy and to write it off his books. And just as with the impedimenta of his various establishments so with their personnel, to a certain extent, where no sense of obligation for long and faithful service existed. Where it did exist no human soul could be kinder or more considerate.

Mr. Munsey's feeling of responsibility to the public was acute. The real as well as titular editor of the New York *Herald*, and later of the *Sun*, he spent hours daily in the direction and preparation of articles. In his latter years he usually began his editorial work at the Ritz Carlton Hotel, where he lived, at eight o'clock in the morning, having proof sheets read to him, scanning the

FRANK A. MUNSEY
Owner of *The Sun*, 1916-1925.

morning newspapers, and deciding what should be printed on the *Sun's* editorial page. In the afternoon he went through the *Sun*, page by page, commenting on news articles, criticizing advertising layouts and press work, and ordering changes here and there.

He was particularly fond of news stories and editorial articles on scientific subjects. A headline on some astronomical or archeological discovery would attract him at once. He insisted on making over the editorial page to get in an article on a total eclipse of the sun. He was fascinated by the excavations in the Valley of the Kings and by the new matter dug up by the Mayan and Chaldean expeditions. The same lively interest was given to medical and surgical discoveries. A piece of news about some new remedy for cancer or consumption interested him more than any political item. Once, when he was commenting on a news article which related to the excellent results of some new derivative of chaulmoogra in leprosy cases, an editorial writer remarked that that drug had been used in treating the disease for at least three thousand years in the Far East.

"Say so," said Mr. Munsey; "nobody but the doctors knows that."

Mr. Munsey, while generally regarded as a Republican, preferred to call himself an independent. He was ever insistent that his papers were independent. He supported the Republican party in national elections for the simple reason, as he often said, that he could not bear the thought of having free trade or anything like it saddled on the country. Beyond the tariff he could see little difference between the two major parties. To him they had become so much alike that their usefulness was impaired. He believed that eventually the United States must have a new political cleavage, with one party radical and the other liberal-conservative. His theory was supported frequently in Congress when the radical Republicans voted with the Democratic minority and the conservative Democrats joined with the Republican majority. Mr. Munsey was not a radical, yet in the summer of 1924 he gave the La Follette conventions a great deal of publicity, much to La Follette's surprise. Mr. Munsey's idea was that the La Follette candidacy should be thoroughly aired, so that if it was a failure the failure would be all the more emphatic. La Follette carried only Wisconsin.

Mr. Munsey never went blindly with any party. He strongly opposed certain sections of the Fordney-McCumber tariff, although he was a lifelong protectionist. He fought the Dillingham immigration bill and other Republican immigration measures, insisting that the quota method was an injustice to the peoples on both sides of the Atlantic and that the only right system was a selective one by which the United States could choose exactly the immigration it needed. He opposed American entrance into the World Court, although it had been made a part of the Republican national platform. In issues like this he could not be moved by party policies or presidents. Once his mind was made up he was a rock. His greatest fight was against American membership in the League of Nations. The Munsey newspaper policy, expressed in the masterly editorial articles of Edward P. Mitchell, did more to overwhelm the League idea at the polls in 1920 than any other force. Later, in opposing the soldier bonus, Mr. Munsey risked circulation and friendships for the sake of his principles.

CHAPTER XIV

WILLIAM T. DEWART BUYS "THE SUN"

His Mutualization Plan Hailed by Newspapers Everywhere as a Forward Step in Journalism.—A Herculean Task to Carry Out.

MR. MUNSEY died on December 22, 1925, after an illness of ten days. His will, filed on December 30, 1925, disposed of an estate the estimated value of which was between $20,000,000 and $40,000,000. Executed nearly five years before he died, the will left approximately $2,000,000 to relatives, friends, business associates, and Maine institutions, including $250,000 to Bowdoin College, $100,000 to the Maine State Hospital, and $50,000 to the Central Maine General Hospital. The residue was bequeathed to the Metropolitan Museum of Art. Mr. Munsey appointed as his executors William T. Dewart, his most intimate friend and for many years his general manager; Richard H. Titherington, who had been associated with him in magazine work and as secretary of his companies for forty years, and the Guaranty Trust Company of New York. These executors were clothed with broad powers in regard to the disposition of the Munsey newspapers, for the will said:

> Newspapers, periodicals and merchandising properties are not easily sold. To dispose of them to advantage means finding customers for them. This might be done quickly or might call for five or eight

years. I should need as much time to turn them into cash myself. To expect my executors to accomplish this in less time than I should require would be asking of them something they would doubtless fail to perform. I therefore direct that my executors have five years in which to convert my property into cash, and more time if in the discretion of the court they should have it.

Coincident with the publication of the will Mr. Dewart made this significant announcement:

Within the last five years Mr. Munsey's newspapers and business properties have almost doubled in value, notwithstanding Mr. Munsey's absences in Europe and elsewhere, during which matters of policy as well as business details were handled by an extraordinarily efficient organization of men. Within the next five years, by a continuation of policies now familiar and firmly established, the value of these properties should be still further enhanced. None of the officers, editors or those associated in any of these active and successful enterprises, to many of whom Mr. Munsey was sincerely attached, need be apprehensive of any sudden sale or change. Had Mr. Munsey lived, or had his passing not been so sudden, these large and profitable businesses would have been mutualized, or partially so, in a way beneficial to all of those who have of late years made substantial contributions to their great success. This intention Mr. Munsey expressed to me with great earnestness only a few weeks before he was stricken. But, now that Mr. Munsey is gone from us, his written testament must be our chart and guide, but under its broad discretionary provisions the trustees will do what is legally permissible to carry out Mr. Munsey's known desires.

Notwithstanding this intimation that Mr. Dewart and his fellow executors intended to mutualize the *Sun* if that were possible, they immediately received many offers from would-be purchasers of the newspaper property. It was generally conceded that the *Sun* was the most desirable evening newspaper in New York City and, with the possible exception of the Chicago *Daily News*, the most valuable evening newspaper property in the United States. The bids ranged from $10,000,000 upward.

On September 30, 1926, nine months after the filing of the will, Mr. Dewart, who had been elected president of all the Munsey companies, announced that he had purchased the *Sun*, the New York *Telegram* and certain other Munsey interests from the Metropolitan Museum of Art for $13,000,000 and that he intended to mutualize the properties, wherever possible, as Mr. Munsey would have done if he had lived. On this point the *Sun* made the following editorial statement:

> To bring this about would have been difficult if the executors had not received the sympathetic understanding and aid of the trustees of the Metropolitan Museum of Art, the residuary legatee of Mr. Munsey's fortune. A beneficiary less unselfish might have insisted upon putting the *Sun* on the auction block, thereafter to be the plaything of some personal ambition or to become a mere commercial organ. But President Robert W. De Forest of the Metropolitan and his fellow trustees were quick to appreciate the plan which Mr. Munsey had been making;

quick to realize the importance of the *Sun* as it was, and is, and will be, to this community.

The outcome, briefly, is that the *Sun*, now purchased by Mr. Dewart from the Metropolitan Museum of Art as the first step toward mutualization, will continue to be conducted by those who under Mr. Munsey's guidance brought it to eminence and who, under the direction of Mr. Dewart, since Mr. Munsey's death have carried on. In this connection it is pleasant to record that in the nine months since Mr. Munsey died the *Sun* has not lost a single department head or, in fact, any man whose work was vital to the paper. Under the leadership of Mr. Dewart as president of the Sun Printing and Publishing Association the organization has worked in perfect harmony. The *Sun's* advance in circulation, advertising and general excellence, rapid as it was in the final years of Mr. Munsey's guidance, has continued steadily. Nothing could be better proof than this that the way to keep the *Sun* in its high place as the greatest evening newspaper is to leave it in the hands that have sustained it since Mr. Munsey turned away from his desk for the last time.

On October 16, 1926, Mr. Dewart incorporated at Albany, New York, The New York Sun, Inc., with 30,000 shares of preferred (or A) stock, 20,000 shares of second preferred (or B) stock, all of the par value of $100 a share, and 100,000 shares of common stock of no par value. To this new corporation he transferred the *Sun* and the *Telegram*. The employees of the *Sun* were permitted to buy the preferred (or A) stock and, as only 20,000 shares were offered (10,000 being held in reserve) the $2,000,000 for these securities, bearing interest at 8 per cent, was quickly subscribed among 500 or more *Sun* employees. Portions of the second preferred and common stocks were later distributed among *Sun* employees according to the importance of the recipients to the organization, a large amount of the common stock being retained to provide future rewards.

Thus, within a year of Mr. Munsey's death his wish, omitted from the will of 1921, that his employees might participate in the profits of some of his enterprises was carried out by Mr. Dewart. This naturally was a Herculean task to accomplish so quickly or even to accomplish at all. In the case of the *Sun* the huge value of the property was an apparent handicap in the effort to keep it in the hands of its producers.

Fortunately for the *Sun*, Mr. Dewart, whose business ability was known in the world of finance, could augment his own personal fortune with ample credit. His familiarity with the *Sun's* structure was recognized. For years he had acted as the fiscal representative of Mr. Munsey in all his huge transactions in newspapers, real estate, banking, and trade. Mr. De Forest and his fellow trustees of the Metropolitan Museum of Art quickly agreed with Mr. Dewart that the *Sun* was too much a part of the life of the city to be allowed to drift into alien hands.

Mr. Dewart's announcement that he had bought the *Sun* and would mutualize it was received in the world of journalism with warm approbation. The following extracts from the editorial comment on the decision indicate the general view:

> New York *Times:* The step taken is the one best fitted to maintain the spirit and energy of all connected with the *Sun*. . . . It is a real achievement

upon which Mr. Dewart and his associates are to be congratulated.

New York *Herald Tribune:* Now comes the welcome news that the *Sun*, an institution of eminence and power in this community, is to come into the hands of Mr. William T. Dewart. There are strong personal reasons for rejoicing at this result; he possesses a thorough training, great executive ability and high principle. There is the equally important fact that Mr. Dewart's proprietorship means a continuance of personalities and personnel and a preservation of the standards of accuracy, dignity and intelligence that have long distinguished the *Sun*. We congratulate Mr. Dewart and the men of the *Sun* and not less the community in which they serve.

New York *World:* The mutualization of a paper of the wealth and importance of the *Sun* . . . is an experiment that is much needed.

New York *Evening Post:* We congratulate the *Sun* and its men on this fortunate adjustment of its affairs.

Kansas City *Times:* The staffs headed by Mr. Dewart have shown editorial ability of high order and business acumen. They are the natural owners of the newspaper.

New Orleans *Times-Picayune:* The mutualization of the *Sun* will be a benefit to American journalism.

Syracuse *Herald:* This means that the prestige of the *Sun* of Dana's time will be perpetuated in some of its best and most marked characteristics. It ranks high among metropolitan journals and its editorial page in particular remains, as it was under the Dana régime, a source of varied delight to discriminating readers.

Syracuse *Post-Standard:* This holds together a

group which has worked together having common concerns, and assures continuance of the spirit which has actuated the organization.

Atlanta *Constitution:* It is the most notable experiment of the kind ever undertaken in the journalism of America.

Brooklyn *Citizen:* In adopting this plan Mr. Dewart has placed the *Sun* in the foreground of American newspapers in the relations between the owners of the paper and its employees.

Paris (France) *Herald:* The purchase of the *Sun* by William T. Dewart is of great interest both to the profession of journalism and to the vast reading public, since it will inaugurate a system of ownership and management which will exemplify an altruistic and economic principle which is gaining an ever widening vogue. The *Sun* is one of the world's newspapers richest in fine tradition and with an influence on all worthy human activities. This newspaper congratulates Mr. Dewart on an event that should assure the future usefulness of an invaluable institution.

New London (Connecticut) *Day:* In Mr. Dewart the paper will have a powerful director. He has shown his capacity and business sagacity.

Asheville (North Carolina) *Times:* Mr. Dewart is no stranger to the traditions and policies of the *Sun.* He can, for that reason, be trusted to see to it that the *Sun* continues to fill with credit and power the unique place which it has always occupied in American journalism.

Macon (Georgia) *Telegraph:* Under Mr. Dewart and his associates the *Sun* will be a greater newspaper than it has been.

Des Moines *Capital:* Mr. Dewart's purchase of the *Sun,* with his plan for general association of employees as shareholders, gives to this justly proud veteran of American journalism the assurance of a future in keeping with its brilliant past.

Brooklyn *Eagle:* The bargain will doubtless prove profitable to Mr. Dewart, whose ability and experience should increase the value of the investment. But beyond the profit that may accrue to him personally is the promise that the property will be mutualized for the benefit of the employees.

Camden (New Jersey) *Courier:* The *Sun* shines more brightly for all newspaper men with the news of its mutualization. William Dewart must be a wise, big man.

St. Louis *Star:* The experiment will be watched with a great deal of sympathetic interest, not only by newspapermen the country over, but by business and the public at large.

Providence *News:* Mr. Dewart was for years Mr. Munsey's chief business associate. He is an executive of great ability and has a most scrupulous sense of business honor.

Superior (Wisconsin) *Telegram:* The newspaper fraternity will note with a good deal of satisfaction the disposal of the late Frank Munsey's newspaper properties in New York to William T. Dewart.

Miami *Herald:* Mr. Dewart, who was associated with Mr. Munsey for twenty-eight years, serving in all branches, established a record of intelligent faithfulness to his chief.

Hartford *Times:* It means that instead of falling into the hands merely of some one who has the money to buy them, the properties will be owned by men who have been virtually their life blood.

Macon (Georgia) *Telegraph:* Mr. Dewart's plan is not only good economics, it is also good newspaper judgment. . . . Under Mr. Dewart and his associates the *Sun* will be a greater newspaper than it ever has been.

Atlanta *Journal:* Mr. Dewart has both the courage and the perseverance to bring dreams to pass and to forge imagination into fact.

Scranton *Times:* The purchase of the *Sun* by William T. Dewart . . . gives assurance that the magnificent evening paper which the late Frank Munsey built up will be continued under the management of the able and competent gentlemen whom Mr. Munsey gathered about him in his lifetime.

Editor and Publisher: It is a feat that is but another proof of the singular ability of the man whom Mr. Munsey chose to carry on his policies and effect his desires.

Lincoln (Nebraska) *Star:* There was fear that the *Sun,* with all its fine traditions and honorable record, might fall into hands which would inaugurate sweeping and radical changes. These fears have been dissipated by the announcement that a group of the *Sun* executives, under the leadership of William T. Dewart, have acquired the property. . . . The *Sun* is a national institution.

Watertown (New York) *Times:* Mr. Dewart is a thorough newspaper man and he will continue to uphold the high standards which have so long characterized the *Sun.*

Rochester *Democrat Chronicle:* Mr. Dewart appears to have evolved a plan that will be of continuing benefit not only to the *Sun* organization and readers but to the community which that newspaper has served for many years.

The *Fourth Estate:* As pilot of the *Sun* and the *Telegram* Mr. Dewart has wrought wonders.

Louisville (Kentucky) *Times:* Mr. Dewart was Frank A. Munsey's right-hand man. He did as much as any one to build up the great property that the *Sun* now constitutes.

Manchester (England) *Guardian:* It is so rare a thing for a working journalist—as Mr. Dewart is—to acquire a big newspaper in these days that the announcement of the sale has aroused interest throughout the world of journalism.

London (England) *Star:* With his acquisition of the two Munsey newspapers Mr. Dewart becomes one of the outstanding figures of the American newspaper world.

Paris (France) *Times:* No one but William T. Dewart could have effected the purchase with such despatch. He had been general manager of the Munsey properties for several years and was more conversant with some sides of their control than the owner himself.

Montreal *Star:* All working newspapermen will watch with keen interest Mr. William T. Dewart's daring experiment in purchasing so great a property as the *Sun* with the intention of mutualizing it.

Toronto *Globe:* The experiment will be watched with keen interest and the result will be instructive for the newspaper business everywhere.

The word "experiment," which appeared occasionally in newspaper comment on the mutualization of the *Sun,* was never heard in the *Sun* office. A ship's crew taking its vessel out for the hundredth time, but under new arrangements for sharing the profits of the voyage, would not regard itself as entering upon an experiment. So with the *Sun's* crew. Never, from the first intimation by Mr. Dewart that he would put in force the idea which

Mr. Munsey had discussed with him, was there a doubt in the *Sun* office that the departure would be successful. This was not a matter of gathering together a new organization. In every department of the paper the personnel had been tried by long association and experience. This volume goes to press nearly two years after the death of Mr. Munsey and nearly a year after Mr. Dewart threw open the doors of stock ownership; yet the *Sun* has not lost a single department head or any other employee of high importance.

Another misconception which crept into a few newspapers was in respect to what "mutualization" meant. A few editors, unacquainted with the real plan, exhibited a fear for what they termed the "abandonment of central control." They may have visualized a sort of bolshevism, with the editorial, news, and business policies of the *Sun* determined in a mass meeting of the stockholders. Nothing was further from Mr. Dewart's thought. Nothing, indeed, was further from the thoughts of the stockholders.

Probably no newspaper has a more definite organization than the *Sun's*. The president of the company appoints the editor, the managing editor, and the business manager and holds them responsible for the conduct of their departments, consulting and advising with each on problems and policies. When there are questions which concern all three departments, the conferences grow according to the number of branches involved. The employees in general have contact with Mr. Dewart, not only through their particular chiefs, but directly whenever they desire. A truck driver not only is free to make suggestions to the president, but is invited to make them; yet he would no more wish to vote on the policies of the *Sun* than the president would desire to take the truck out for a joy ride. Caprice is excluded from the *Sun* establishment. The paper is not ruled by the personal eccentricities of any individual. It is the history of really great newspapers of a certain age, reputation, and clientele that the paper itself becomes, as Mr. Mitchell wrote in the introduction to this book, "an individuality apart from and in a degree independent of the dozens or hundreds or thousands of personal values entering at a given time into the composite of its gray pages." Even the most egotistic individual owner of a newspaper cannot but rejoice when that newspaper becomes bigger than himself; when it has come to be guided largely by the tradition it has made and the opinion it has created.

In the case of the *Sun,* it had the good fortune to find its principal ownership vested in a man not only familiar with the newspaper's traditions but deeply sympathetic with them. It was more significant that he was endowed with unusual journalistic ability, the previous decade of his life having been spent in studious application to the development of newspaper properties and their relation to the reading public. Mr. Dewart's long connection with the *Sun* and his intimacy with its men and its views, stimulated by his own high ideals and an uncanny gift, which, twenty years ago, would have been called a nose for news, guaranteed the continuation of *Sun* quality. There is no part of the institution with which he is not perfectly acquainted. He holds in reserve, subject to instantaneous demand, a familiarity with editorial policy, news handling, advertising, production, and distribution. His regard for the principle of coöperation between all departments of the *Sun,* in which he is ever ready to participate with an open mind, is the greatest inspiration for his associates.

William Thompson Dewart was born in Fenelon Falls, Ontario, Canada, on January 29, 1875. His father was William Dewart, whose ancestors came from Duart Castle, Mull, Scotland, and whose essays on political economy, particularly those supporting protection, were familiar to Canadians of the sixties and seventies. William T. Dewart's mother was Jessie Graham, the daughter of a Scottish banker and landowner. The Dewarts moved to Rochester, New York, when the younger William was six years old. The family was not rich, and most of the eleven children struck out early to make a living. At the age of fourteen William went to work in a button factory and, soon realizing the importance of chemistry in the button business, took a special course in it at the University of Rochester. With his brother Robert he started a button company, but the low tariff law of the Cleveland administration compelled them to sell out. He tried the railroad business, working on a Buffalo, Rochester and Pittsburgh wrecking train at thirteen cents an hour. Later, in the machine shops, he learned to operate every planer and lathe. Railroading, he soon found, held out no high hope to the ambitious lads of that period. He studied accountancy and found that it suited his natural liking for figures.

In January, 1898, he heard that Frank A. Munsey, who had built a great printing establishment in New London, Connecticut, was turning the building into a hotel, with a department store on the ground floor. He heard also that the Second Congregational Church of New London was in need of a good tenor. He applied to Mr.

Munsey for a place as office manager and to the church for a place in the choir. He got both jobs, the choir salary eking out the twelve dollars a week which Mr. Munsey paid him. So well did Dewart suit Munsey—who was only too eager to have somebody lift from him the burden of financial detail—that within eighteen months Dewart became head bookkeeper of Munsey's Red Star News Company, assistant superintendent of the Munsey publishing plant, and auditor of the Munsey businesses. In 1902, he was made treasurer, without bond, of the Frank A. Munsey Company, and in 1903, when E. J. Ridgway retired as general manager of the company Mr. Dewart, then twenty-eight years old, succeeded him as vice president, general manager, and treasurer. In 1907, when Mr. Munsey raised his salary to fifteen thousand dollars a year, he wrote to his young lieutenant: "Your advance over the heads of all others in the business, starting at $12 a week a few years ago, tells its own story."

For the next eighteen years Mr. Dewart's responsibilities grew with the rise of Mr. Munsey's fortune and the widening of his activities. He personally developed from a small beginning the Mohican stores, now in more than fifty cities. He was the financial director of enterprises which included a dozen newspapers and magazines, the Mohican stores, the Mohican Hotel in New London, the Munsey Trust Company in Washington, and a vast amount of real estate. Mr. Munsey's faith in his general manager was such that when he was in Europe and money panics swept the United States he did not even offer advice to Mr. Dewart. When he wished to buy another newspaper—he spent nearly $20,000,000 in this direction—he would merely say to Dewart: "I shall need a million dollars this week to pay on the ——."

Mr. Dewart was married on April 21, 1908, to Miss Mary Louise Wheeler, daughter of Commodore and Mrs. Thomas H. Wheeler. They have three children, William T., Jr., Thomas Wheeler, and Mary. Mr. Dewart was little known to the public until his purchase of the *Sun*. He was, however, extremely well acquainted with the *Sun* and its people. He and Mr. Mitchell were particularly fond of each other. When it was announced that Mr. Dewart had acquired the *Sun*, he received hundreds of telegrams from noted men, beginning with President Coolidge, but the message which probably pleased him most came from Mr. Mitchell, who was at his farm near Kenyon, Rhode Island:

My dear Friend:

Your telegram makes this one of the happiest days of my life. It is a magnificent achievement, in loyal purpose and generous aim entirely worthy of yourself. My heartiest congratulations to you and all. The old *Sun* in particular, along with several properties, will live on to further success and distinction under management the most capable.

E. P. Mitchell

Watchapey Farm,
Kenyon, R. I.
September 30, 1926

When on October 14, 1926, the staffs of the *Sun* gave a dinner in Mr. Dewart's honor to celebrate his purchase of the *Sun*, Mr. Mitchell sent the following telegram to the Chairman:

I wish I could be at table with the other *Sun* men to-night to say via my own larynx what is in my heart.

No newspaper event within memory has won the attention of the world of journalism and the observers of journalism to the same extent as this. No newspaper man has ever received a finer tribute of confidence and good will.

I think we may express ourselves to-night without much reserve. Surely, at this safe distance that privilege is mine.

Your guest of honor has done more than capture well-nigh universal admiration for an achievement notable beyond record; he has also succeeded in fastening genuine affection among the most unsentimental, offish and even cynical species of human beings existing on earth—the case-hardened working newspaper men around him; and that love is his honestly acquired capital and treasure—perhaps the best of all his treasures.

That is the main thought in this brief message of greeting from a person most of whose life has been of happiness with the *Sun*. It adds but a single voice to the impressive volume of appreciation and congratulation now coming to you, Mr. Dewart, by good right as a man who has done a great and loyal and noble thing.

E. P. Mitchell

New London, Conn.
October 14, 1926

In a letter to Mr. Dewart, written on December 21, 1926, Mr. Mitchell said:

I am moved to say how proud I am of every step

you have conceived and taken during this most difficult of years since Frank Munsey's death.

Mr. Dewart's personal interest in the *Sun*, not merely as its president and principal owner, but as one whose contacts with it were of the closest, led him in February, 1927, to dispose of the New York *Telegram*. This decision, he said, "was reached because the growth of the *Sun* demands, so far as my newspaper interests are concerned, that I devote my time to one newspaper, the *Sun*." The *Telegram* was not sold to the highest bidder. "A factor in the consideration," said Mr. Dewart, "was my knowledge that under the Scripps-Howard system of operation a very considerable block of the *Telegram* stock will be set aside for the management and for the concern's investment companies in which all employees are permitted to acquire holdings."

On December 1, 1926, Mr. Dewart, who since Mr. Munsey's death had been editor as well as president, ordered the personnel section of the *Sun's* editorial masthead to read as follows:

WILLIAM T. DEWART
President and Treasurer

R. H. TITHERINGTON
Vice-President

CLARMAN T. DIXON
Secretary

Editor: FRANK M. O'BRIEN
Managing Editor: KEATS SPEED
Business Manager: EDWIN S. FRIENDLY

In the spring of 1926, Mr. Dewart remodeled the editorial and newsrooms and apportioned to the Sun Club a large room overlooking City Hall Park. This club, whose members include nearly all the employees of the newspaper, is a haven for rest, reading, smoking, and checker playing. There the club receives distinguished men and women (Lindbergh was its guest on June 16, 1927). The club's Christmas Eve parties, flower shows, dances, and outings are enjoyable affairs. Mr. Dewart also established throughout the organization a system of life insurance by which employees obtain policies at a nominal premium, the *Sun* itself sharing the cost.

CHAPTER XV

THE EDITORIAL PAGE

Edward P. Mitchell and His Half Century of Service.—Men of Dana's Time and Afterward.—"Is There a Santa Claus?" and "Lindbergh Flies Alone."

THE editorial writers who contributed most to Dana's success were Edward Page Mitchell, Mayo W. Hazeltine, W. O. Bartlett, John Swinton, Henry B. Stanton, N. L. Thieblin, James S. Pike, Fitz-Henry Warren, Thomas Hitchcock, Francis P. Church, and Edward M. Kingsbury. The greatest of these and, in certain respects, the finest figure in all the *Sun's* history, was Mr. Mitchell. He was born in Bath, Maine, on March 24, 1852, was graduated from Bowdoin in 1871, and became a member of Dana's staff in 1875. For more than half a century thereafter he was in the service of the *Sun* and, more than any other man, his life was entwined with the paper. He became the greatest editorial writer of his generation. The *Sun* said after his death on January 22, 1927:

> In substance and style the articles with which Mr. Mitchell adorned the *Sun* for half a century were unequaled by any contemporary. Substance was assured, for he never wrote anything merely to say something. He shared Mr. Dana's contempt for the editor who rushed to give an opinion on every available subject. The importance of a theme had due consideration from him, but it was the interest

of it that weighed most. Under Mr. Dana and Mr. Mitchell—and their control of the editorial page of the *Sun* lasted almost without interruption from 1868, when Dr. Dana bought the paper, until 1920, when Mr. Mitchell retired from everyday labors—the readers were treated to the richest offerings that these two masters of journalism could furnish. These two, above all others, were responsible for the quality and fame of the page. Mr. Mitchell lacked Mr. Dana's personal interest in politics, but he excelled Mr. Dana in style and color and had the advantage of a wider and more human view of life.

Much of Mr. Mitchell's editorial activities was devoted to political matters. Personally, however, he was free from the slightest partisan bias. The political quarter was the smallest zone of his interests. His field was all of life. He traveled widely and knew his fellows, whether they were in front of the City Hall or at the end of the Street Called Straight. His curiosity was as broad as the earth. He would explore Rhode Island for a new vestige of King Philip or cross the Caribbean to see the house where some South American dictator lay dying in exile. He could identify the rarest Turkish carpet or trace to its beginnings a classic yarn of the Nantucket whaling ships. He could guide the inquirer to the finest Corot in America or direct him to the best omelette soufflée to be had on the Breton coast. Never for him the academic air of the cloistered scholar; his subject was Man and Man's background.

Yet he never underestimated political issues of real importance. When the proposal that America enter the League of Nations was first laid before the people in the idealistic and alluring manner of which President Wilson was master, Mr. Mitchell, with Mr.

Munsey's complete and fervent approval, began the series of expository editorial articles which showed the country in general, and the United States Senate in particular, the perils of American entrance into a supergovernment. Mr. Mitchell was then nearly seventy years old, but his pen was as forceful as it had been in earlier days against the Cleveland policy in Hawaii. Until his articles on the Wilson Covenant were started the League idea was on the way to victory. When they were finished it was beginning the retreat that ended in the rout of 1920.

Mr. Mitchell wrote for the *Sun* many short stories, including "The Ablest Man in the World" and "The Tachypomp," scientific fantasies. As another change from his strictly editorial work he might write a description of Mark Twain in his observatory, armed with a boat hook and preparing to fend off a comet; or, becoming Mr. Dana's reporter, he would expose a spiritualistic séance of the Eddy Brothers somewhere up in Vermont, or go to Madison Square to record the progress of George Francis Train toward world dictatorship by self-evolution on a diet of peanuts; or he would write a dramatic criticism of the appearance of the *Sun's* droll friend, George, the Count Joannes, as Hamlet.

These few instances, a dozen out of twenty thousand articles that Mr. Mitchell wrote for the *Sun,* are not mentioned as a key to the general tenor of his work—which has covered everything from the definition of a mugwump to the interpretation of a president's constitutional powers—but rather as an indication of the *Sun's* catholicity in subjects. If incidentally they serve to counteract the impression that the editorship of a great newspaper is gained through mere erudition, as opposed to a fine understanding of the very human reader, so much the better.

From his first day with the *Sun*, Mr. Mitchell absorbed his chief's lifelong belief that the range of public interest was infinite. As he said in 1916, in an address to the students of the Pulitzer School of Journalism on "The Newspaper Value of Non-Essentials":

> Sometimes people are as much interested in queer names, like Poke Stogis, for example, or in the discussion of a question such as "What Is the Best Ghost in Fiction?" or "How Should Engaged Couples Act at the Circus?" or "What Is a Dodunk?" or "Do the Angels Play Football?" as some other people are interested in the conference of the great powers.
>
> It is well to remember always this psychological factor. Both the range of the newspaper and the attractive power of the writer for the newspaper in any department depend upon the breadth of sympathy with human affairs and the diversity of things in which he, the writer, takes a genuine personal interest.

In that speech the *Sun's* judgment of what the people want, whether it be in news, editorial, or fiction, is restated exactly as it might have been stated at any time within the last fifty years.

Mayo Williamson Hazeltine was a fine example of the scholar in newspaper work; an example of the way in which Dana, with his intellectual magnificence, found the best for his papers. Educated at Harvard and Oxford and in continental Europe, Hazeltine came to the

EDWARD P. MITCHELL
Editor of *The Sun*, 1903-1920.

Sun in 1878, and was its literary critic until his death in 1909. During the same period he was also one of its principal writers of articles on foreign politics and sociology. His book reviews, published in the *Sun* on Sundays, which made the initials "M. W. H." familiar to the whole English-reading world, were marvels of comprehension. Many a publisher of a three-volume historical work lamented when it attracted Hazeltine's attention, for his review, whether two columns or seven, usually compressed into that space all that the average student cared to know about the book, reducing the high cost of reading from six or eight dollars to a nickel.

Hazeltine enjoyed, under both Dana and Mitchell, practically his own choice of subjects, a free hand with them, and a generous income; and in return, for more than thirty years, he poured into the columns of the *Sun* a wealth of erudition which was his by right of education, travel, an intense interest in all things intellectual, and a wonderful memory.

W. O. Bartlett, a lawyer by profession and a writer by inclination, was associated with Dana from 1868 until his death in 1881. He wrote the eight immortal words, "No king, no clown, to rule this town!" and the devastating paragraph describing General Hancock, the Democratic candidate for president in 1880, as "a good man, weighing 240 pounds."

John Swinton, whose specialty was Central American affairs and paragraphing, was a Socialist outside the *Sun* office. He delighted to denounce the "capitalistic *Sun*" in a speech at night and tell Mr. Dana about it the next morning.

Henry B. Stanton was a political writer with whom

Dana became acquainted in his *Tribune* days. He married Elizabeth Cady, one of the early group of advocates of women's rights.

Napoleon Leon Thieblin, who was of French blood, was born in St. Petersburg in 1834. He was graduated at the Russian Imperial Academy of Artillery and commanded forty pieces of cannon at the siege of Sebastopol. At the close of the Crimean War he went to London and became a member of the staff of the *Pall Mall Gazette*, reporting for that journal the French side of the war with Germany in 1870-71, and the atrocities of the Commune, over the pen name of "Azamet Batuk." He reported the Carlist War in Spain for the New York *Herald*, and then came to America to lecture, but Dana persuaded him to join the *Sun* staff. He contributed to the *Sun* many articles on foreign affairs, including a series on European journalism; "The Stranger's Note Book," which was made up of New York sketches; letters from the Centennial Exposition at Philadelphia; and the Wall Street letters signed "Rigolo."

James S. Pike was one of the group that supported Greeley for the presidency in 1872. He was one of the really great publicists of his day. He wrote *The Restoration of the Currency*, *The Financial Crisis*, *Horace Greeley in 1872*, *A Prostrate State*, which was the description of the reconstruction era in South Carolina; and *The First Blows of the Civil War*, this last a volume of reminiscent correspondence, some newspaper, some personal. The friendship and literary association of Pike and Dana lasted more than thirty years, and ended only with Pike's death, in 1882, just after he had passed threescore and ten.

Fitz-Henry Warren, the author of the *Tribune's* cry, "Forward to Richmond!" wrote many editorial articles for Dana, who had conceived a great admiration for Warren, when both were in the service of the *Tribune,* Dana as managing editor and Warren as head of the Washington bureau. Warren emerged from the Civil War not only a major-general, but a powerful politician, and it was not until several years later, after he had served in the Iowa Senate and as minister to Guatemala, that Dana was able to bring the pen of this transplanted New Englander to the office of the *Sun.* Once there, it did splendid work.

Thomas Hitchcock was a young man of wealth and scholarship who had become acquainted with Dana when both were interested in Swedenborgianism. He wrote, among other books, a catechism of that doctrine. For many years he contributed to the *Sun,* under the name "Matthew Marshall," financial articles which appeared on Mondays, and which were regarded as the best reviews and criticisms of their kind.

Francis Pharcellus Church was born in Rochester, New York, on February 22, 1839, and died in this city on April 11, 1906. He was graduated with honor from Columbia College in 1859 and began the study of law, but put it aside to write. He was the editor of the *Galaxy Magazine* and was associated with his brother, Colonel William C. Church, in the management of the *Army and Navy Journal.* His finest work, however, was done for the *Sun.*

Edward M. Kingsbury, whose service on the *Sun* was from 1881 to 1915, gave to the editorial page, in the words of Mr. Mitchell, "the rich quality of a personality almost unique for exquisite humor, fine wit, broad literary appreciation, and originality of idea and phrase."

At the present writing (July, 1927) the editorial staff includes Harold M. Anderson, a *Sun* man since 1894 and an executive and editorial writer under Mr. Mitchell and Mr. Munsey; Lawrence Reamer, whose *Sun* service as reporter, dramatic critic, and editorial writer began in 1893; Louis A. Springer, who came to the *Sun* in 1903; James E. Craig, whose highly competent pen Mr. Munsey acquired when he purchased the *Evening Mail;* Frederick James Gregg, an *Evening Sun* editorial writer as early as 1891; Robert H. Davis, whose "Bob Davis Recalls" articles are a *Sun* feature; Henry Hazlitt, a writer on literature and finance for the Munsey papers since 1923; Philip H. Scott, who first entered the Munsey employ in 1912; and the present writer, who was a *Sun* reporter in 1904 and 1905 and joined the Munsey forces in 1912, going to the *Sun* as an editorial writer under Mr. Mitchell in 1916 and receiving the appointment of editor from Mr. Dewart on December 1, 1926.

Of all the editorial articles that have appeared in the *Sun,* the authorship of only two have been announced by the *Sun* itself. These are "Is There a Santa Claus?" written by Francis P. Church, and "Lindbergh Flies Alone," written by Harold MacDonald Anderson. The origin of the Santa Claus article is thus described by Mr. Mitchell in his *Memoirs of an Editor:*

> One day in 1897 I handed to him a letter that had come in the mail from a child of eight, saying: "Please tell me the truth, is there a Santa Claus?" Her little friends had told her no. Church bristled and pooh-poohed at the subject when I suggested

that he write a reply to Virginia O'Hanlon; but he took the letter and turned with an air of resignation to his desk. In a short time he had produced the article which has probably been reprinted during the past quarter of a century, as the classic expression of Christmas sentiment, more millions of times than any other newspaper article ever written by any newspaper writer in any language. Even yet no holiday season approaches without bringing to the newspaper requests from all over the land for the exact text for repeated use on Christmas Day.

The article, which first appeared in the *Sun* on September 21, 1897, follows:

IS THERE A SANTA CLAUS?

We take pleasure in answering at once and thus prominently the communication below, expressing at the same time our great gratification that its faithful author is numbered among the friends of the *Sun:*

DEAR EDITOR:

I am eight years old.

Some of my little friends say there is no Santa Claus.

Papa says "If you see it in the *Sun* it's so."

Please tell me the truth, is there a Santa Claus?

VIRGINIA O'HANLON

115 West Ninety-fifth Street

Virginia, your little friends are wrong. They have been affected by the skepticism of a skeptical age. They do not believe except they see. They think that nothing can be which is not comprehensible by their little minds. All minds, Virginia, whether they be men's or children's, are little. In this great universe of ours man is a mere insect, an ant, in his intellect, as compared with the boundless world about him, as measured by the intelligence capable of grasping the whole of truth and knowledge.

Yes, Virginia, there is a Santa Claus. He exists as certainly as love and generosity and devotion exist, and you know that they abound and give to your life its highest beauty and joy. Alas! how dreary would be the world if there were no Santa Claus! It would be as dreary as if there were no Virginias. There would be no childlike faith then, no poetry, no romance to make tolerable this existence. We should have no enjoyment, except in sense and sight. The eternal light with which childhood fills the world would be extinguished.

Not believe in Santa Claus! You might as well not believe in fairies! You might get your papa to hire men to watch in all the chimneys on Christmas eve to catch Santa Claus, but even if they did not see Santa Claus coming down, what would that prove? Nobody sees Santa Claus, but that is no sign that there is no Santa Claus. The most real things in the world are those that neither children nor men can see. Did you ever see fairies dancing on the lawn? Of course not, but that's no proof that they are not there. Nobody can conceive or imagine all the wonders there are unseen and unseeable in the world.

You tear apart the baby's rattle and see what makes the noise inside, but there is a veil covering the unseen world which not the strongest man, nor even the united strength of all the strongest men that ever lived, could tear apart. Only faith, fancy, poetry, love, romance, can push aside that curtain and view and picture the supernal beauty and glory

beyond. Is it all real? Ah, Virginia, in all this world there is nothing else real and abiding.

No Santa Claus! Thank God! he lives, and he lives forever. A thousand years from now, Virginia, nay, ten times ten thousand years from now, he will continue to make glad the heart of childhood.

"Lindbergh Flies Alone" was written by Mr. Anderson a few hours after the post office pilot had taken off for Paris. It was printed in the *Sun* on May 21, 1927, while Lindbergh was still in flight. Its poetic quality, simplicity, and beauty of expression touched the chords of public sympathy more quickly and widely than any other editorial expression I have ever heard of. The *Sun* received thousands of requests for copies of it. The authorship was revealed, in spite of Mr. Anderson's demurrer, on June 16, 1927, when Colonel Lindbergh was the guest of the Sun Club and, after receiving from Mr. Dewart a copy of the editorial article in silver, presented to Mr. Anderson an illuminated copy signed by himself. The article follows:

"LINDBERGH FLIES ALONE"

Alone?

Is he alone at whose right side rides Courage, with Skill within the cockpit and Faith upon the left? Does solitude surround the brave when Adventure leads the way and Ambition reads the dials? Is there no company with him for whom the air is cleft by Daring and the darkness is made light by Emprise?

True, the fragile bodies of his fellows do not weigh down his plane; true, the fretful minds of weaker men are lacking from his crowded cabin; but as his airship keeps her course he holds communion with those rarer spirits that inspire to intrepidity and by their sustaining potency give strength to arm, resource to mind, content to soul.

Alone? With what other companions would that man fly to whom the choice were given?

No list of former *Sun* editorial writers would be complete without mention of such skilled writers as Frank H. Simonds, war expert and student of international affairs; Henry M. Armstrong, later of the New York *Times;* Winfield Moody, long with the *Evening Sun;* Henry J. Wright, who was the editor of the *Globe* when Mr. Munsey united that old journal with the *Sun;* Grant M. Overton, Willis J. Abbot, now editor of the *Christian Science Monitor;* William L. Chenery, who went to *Collier's,* and Frank Ernest Hill, who turned his immense energy to the publishing field.

Judge Willard Bartlett, who contributed to the editorial page until his death at the age of seventy-three, was the inventor of the *Sun's* celebrated office cat. One night in the eighties the copy of a message from President Cleveland to Congress came to the desk of the telegraph editor. It was a warm evening, and the window near the telegraph desk was open. The message fluttered out and was lost in Nassau Street. The *Sun* had nothing about it the next morning, and in the afternoon, when Mr. Bartlett called on Mr. Dana, the matter of the lost message was under discussion. The editor remarked that it was a matter difficult to explain to the readers.

"Oh, say that the office cat ate it up," suggested Bartlett.

Dana chuckled and dictated a paragraph creating the cat. Instantly the animal became famous.

CHAPTER XVI

THE NEWS DEPARTMENT

Managing and City Editors and Star Reporters.—The Staff That Makes the "Sun" To-Day.—The Paper's Circulation and Advertising Growth.

NEW YORK newspapers had no managing editors until Dana received that title on the *Tribune.* The *Sun's* first managing editor was Isaac W. England, who was appointed by Dana in 1868. After a year England became publisher and Amos J. Cummings succeeded him as managing editor. Cummings, who was born in 1842, had been a boy filibuster with Walker in Nicaragua, a printer on the *Tribune,* a soldier in the Union Army—he won the Medal of Honor at Fredericksburg—and a political writer on the *Tribune.* "I am leaving the *Tribune,*" he said to Dana, "because they say I swear too much." And Dana replied, according to Cummings' version, "Just the man for me!"

Cummings was the best all-round news man of his day. He was the first real human-interest reporter. He knew the news value of the steer loose in the streets, the lost child, the Italian vendetta. He was a good copy handler and an expert adviser of the *Sun's* young men. In 1876, John Kelly, who was then trying to reform Tammany Hall, persuaded Cummings to become managing editor of the New York *Express,* but after a year of that he went back to the *Sun.* In 1887 he became editor of the *Eve-*

ning Sun. He served fifteen years in the House of Representatives.

Cummings' successors as managing editor of the *Sun* were in turn William Young and Ballard Smith. Then came Chester Sanders Lord, who served from 1880 to 1913. Born in 1850, Mr. Lord went on the *Sun* as a reporter in 1872. He was successively suburban editor, assistant night city editor under Ambrose W. Lyman, and assistant managing editor under Ballard Smith. As managing editor he organized the Laffan Bureau, which fought the Associated Press for twenty years; built up a model system of collecting election returns, and hired (or fired) more genius and near-genius than any other managing editor that ever lived. Dana called him "the John L. Sullivan of newspaperdom," but personally he was the mildest, most unruffled of men.

The *Sun's* managing editors since the retirement of Mr. Lord have been James Luby, William Harris, and Keats Speed. Mr. Speed, who was managing editor of the *Evening Journal* from 1907 to 1912 and editor of the Atlanta *Georgian* from 1912 to 1914, joined the Munsey forces in 1914 as managing editor of the New York *Press*, which two years later was consolidated with the *Sun*. He was for a time managing editor of the New York *Herald* and he has been managing editor of the *Sun* since 1924.

The city editors of the *Sun* since 1868 have been John Williams, Larry Kane, W. M. Rosebault, William Young, John B. Bogart (1873-90), Daniel F. Kellogg (1890-1902), George Barry Mallon (1902-12), Kenneth Lord (1912-22), son of Chester S. Lord, and the present incumbent, Edmond Bartnett. Brisbane, who learned his trade under Bogart, said that he was "the best teacher of

Amos J. Cummings

John B. Bogart

Chester S. Lord

S. M. Clarke

journalism that America had produced. He could tell young men where to go for their news, what questions to ask, what was and what was not worth while. Above all, he could give enthusiasm to his men."

The list of night city editors in the period when the *Sun* was issued in the morning includes Henry W. Odion, E. M. Rewey, Ambrose W. Lyman, Selah Merrill Clarke, Warren Bishop, J. W. Phoebus, Eugene Doane, and Marc A. Rose. Clarke and his genius remain as lasting traditions of Park Row. Dana was attracted to him by a story which Clarke wrote for the *World* of a milkman's ride down the valley of the Mill River when the dam broke at the Ashfield reservoir, near Northampton, Massachusetts, in May, 1874. On the *Sun* Clarke's gifts as news handler immediately appeared. His touch put life into a dull story. His headlines, whether dramatic or humorous, were jewels. His memory was uncanny. Twenty-five years after the Beecher-Tilton trial a three-line death notice came to his desk. He read the dead man's name and summoned a reporter. "This man was a juror in the Beecher case," he said. "Look in the file of February 6 or 7, 1875, and I think you'll find that he stood up and made an interruption. Write a little piece about it."

Among the night editors of the *Sun* in the same period were Dr. John B. Wood, the Great American Condenser, who edited copy after his sight failed by having a cub reporter read it to him; Garret P. Serviss, Charles M. Fairbanks, Carr V. Van Anda, who has been the managing editor of the *Times* since he left the *Sun* in 1904; and George M. Smith, who succeeded Mr. Van Anda and who in 1912 was made managing editor of the *Evening Sun*, a place which he held until 1919.

One of the first reporters under Dana and Cummings was Franklin Fyles. In 1875, five years after he went on the paper, he was the star reporter. He wrote about ten thousand words a day on the Beecher trial. In 1885 he was made dramatic critic and continued as such until 1903. He collaborated with David Belasco in "The Girl I Left Behind Me" and was the author of "Cumberland '61." Another famous reporter of the period was Edward Payson Weston, the best "leg man" in the history of journalism. What he lacked in style he made up in swiftness. Other news writers of the period were Henry Mann, who covered the Tweed and Stokes trials and the impeachment of Judge Barnard for the *Sun;* Tom Cook, a Californian; the McAlpin brothers, Robert and Tod, and Chester S. Lord, later to serve as managing editor for a third of a century. The chief sporting writer was Mark McGuire, commonly called "Toppy," an ex-newsboy who had sold papers to Jackson, Webster, and Clay and who, in the days of Dexter and Maud S., was an intimate of Robert Bonner.

Arthur Brisbane, whose father had been with Dana at Brook Farm and on the *Tribune,* became a *Sun* reporter on December 12, 1882—his eighteenth birthday. For three or four months he was a puzzle to his city editor, appearing not to know what it was all about. "After that," said Mr. Bogart, "he seemed to know all about everything." In 1884 Brisbane went to France to continue his studies, but presently became the *Sun's* London correspondent. At the age of twenty-three he was named as managing editor of the *Evening Sun.* In 1890 he went to the *World* as Sunday editor and in 1897 to the *Evening Journal* as editor.

In Brisbane's decade the *Sun* staff included Henry R. Chamberlain, who in 1892 became the London correspondent of the paper with general supervision over the *Sun's* European news; William McMurtrie Speer, Charles W. Tyler, Robert Sterling Yard, Paul Drane, Willis Holly, S. S. Carvalho, and E. J. Edwards.

The *Sun's* reportorial staff in 1893 included more than twenty men who, if not stars then, were to make their names in the profession later. They included:

Julian Ralph, who went on the *Sun* in 1875 and became the greatest individual reporter of his time. He could handle any story alone. He wrote a full page of agate on the funeral of General Grant in August, 1885; wrote it with a pencil and in seven hours. He made copy of everything he saw and was the author of several books, including *Our Great West, Chicago and the World's Fair, War's Brighter Side,* with Conan Doyle; *Towards Pretoria,* and *People We Pass.* He was on the staff of the London *Daily Mail* during the Boer War and died in London in 1903.

John R. Spears, who went to West Virginia and Kentucky to report for the *Sun* the feuds of the Hatfields and the McCoys, told of the wildness of no man's land before it became part of Oklahoma, covered the international yacht races in the eighties, and wrote *The History of Our Navy, The Story of the American Merchant Marine, The History of the American Slave Trade,* and other books.

Wilbur J. ("Jersey") Chamberlin, a man of the Ralph type. He wrote eleven columns, longhand, about the Dewey parade of 1899. In the Spanish War he was the captain of the *Sun's* shore force in Cuba, his staff including Harold M. Anderson, Dana Carroll, and Walstein Root of the *Sun*, and Henry M. Armstrong and Acton Davies of the *Evening Sun*. Chamberlin sent the first news of the formal surrender of Santiago, but the government censor commandeered the cablegram and gave it out as an official bulletin. Incidentally, the first American flag hoisted over the Morro at Santiago was the *Sun's*. It was a boat ensign from the *Sun's* yacht, the *Kanapaha*. Anderson and Davies gave it to some soldiers of the *Texas*, who fastened it to the bluejackets' staff.

Oscar King Davis, immortal in *Sun* history as the author of the two-page article on the capture of Guam on June 21, 1898. He had the luck to be on the cruiser *Charleston*, the crew of which, after seizing the isolated Pacific island, learned that the people of Guam were not aware that a war existed.

Edward G. Riggs, later to become the greatest of American political corespondents and the friend and confidant of presidents from Harrison to Taft. He went for the *Sun* to every national convention from 1888 to 1912. It was through Riggs that Thomas C. Platt sent word to Dana that he would like to have the *Sun's* idea of a financial plank for the Republican state convention of 1896. Dana and Laffan wrote the plank, which denounced free silver and declared for the gold standard. The state convention adopted the plank and the Republican national convention put the same idea in the platform on which McKinley defeated Bryan.

Edward W. Townsend, the author of the Chimmie Fadden stories and an excellent all-round writer.

David Graham Phillips, remembered by the general public for his novels but distinguished in *Sun* tradition as the author of a remarkable story about the search for a child lost in the Catskills.

Christopher J. FitzGerald, a first-class news man who later wrote racing for the *Sun* and who left the paper to become an official of the Jockey Club.

Victor Speer, who learned his art on the *Sun* and later on the Buffalo *Express,* for which he covered the McKinley tragedy, the Burdick murder, and the Tonawanda murders, showed himself as one of the greatest reporters of all time. He was an untiring giant who wrote by hand, in nine hours, twelve columns about the parade at a national encampment of the Grand Army of the Republic.

Daniel F. Kellogg and George B. Mallon, later city editors of the *Sun.* Mr. Mallon resigned in 1912 to enter the magazine, and afterward the banking, field.

Erasmus Darwin Beach, who became a distinguished book reviewer.

Samuel Americus Wood, whose prose in rime stories of ships and weather began in the *Sun* in the early eighties.

Lawrence Reamer, later a dramatic critic and now of the editorial staff.

Samuel Hopkins Adams, who became a fiction writer.

Rudolph E. Block, the "Bruno Lessing" of the Hearst papers.

Collin Armstrong, who found wealth in the advertising field.

William A. Willis, afterward of the *Evening World* and the New York *Herald.*

In a later period, the first and second decades of the twentieth century, the list of *Sun* reporters shows some well-known names:

Lindsay Denison, famous for his story of the burning of the steamer *Slocum.*

Will Irwin, afterward a distinguished war correspondent, who wrote a page for the *Sun* on "The City That Was" when the earthquake wrecked San Francisco.

Edwin C. Hill, the *Sun's* topsawyer on the story of the *Titanic* disaster and still a *Sun* star.

Frank Ward O'Malley, whose humor and pathos, whether expressed in an account of the doings of the Duke of Essex Street or in the story of the killing of Policeman Sheehan, marked the *Sun* indelibly.

Laurence Hills, who became the *Sun's* principal Washington correspondent and at this writing is editor and general manager of the Paris *Herald.*

Charles Selden, whose vein of structural humor was perhaps unsurpassed in journalism.

Joseph Fox, the man to whom the night desk turned when some story "must be got."

Eltinge A. Fowler, one of the greatest and most modest of the Washington correspondents.

There have been few changes in the staff of the *Sun* during the last several years. The news executives under the managing editor, Mr. Speed, are Edmond Bartnett, city editor; Peter A. Dolan, news editor; Charles E. Still, assistant city editor; William Keats, make-up editor; Herrick Brown, assistant make-up editor; James C. Grey, cable editor; Owen Oliver, telegraph editor; Gustave Zismer, real estate editor.

Among the reporters of long service are George Van Slyke, the foremost political correspondent of the country; Gavin D. High, Mary Watts, W. G. Olson, John H. Barlow, William Bolger, Harry Factor, and Robert J.

Patterson. The staff also includes Dorothy Dayton, Robert Mountsier, Fairfax Downey, Phelps Adams, R. C. McManus, and Edmund De Long. The *Sun's* rewrite staff is one of its greatest prides. Its principal writers are Richard Lockridge, E. H. Blanchard, and Frank Curtis. The copy desk, headed by James Hickey, has remained almost intact for years.

The famous "Sun Dial," printed every day on the editorial page, is conducted by H. I. Phillips.

Franz Schneider, Jr., is financial editor, having come to the *Sun* from the *Evening Post* three years ago. Mr. Schneider's assistant is Carleton A. Shively, and on his staff are Harry Bunce, Preston B. Krecker, Arthur J. Meyers, Frank E. Tyng, Jr., Thomas H. Gammack, Lloyd Churchill, and Benjamin S. Bostick.

William J. Henderson, dean of American musical critics, and Henry McBride, art critic, have been with the *Sun* for a score of years. Gilbert W. Gabriel, dramatic critic, is assisted by Stephen Rathbun and Ward Morehouse. John S. Cohen and Eileen Creelman, are the critic and news writer, respectively, on motion pictures. Eleanor Stanton, who came from the Providence *Journal,* has been in charge of the magazine page for seven years.

The school page, which is read by almost every teacher in the public schools of New York, is conducted by Jacob Jacowitz, with John C. Draper as his assistant.

Joe Vila, known from coast to coast, has been sporting editor of the *Sun* for more than twenty-five years. Fred Steimer, long sporting editor of the *Herald,* is his assistant, and the sports department is probably the ablest ever collected. It includes George Trevor, football and golf writer; Wilbur Wood, boxing; Henry D. King, racing; Frank Graham, Will Wedge, Edward Murphy and Sam Murphy, baseball; Lawrence Perry and John Foster, college sports; Alfred Dayton, cycling; and Edward P. Duffy, soccer.

The radio department is headed by E. L. Bragdon, who started the radio section on the *Globe*. He is assisted by Fred Ehlert, George Hoppert, Katherine Trenholm, and a large staff of contributors.

Maurice Judd and Ralph A. Collins have represented the *Sun* in Washington for more than ten years. The political correspondent at Albany is John C. Crary. The paper's special representative in Europe is Joseph Grigg, with headquarters in London.

The society editor is C. J. Allen, with W. S. Shoemaker and E. C. Gibney as his assistants.

The art director is C. Howard Tate, a veteran in the Munsey-Dewart organization. The chief photographer is Joseph Lyons. The *Sun's* library is in the charge of Paul Drane, whose *Sun* service began in 1887, and Charles Stolberg is the head of the reference department, or "morgue."

The business department is under the leadership of Edwin S. Friendly, who came from the New York *Times* to the *Sun* as business manager in 1923. His staff is as follows:

Advertising department: Herbert B. Fairchild, advertising manager; Conrad F. Colborn, assistant advertising manager; Edwin A. Sutphin, manager, national advertising; Einar O. Petersen, manager, local advertising; Harold L. Goldman, manager, classified advertising; George Benneyan, manager, promotion-statistical department.

Business office: Charles E. Luxton, office manager; Hans Muller, manager, general bookkeeping department; Samuel Wolfenden, manager, advertising bookkeeping department; Howard F. Rhoads, manager, circulation bookkeeping department; Hilson Munsey, auditor; Emma André, cashier; John E. Dier, purchasing agent; Margaret Dusseau, chief telephone operator.

Circulation department: James E. Hasenack, circulation manager; George L. Yaisle, assistant circulation manager; Cornelius J. Daly, mail room, foreman; Cornelius Neilson, mail room, assistant foreman; Saul D. Rubinstein, delivery department, foreman; Abraham Silverman, delivery department, assistant foreman; Thomas F. Brady, delivery department, assistant foreman.

Mechanical department: John Edgar Martin, production manager; Donall O'Neill, assistant production manager; Ralph J. Groff, composing room, day foreman; Andrew Gilchrist, composing room, day assistant foreman; John Heaney, composing room, day assistant foreman; John H. Fichtel, composing room, night foreman; Joseph First, composing room, night assistant foreman; John F. Ryan, composing room, third shift foreman; Harry P. Smith, composing room, third shift assistant foreman; John J. Cunningham, stereotype room, foreman; Richard M. Wharry, stereotype room, assistant foreman; Joseph E. Kohlberger, engraving room, foreman; Alexander Zeese, engraving room, assistant foreman (day); Henry Collins, engraving room, assistant foreman (third shift); William J. Brand, press room, foreman; William J. French, press room, assistant foreman; James McConnell, chief electrician; John Heffernan, paper handlers, foreman.

Publication office: Henry Buggeln, manager; Charles F. Seaquist, assistant manager.

The *Sun* in the last five years has won the title of "the greatest of evening newspapers in quality." It has not the largest circulation in the evening field, although the average daily net has risen from 180,000 in 1923 to 280,000 in 1927. This circulation is among the best class of readers in the Metropolitan zone, for the *Sun* has not resorted to prizes, puzzle contests, or any of the other artificial stimulants with which the yellow or near-yellow newspapers inflate their sales. The *Sun* has the services of five great news agencies and its own bureaus in many cities. A survey of one issue in May, 1927, showed that the 52 pages held 162 columns of news, editorial articles, and features, and 254 columns of advertisements. Although advertising predominated the space, the printing of 162 columns of reading matter meant that the *Sun* gave to its readers, for three cents, twice as much material as is found in the average novel. It included 26 columns of local news, 25 columns of telegraph and cable news, 36 columns of financial news, 23 columns of sport news, 20 columns devoted to the theater, music, social affairs, and women's activities; an editorial page filled with opinions, essays, Mr. Phillips's humor, Bob Davis's reminiscences and the letters of readers; pages given to automobile, radio, shipping, and real estate news; and many cartoons and pictures.

In July, 1925, the *Sun* for the first time in its history published more advertising than any other New York evening newspaper. For the year ended June 30, 1926, the *Sun* printed 16,095,514 agate lines of advertising, having recorded a lead over its nearest competitor of

1,064,676 agate lines and having gained 2,630,530 agate lines over its own record for the previous year. For the year ended June 30, 1927, the *Sun* printed 16,308,659 agate lines, or 213,145 agate lines more than in the previous year, leading the second evening newspaper by 1,979,062 agate lines. As this book goes to press the *Sun* has completed its second year of advertising leadership among the evening papers of New York.

CHAPTER XVII

SOME "SUN" STORIES

Examples of the Styles of Reporters from Dana's Time to the Present, Including the Saga of the Snyg and the Accounts of Notable Trial Scenes.

IT would take a small book to give a list of the "big" stories that the *Sun* has printed, and a five-foot shelf of tall volumes to reprint them all. Some of them were written leisurely, like Spears's stories of the Bad Lands, some in comparative ease, like Ralph's stories of presidential inaugurations and the Grant funeral, or W. J. Chamberlin's eleven-column report of the Dewey parade in 1899. In these latter the ease is only comparative, for the writer's fingers had no time to rest in the achievement of such gigantic tasks. And the comparison is with the work done by reporters on occasions when there was no time to arrange ideas and choose words, when the facts came in what would be to the layman hopeless disorder.

Such an occasion, for instance, was the burning of the excursion steamer *General Slocum,* the description of which—in the end a marvelous tale of horror—was taken page by page from Lindsay Denison as his typewriter milled it out. Such an occasion was Richard Lockridge's story of the start of Lindbergh's Atlantic flight, dictated by telephone from Roosevelt Field, and in print and on the street in less than two hours after Lindbergh flew.

Introductions to big stories tell the pulse of the paper.

Read, for example, the *Sun* introduction to the great ocean tragedy of 1898:

HALIFAX, NOVA SCOTIA, July 6—The steamship *La Bourgogne* of the Compagnie Générale Transatlantique, which left New York on Saturday last bound for Havre, was sunk at five o'clock on Monday morning after a collision with the British ship *Cromartyshire* in a dense fog about sixty miles south of Sable Island. The ship had 750 persons aboard. The number of first- and second-cabin passengers was 220 and of the steerage passengers 297, a total of 517. The number of officers was 11, of the crew 222. Eleven second-cabin and 51 steerage passengers and 104 of the crew, a total of 166, were saved. All the officers but four, all the first-cabin passengers, and all but one of the more than one hundred women on board, were lost. The number of lost is believed to be 584.

This was more detailed, but not more calm than the opening of Edwin C. Hill's story on the loss of the *Titanic:*

The greatest marine disaster in the history of ocean traffic occurred last Sunday night, when the *Titanic* of the White Star Line, the greatest steamship that ever sailed the sea, shattered herself against an iceberg and sank with, it is feared, fifteen hundred of her passengers and crew in less than four hours. The monstrous modern ships may defy wind and weather, but ice and fog remain unconquered.

Out of nearly twenty-four hundred people that the *Titanic* carried, only eight hundred and sixty-six are known to have been saved, and most of these were women and children.

Probably the most restrained lead on a *Sun* account of a great disaster was the introduction to the article on the Brooklyn Theater fire of 1876:

> The Brooklyn Theater was built in September, 1871, opened for public entertainment October 2, 1871, and burned to the ground with the sacrifice of three hundred lives on the night of Tuesday, December 5, 1876.

Of a more literary character, yet void of excitement, was the way Julian Ralph began his narrative of the blizzard of March, 1888:

> It was as if New York had been a burning candle upon which nature had clapped a snuffer, leaving nothing of the city's activities but a struggling ember.

A patient historian of American journalism, armed with a file of the *Sun,* could dig out volumes of examples of perfect reportorial work, the product of men who threw the whole vigor of their youth into the collection and writing of news. He would find Julian Ralph's story of Grant's funeral in 1885, beginning with this dignified paragraph:

> There have not often been gathered in one place so many men whose names have been household words, and whose lives have been inwoven with the history of a grave crisis in a great nation's life, as met yesterday in this city. The scene was before General Grant's tomb in Riverside Park; the space

was less than goes to half an ordinary city block, and the names of the actors were William T. Sherman, Joe Johnston, Phil Sheridan, Simon B. Buckner, John A. Logan, W. S. Hancock, Fitz John Porter, Chester A. Arthur, Thomas A. Hendricks, John Sherman, Fitzhugh Lee, John B. Gordon, David D. Porter, Thomas F. Bayard, John L. Worden, and a dozen others naturally linked in the mind with these greater men. Among them, like children amid gray-heads, or shadows beside monuments, were other men more newly famous, and famous only for deeds of peace in times of quiet and plenty—a President, an ex-President, Governors, mayors, and millionaires. And all were paying homage to the greatest figure of their time, whose mortal remains they pressed around with bared, bowed heads.

That was the beginning of a story of about eleven thousand words, all written by Ralph in one evening. It told everything that was worth reading about the burial —the weather, the crowded line of march, the people from out of town, the women fainting at the curbs, the uniforms and peculiarities of the Union and Confederate heroes who rode in the funeral train; told everything from eight o'clock in the morning, when the sight-seers began to gather, until the bugler blew taps and the regiments fired their salute volleys. It was a story typical of Ralph, who saw everything, remembered everything, wrote everything. In detail it is unlikely that any reporter of to-day could surpass it. In dramatic quality it has been excelled by a dozen *Sun* reporters, including Ralph himself.

For example, there is the story of a similar event—Admiral Dewey's funeral—written in January, 1917, by

Thoreau Cronyn, of the *Sun,* with a dramatic climax such as Ralph did not reach. This is the end of Cronyn's story—the incident of the old bugler whose art failed him in his grief:

> Chattering of spectators in the background hushed abruptly. A light breeze, which barely rumpled the river, set a few dry leaves tossing about the tomb of Farragut, Dewey's mentor at Mobile. The voice of Chaplain Frazier could be heard repeating a prayer, catching, and then going on smoothly.
>
> A second silence, then the brisk call of the lieutenant commanding the firing squad of Annapolis cadets.
>
> "Load!"
>
> Rifles rattling.
>
> "Aim!"
>
> Rifles pointed a little upward for safety's sake, though the cartridges had no bullets.
>
> "Fire!"
>
> Twenty rifles snapped as one. This twice repeated—three volleys over the tomb into which the twelve sailors had just carried the admiral's body.
>
> And now came the moment for Master-at-Arms Charles Mitchell, bugler on the *Olympia* when Dewey sank the Spanish fleet, to perform his last office for the admiral. Raising the bugle to his lips and looking straight ahead at the still open door of the tomb, he sounded "taps." The first three climbing notes and the second three were perfect. Then the break and the recovery, and the funeral was over.

The browsing historian would find the picturesque account written by Arthur Brisbane of the fight between John L. Sullivan and Charley Mitchell:

Deeply interested were the handfuls of Frenchmen who gathered and watched from such a safe and distant pavilion as we would select to look upon a hyena fight.

And, when other reporters were deafened by the battle, Brisbane heard the plaintive appeal of Baldock, Mitchell's tough second:

> "Think of the kids, Charley, the dear little kids, a-calling for you at home and a-counting on you for bread! Think what their feelings will be if you don't knock the ear off him, and knock it off him again!"

Not but what the correspondent paid conscientious attention to the technic of the fray:

> A detailed report of each of the thirty-nine rounds taken by me shows that out of more than a hundred wild rushes made by Sullivan, and of which any one would have been followed by a knockout in Madison Square, not half a dozen resulted in anything.

He would find Erasmus D. Beach's description of the football game of 1890 between Yale and Princeton, with the introduction which Mr. Dana called classic:

> Great in the annals of Yale forever must be the name of McClung. Twice within a few minutes this man has carried the ball over the Princeton goal-line. He runs like a deer, has the stability of footing of one of the pyramids, and is absolutely cool in the most frightfully exciting circumstances.
>
> A curious figure is McClung. He has just finished a run of twenty yards, with all Princeton shoving

against him. He is steaming like a pot of porridge, and chewing gum. His vigorously working profile is clearly outlined against the descending sun. How dirty he is! His paddings seem to have become loosed and to have accumulated over his knees. He has a shield, a sort of splint, bound upon his right shin. His long hair is held in a band, a linen fillet, the dirtiest ever worn.

He pants as a man who has run fifty miles—who has overthrown a house. He droops slightly for a moment's rest, hands on knees, eyes shining with the glare of battle, the gum catching between his grinders. A tab on one of his ears signifies a severe injury to that organ, an injury received in some previous match from an opposition boot-heel, or from a slide over the rough earth with half a dozen of the enemy seated upon him. He has a little, sharp-featured face, squirrel-like, with a Roman nose and eyes set near together. Brief dental gleams illuminate his countenance in his moments of great joyfulness.

In his collections of sea idylls the historian would include many of the prose poems of Sam Wood, for instance the story over which Mr. Clarke wrote the head:

SNYGLESS THE SEAS ARE—WIIG RIDES THE WAVES NO MORE—BACK COME BANANA MEN—SKAAL TO THE VIKINGS!

This is the text:

While off the Honduranean coast, not far from Ruatan, the famous little fruiter *Snyg* on dirty weather ran. Her skipper, Wiig, was at the helm, the boatswain hove the lead; the air was thick; you could not see a half-ship's length ahead. The mate said:

"Reefs of Ruatan, I think, are off our bow."

The skipper answered:

"You are right; they're inside of us now."

The water filled the engine-room and put the fires out, and quickly o'er the weather rail the seas began to spout.

When dawn appeared there also came three blacks from off the isle. They deftly managed their canoe, each wearing but a smile; but, clever as they were, their boat was smashed against the *Snyg*, and they were promptly hauled aboard by gallant Captain Wiig.

"We had thirteen aboard this ship," the fearful cook remarked. "I think we stand a chance for life, since three coons have embarked. Now let our good retriever, Nig, a life-line take ashore, and all hands of the steamship *Snyg* may see New York once more."

But Nig refused to leave the ship, and so the fearless crew the life-boat launched, but breakers stove the stout craft through and through. Said Captain Wiig:

"Though foiled by Nig, our jig's not up, I vow; I've still my gig, and I don't care a fig—I'll make the beach somehow!"

And Mate Charles Christian of the *Snyg* (who got here yesterday) helped launch the stanch gig of the *Snyg* so the crew could get away. The gig was anchored far inshore; with raft and trolley-line all hands on the *Snyg*, including Nig, were hauled safe o'er the brine.

Although the *Snyg*, of schooner rig, will ply the

waves no more, let us hope that Wiig gets another *Snyg* for the sake of the bards ashore.

Surely a collection of *Sun* stories would include the masterpiece of Thomas M. Dieuaide on the destruction of St. Pierre in 1902, beginning:

> Fort de France, Martinique, May 21—To-day we saw St. Pierre, the ghastliest ghost of the modern centuries. But yesterday the fairest of the fair of the wondrous cities of the storied Antilles, bright, beautiful, glorious, glistening and shimmering in her prism of tropical radiance, an opalescent city in a setting of towering forest and mountain, now a waste of ashen-gray without life, form, color, shape, a drear monotone, a dim blur on the landscape—it seems even more than the contrast between life and death.
>
> The dead may live. St. Pierre is not alive, and never will be. Out of shape has come a void. It is the apotheosis of annihilation. To one who sits amid the ruins and gazes the long miles upward over the seamed sides of La Pelée, still thundering her terrible wrath, may come some conception of the future ruin of the worlds.
>
> It has been a day of sharp impressions, one cutting into another until the memory-pad of the mind is crossed and criss-crossed like the fissured flanks of La Pelée herself; but most deeply graven of all, paradoxically, is the memory of a dimness, a nothingness, an emptiness, a lack of everything—the gray barrenness unrelieved of what was the rainbow St. Pierre. Mont Pelée, the most awful evidence of natural force to be seen in the world to-day—La Pelée, majestic, terrible, overpowering, has been in evidence from starlight to starlight, but it is the ashen blank that was once the city of the Saint of the Rock that

stands out most clearly in the kaleidoscopic maze slipping backward and forward before our eyes.

Another unforgettable article related to disaster was Will Irwin's striking story, "The City That Was," printed the day after the San Francisco earthquake. These were introductory lines:

> The old San Francisco is dead. The gayest, lightest-hearted, most pleasure-loving city of this continent, and in many ways the most interesting and romantic, is a horde of huddled refugees living among ruins. It may rebuild; it probably will; but those who have known that peculiar city by the Golden Gate, and have caught its flavor of the *Arabian Nights* feel that it can never be the same.
>
> It is as though a pretty, frivolous woman had passed through a great tragedy. She survives, but she is sobered and different. If it rises out of the ashes it must be a modern city, much like other cities and without its old flavor.

There were less than five columns of the article, but it told the whole story of San Francisco; not in dry figures of commerce and paved streets, but of the people and places that every Eastern man had longed to see, but now never could see.

As examples of the work of *Sun* reporters in murder trials, let us take three widely separated examples, beginning with the verdict rendered January 5, 1873, against Edward S. Stokes for the murder of Jim Fisk:

> Stokes took his accustomed place, and his relatives sat down facing the jurors. The judge entered and took his place. Then, amid the most solemn silence,

the twelve jurymen filed in and seated themselves. The awful conclusion at which they had arrived could be read in their faces. Each juror's name was called, and with the usual response.

The judge turned toward them, and in a low, clear voice asked:

"Gentlemen, have you agreed on a verdict?"

The foreman of the jury arose and said, "We have."

Clerk of the Court: "Gentlemen of the jury, rise. Prisoner, stand up. Gentlemen of the jury, look upon the prisoner. Prisoner, look upon the jury. What say you, gentlemen of the jury? Do you find the prisoner at the bar guilty or not guilty?"

Foreman of the Jury: "Guilty of murder in the first degree."

A passionate wail that made men's hearts leap rose from the group that clustered round the prisoner, and the head of the horror-stricken girl from whose bosom the anguished cry was rent fell upon the shoulder of her doomed brother.

The jury was polled by request of the prisoner's counsel. No sooner had the last man answered "Yes" to the question whether all agreed on the verdict than the prisoner, erect and firm, turned his face full upon Mr. Beach (of the prosecution), who at one time had been his counsel in a civil case.

"Mr. Beach," the prisoner said, slowly and in a full-toned voice, "you have done your work well. I hope you have been well paid for it."

Then the prisoner sank slowly into his seat. Mr. Beach made no reply. Mr. Fellows, assistant district attorney, explained that he had refused to try the case unless Mr. Beach and Mr. Fullerton were associated with him. They had consented to join him

Julian Ralph

Edward G. Riggs

W. J. Chamberlin

Frank Ward O'Malley

at the request of District Attorney Garvin, and without any fee from any member of Colonel Fisk's family.

The prisoner half-arose and, sweeping the air with his clenched fist, said:

"Mr. Fellows, say that they were hired by Jay Gould. Please say that!"

The sensation in court was such as is seldom known. You could hear it as you hear the wind stirring the trees of the forest. Then the court discharged the jury and the people began to move.

Next we have an extract from Julian Ralph's story of the acquittal of Lizzie Borden, accused of the murder of her father and stepmother. It appeared in the *Sun* of June 21, 1893:

"Lizzie Andrew Borden," said the clerk of the court, "stand up!"

She arose unsteadily, with a face as white as marble.

"Gentlemen, have you agreed upon a verdict?" said the clerk to the jury.

It was so still in court that the flutter of two fans made a great noise.

"We have," said Foreman Richards boldly.

The prisoner was gripping the rail in front of the dock as if her standing up depended upon its keeping its place.

"Lizzie Andrew Borden," said the clerk, "hold up your right hand. Jurors, look upon the prisoner. Prisoner, look upon the foreman."

Every juryman stood at right-about-face, staring at the woman. There was such a gentle, kindly light beaming in every eye that no one questioned the verdict that was to be uttered. But God save every woman from the feelings that Lizzie Borden showed in the return look she cast upon that jury! It was what is pictured as the rolling gaze of a dying person. She seemed not to have the power to move her eyes directly where she was told to, and they swung all around in her head. They looked at the ceiling; they looked at everything, but they saw nothing. It was a horrible, a pitiful sight, to see her then.

"What say you, Mr. Foreman?" said the gentle old clerk.

"Not guilty!" shouted Mr. Richards.

At the words the wretched woman fell quicker than ever an ox fell in the stockyards of Chicago. Her forehead crashed against the heavy walnut rail so as to shake the reporter of the *Sun* who sat next to her, twelve feet away, leaning on the rail. It seemed that she must be stunned, but she was not. Quickly, with an unconscious movement, she flung up both arms, threw them over the rail, and pressed them under her face so that it rested on them. What followed was mere mockery, but it was the well-governed order of the court and had to be gone through with.

Finally, the conviction of Charles Becker in May, 1914, of the murder of Herman Rosenthal as reported for the *Sun* by Edwin C. Hill:

"Charles Becker to the bar!"

Once more the door that gives entrance toward the Tombs as well as to the juryroom was opened. A deputy sheriff appeared, then Becker, then a second deputy. One glance was all you needed to see that Becker had himself under magnificent control. His iron nerve was not bending. He swung with long strides around the walls and came to a stand at the railing. Those who watched him did not see a sign of agitation. He was breathing slowly—you could see that from the rise and fall of his powerful chest—and smiling slightly as he glanced toward his counsel.

He looked for the first time toward the jurors. There was confidence and hope shining in his eyes. Coolly, without haste, he studied the face of every man in the box. Not one of them met his eye. Foreman Blagden gazed at the floor. Frederick G. Barrett, Sr., juror No. 12, studied the ceiling. The others gazed into space or turned their glance toward the justice.

There was the most perfect silence in the courtroom. The movements of trolley-cars in Centre Street made a noise like rolling thunder. A pneumatic riveter at work on a building close by set up a tremendous din.

And yet such sounds and annoyances were forgotten, ceased to be of consequence, when Clerk Penny bent toward the foreman and slowly put the customary question:

"Gentlemen of the jury, have you agreed upon your verdict?"

Mr. Blagden's reply was barely audible; many in the room sensed its import, but failed to grasp the actual words. It was obvious that the foreman, having to express the will of his associates, was stirred by such feeling as seldom comes to any man.

"Guilty as charged in the indictment," he breathed more than spoke.

Becker's right hand was then gripped to the railing. He held his straw hat in his left hand, which, as his arm was bent backward and upward, rested against the small of his back. It is the plain truth that he took the blow without a quiver. After a second, it may be, he coughed just a little; a mere clearing of the throat. But his mouth was firm. His dark face lost no vestige of color. His black eyes turned toward the jurymen, who still avoided his glance, who looked everywhere but at the man they had condemned.

Frank W. O'Malley's story of the killing of Policeman Gene Sheehan has been reprinted from the *Sun* by several textbooks for students of journalism. Practically all of it—and it was a column long—was a straightforward report of the story told by the policeman's mother. This is a part:

> Mrs. Catherine Sheehan stood in the darkened parlor of her home at 361 West Fifteenth Street late yesterday afternoon and told her version of the murder of her son Gene, the youthful policeman whom a thug named Billy Morley shot in the forehead down under the Chatham Square elevated station early yesterday morning. Gene's mother was thankful that her boy hadn't killed Billy Morley before he died, "because," she said, "I can say honestly, even now, that I'd rather have Gene's dead body brought home to me, as it will be to-night, than to have him come to me and say, 'Mother, I had to kill a man this morning.'
>
> "God comfort the poor wretch that killed the boy," the mother went on, "because he is more unhappy to-night than we are here. Maybe he was weak-minded through drink. He couldn't have known Gene, or he wouldn't have killed him. Did they tell you at the Oak Street Station that the other policemen called Gene 'Happy Sheehan'? Anything

they told you about him is true, because no one would lie about him. He was always happy, and he was a fine-looking young man. He always had to duck his helmet when he walked under the gas-fixture in the hall as he went out the door.

"After he went down the street yesterday I found a little book on a chair—a little list of the streets or something that Gene had forgot. I knew how particular they are about such things, and I didn't want the boy to get in trouble, so I threw on a shawl and walked over through Chambers Street toward the river to find him. He was standing on a corner some place down there near the bridge, clapping time with his hands for a little newsy that was dancing; but he stopped clapping—struck, Gene did, when he saw me. He laughed when I handed him a little book and told him that was why I'd searched for him, patting me on the shoulder when he laughed—patting me on the shoulder.

" 'It's a bad place for you here, Gene,' I said. 'Then it must be bad for you, too, mammy,' said he; and as he walked to the end of his beat with me—it was dark then—he said, 'There are lots of crooks here, mother, and they know and hate me, and they're afraid of me'—proud, he said it—'but maybe they'll get me some night.'

"He patted me on the back and turned and walked east toward his death. Wasn't it strange that Gene said that?

"You know how he was killed, of course, and how—now let me talk about it, children, if I want to. I promised you, didn't I, that I wouldn't cry any more or carry on? Well, it was five o'clock this morning when a boy rang the bell here at the house, and I looked out the window and said:

" 'Is Gene dead?'

" 'No, ma'am,' answered the lad; 'but they told me to tell you he was hurt in a fire and is in the hospital.'

"Jerry, my other boy, had opened the door for the lad, and was talking to him while I dressed a bit. And then I walked down-stairs and saw Jerry standing silent under the gaslight; and I said again, 'Jerry, is Gene dead?' And he said 'Yes,' and he went out.

"After a while I went down to the Oak Street Station myself, because I couldn't wait for Jerry to come back. The policemen all stopped talking when I came in, and then one of them told me it was against the rules to show me Gene at that time; but I knew the policeman only thought I'd break down. I promised him I wouldn't carry on, and he took me into a room to let me see Gene. It was Gene."

As an example of "action" writing nothing could be more typical of the *Sun* style than W. J. Chamberlin's report of the breaking of the suspenders of the sergeant-at-arms at the Populist Convention in 1896:

He clutched, but he clutched too late. He dived and grabbed once, twice, thrice, but down those trousers slipped. Mary E. Lease was only three feet away. Miss Mitchell, of Kansas, was less than two feet away. Helen Gougar was almost on the spot. Mrs. Julia Ward Pennington was just two seats off, and all around and about him were gathered the most beautiful and eloquent women of the convention, and every eye was upon the unfortunate Deacon McDowell.

Then he grabbed, and then again, again, and again they eluded him. Down, down he dived. At last victory perched on him. He got the trousers, and, with a yank that threatened to rip them from stem to stern, he pulled them up. At no time had the applause ceased, nor had there been any sign of a let-up in the demonstration. Now it was increased twofold. The women joined in.

McDowell, clutching the truant trousers closely about him, attempted to resume his part in the demonstration, but it was useless, and after frantic efforts to show enthusiasm he retired to hunt up ten-penny nails. When it was over, an indignant Populist introduced this resolution:

"Resolved that future sergeants-at-arms shall be required to wear tights."

The chairman did not put the resolution.

That was a "fast" story, yet we find it outdone in speed by Richard Lockridge in his report of Captain Lindbergh's take-off for Paris at Roosevelt field on May 20, 1927:

Lindbergh got into the plane at 7:40 o'clock and the crowd cheered. His motor was started at once and for ten minutes droned as it tuned. At 7:50 the blocks were knocked from the wheels and, slowly, heavily, the plane started. It sank into the soft turf of the field, bearing down with its weight of 5,150 pounds. It started very slowly.

The crowd hurled its hats into the air and stepped on its motor sirens. Through the side openings in the cockpit those closest saw Lindbergh's hand go up stiffly in an army salute. The plane rolled on, its Wright Whirlwind motor rising gradually in the tune it was singing to itself. The crowd was breathless. Never before had a single motor of 225 horsepower, such as this, taken into the air a load of more than 5,000 pounds. And the ambulance waited.

The plane's speed increased—but not rapidly. It lunged and swayed. It hit a bump and staggered into the air a few feet. The watchers could see light under its wheels. Then it went down again, solidly, sulkily, into the mud. The motor's drone increased.

It jumped out again a little further on. It lunged and swayed in the air—now he'd done it! The crowd yelled, and the plane slumped down again into the mud. Behind it lay most of the course it had on land—ahead lay a cornfield, some buildings and an ambulance. Its speed increased, but not fast enough. It lunged up again; it clung to the air, ten feet above the soggy earth which fought to hold it. Now he'd done it! And now, indeed, he had.

He rose very slowly in the air. He cleared the cornfield. He cleared the telegraph wires. He cleared the trees. They could trundle the ambulance away, then; Lindbergh was on his way to Paris.

There is hardly a man who has lived five years as a *Sun* reporter but could write his own story of the *Sun* just as he has written stories of life. Here but a few of these men and their work have been touched. Many of the great reporters are dead, and of some of these it may be said that their lives were shortened by the very fever in which they won their glory. Some passed on to other fields of endeavor. Others are waiting to write "the best story ever printed in the *Sun*."

What was the best story ever printed in the *Sun?* It may be that the story has been quoted from in these articles; and yet, if a thousand years hence some super-scientist should invent a literary measure that would answer the question, the crown of that high and now unbestowable honor of authorship might fall to some man here unmentioned and elsewhere unsung. Perhaps it was an article only two hundred words long.

INDEX

www.ingramcontent.com/pod-product-compliance
Lightning Source LLC
LaVergne TN
LVHW010156110826
845151LV00002B/531
* 9 7 8 1 4 2 5 5 3 8 6 3 7 *